Throughout her time as an Executive Leadership Coach, Adele began to notice regular patterns with her clients. The root cause of these patterns was low self-belief, low self-confidence and low self-esteem. Adele also noticed that people don't really know themselves too well and that they let fear hold them back and she wanted to help! Using her expertise, instinct and experience, she decided she could really help others by creating the formula for true internal self-confidence. Adele then put down in writing what she believes as the true equation to total inner and outer confidence.

This work was inspired by all my amazing coachees – for trusting me, trusting the process and allowing yourself to be vulnerable, to unlock all of your incredible potential. I have watched you grow and blossom and I am proud of you all for dedicating yourself to your personal and professional self-development. It's a brave thing to do. Thank you to all those who believed in me, encouraged me and loved me – this book is for everyone who is in my life. You are loved dearly.

Adele Bradley

EQUATION TO CONFIDENCE

AUSTIN MACAULEY PUBLISHERS™

LONDON • CAMBRIDGE • NEW YORK • SHARJAH

A CIP catalogue record for this title is available from the British Library.

ISBN 9781528973960 (Paperback)
ISBN 9781528973984 (ePub e-book)
ISBN 9781035825325 (Audiobook)

www.austinmacauley.com

First Published 2023
Austin Macauley Publishers Ltd®
1 Canada Square
Canary Wharf
London
E14 5AA

I want to thank Austin Macauley publishers for offering me a chance to work with them.

Table of Contents

Introduction

My name is Adele Bradley – I'm 41 years young and I live in Leeds. I live with my dog, Mia, and I love renovating property (if you love properties and interiors, follow my Instagram page @designbyadele). I'm driven, passionate, enthusiastic, happy and I adore personal growth. I'm passionate about everything that I do and I love life. I actually do! Yes, the world can be crap sometimes but how you live your life is down to your mindset – and you get to choose that mindset, so why wouldn't you make it a great one that helps you grow and flourish every day?

I personally am frustrated that I only get to live life once, as there are so many things I want to do, see and try. I would like to live lots of lives so I could do all types of different things, like be the commander of any army, an award-winning actress, an astronaut, a surgeon, a captain, a pilot, an architect – the list goes on and on! I want to experience as much as I possibly can…after all, isn't that the point of life…experiences?

That's where we make our memories, right? And on our deathbed, our memories will be all we have…I don't ever want to be that person on my deathbed, wishing I had done more or be filled with lots of regrets.

Sometimes, we do hold ourselves back from being the best we can be, creating experiences and making memories because of our own internal thoughts. We tell ourselves we can't do something, that we will be no good at it, that we live in a fantasy world. Or we choose to listen to others – they tell us not to do it or that it's not possible and we listen. That then holds up back and stops us from experiencing as much as possible. What if we were confident enough to listen to ourselves, back ourselves and believe in ourselves? What if nothing stopped us from moving forward creating experiences and making memories? What if we had true self confidence within each and every one of us?

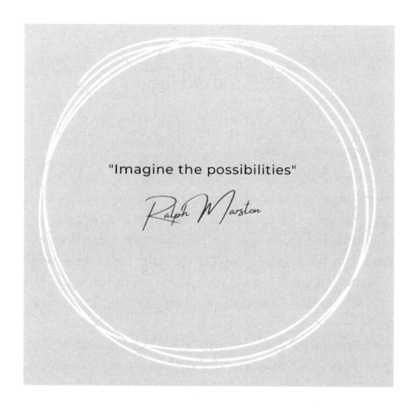

"Imagine the possibilities"

Ralph Marston

I wrote this book because it's a question I get asked a lot – 'How are you so confident?' And I have wanted to write a book for years – so I decided, if not now, when? The subject was a natural one, due to a few factors really. I work as an executive business coach – and as a coach, people come to you with goals they want to work on to enhance and develop their performance. From coaching many, many executives, senior managers and directors, I have found a real theme that sits behind a lot of their issues. Low self-confidence, low self-belief. Low self-esteem. Imposter syndrome.

I have found this theme from listening, observing and understanding root causes that drive the performance issues. The issues stem from lots of things like: assumptions about others' intentions, limiting beliefs, worrying about things out of their control, biases, carrying baggage around, reacting instead of responding, not letting go, and the list goes on.

I coach them around this mindset and I challenge them in thinking in different ways, reframing thoughts and challenging existing behaviours and assumptions. It's such a pleasure when I see them achieve their goals. I absolutely love coaching others and seeing them succeed!

The other factor is my own confidence – I have it in spades and I'm often asked about it. You can get away with quite a lot if you are confident with a cheeky smile on your face, believe me! I enjoy being confident and I wanted to share with you what I believe is the equation to confidence and how you can achieve it from the inside out.

When I piece it all together, what I know from this experience is that you have to **believe in yourself explicitly**, you have to **trust yourself** but most of all you have to **know yourself**. If we spend more time getting to know ourselves, understanding why we behave the way we do, what impact we have on others and raising our levels of self-awareness, our lives will change dramatically for the better.

If you really get to know yourself, that is where true confidence comes from – it will shine bright out of you like a star – your confidence will tell everybody how you feel about yourself.

'SHINING IN YOUR OWN LIGHT, NATURALLY'

I made this book / journal – **a book for life** as you can update it, keep it with you for when you have those light bulb moments. You can note it in this journal book! This book is designed to be with you throughout your journey and it will be an amazing document to look back and see how your journey progressed.

This book is meant to be a friend, a confidant and a place of peace. Learning about yourself is an ongoing journey of self-reflection and self-love and I feel it's important to get all the help you need on this beautiful journey, so use this book as intended, write, scribble and doodle to your heart's content!

Gaining confidence will not happen overnight. And if you put your mind to it, commit to it and practice it, you too will achieve the equation to confidence. There are a few tips throughout the book on body language and voice which will help you start to make immediate external changes whilst working inwardly on the others. You have GOT this. Are you ready to get to know yourself?

To get the best out of this book, lots of self-reflection is required. Hold that mirror up close and be okay with what you find out, use it to evolve and become the best version of you.

I hope you enjoy the book, let me know what you think over on @adelebradleygram Let's connect!

Confidence and Me

Do you know what is beautiful?
What is utterly undeniable?

A woman so confident that she doesn't feel the need to compete. That she doesn't belittle others. That she doesn't judge. A woman who knows her worth is dictated only from within herself and isn't dependent on anyone but herself. A woman who works to build others up rather than tear them down. One who relishes in the success of her sisters and never, not for one minute, wishes ill upon another. A woman who is in love with every single breath that she takes and works to empower others to feel the same.

Becca Lee

I have always been confident; I think it's something I was born with. It's something I've never not had. It is literally part of me. When I was younger, I literally had balls of steel, now was that just a young cocky attitude manifesting as confidence or was I just cocky? What do you think? Either way, I've never been afraid of any situation, any group of people, any one individual and any scenario that might arise. I've always walked confidently into any room and can hold my own with anyone, with ease and no nerves. I enjoy being confident. I enjoy the feeling and I like how it makes me feel.

Being confident makes me feel capable, strong, sexy and powerful. When I walk, I walk with purpose, head high, shoulders back and a confident stride. I know that I can handle any situation (to the best of my ability) as I am confident in myself.

Confidence is sexy. Just ask anyone. Confidence is a presence, energy, a mindset and a way of being. It is who you are. It's owning it. It's your POWER!

People have made comments to my parents before, when I have walked in somewhere 'Is she famous?' It's because I walk with confidence.

I like the feeling of self-assurance I have wrapped around myself. It's not arrogance, it's just warm reassurance that 'I got this' no matter what the situation.

Having internal and external confidence is very important – imagine walking like a king / queen into somewhere and then not being able to answer basic questions or know what you are talking about. It just wouldn't work.

Don't get me wrong, I do get nervous (occasionally) – there have been times in my life where I have been REALLY nervous like my driving test(s). I passed my driving test on my 7th attempt after 4 years. There was something about being in the car under those conditions that just made me go to pieces. I got there though, perseverance and determination after 4 years, I passed on my 7th go. I was 21 back then. What a lesson to learn at that age. Perseverance, determination, resilience and trying!

I did mention above that I had balls of steel when I was younger and it got me thinking about a recent podcast I heard. I was recently listening to a podcast with Fern Cotton and Steven Bartlett (if you haven't heard of him, google him, he has a fascinating story). Fern was saying that when we are younger, we have naivety on our side. We look at something and think 'I could do that' and because we are naive and don't have any experience, we just go for it. I reflected on this and agreed with some of her points – maybe when we don't know any better, we just go for it. Maybe time, experiences, and learning shape our thinking as adults as we get older and this makes us less confident because we do have the experience to back it up. I wonder if being a tiny bit naive sometimes with our mindset would help our confidence?

Something to think about…

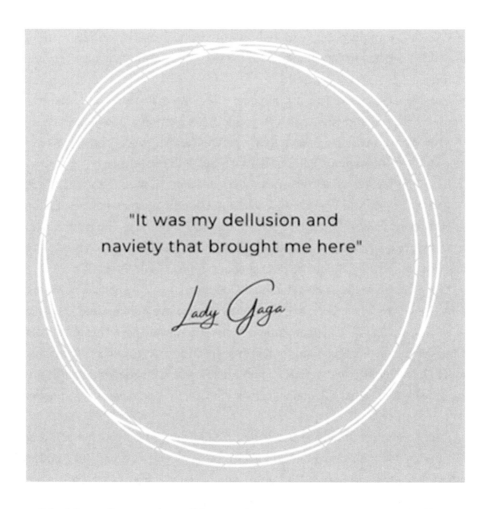

"It was my dellusion and naviety that brought me here"

Lady Gaga

I had lots of external confidence when I was younger. I was a ballsy girl. However recently I have truly learnt inner confidence and it's absolutely liberating, freeing and incredible. If you follow this book to the note, you will too. But it won't happen overnight. This is a process and it takes years. You just have to make the commitment to yourself that you are going to go on this journey of inner self confidence and external confidence and learn as much as you can. Make you make it a lifelong practice. I believe that is what I have committed to now. I know that I can keep learning things about myself and I don't want to stop. I'm committed to being the most incredible version of myself I can possibly be! Mind, body and soul.

I also think there is a thing called "blind confidence" – I have this in spades. It's where you have no data, no experience, no prior knowledge and don't know anything about it but you know 100% that it will get done / give it a go. Does that sound familiar? It's like naivety and confidence all rolled up in one.

Let me give you an example – when I split up with my ex-husband, I decided I wanted to renovate properties. I have ever done it before, no experience in it to draw from and no data to back this up but my gut told me I could do it, it told me I am resourceful and switched on, I believed in myself and I knew implicitly I would not fail = blind confidence.

And guess what? I did it but not only did I do it, a full house renovation, I did it in 4 months. I knew I could do it and I proved it to myself and to everyone who was watching and doubting me. I **believed in myself** because I **knew myself** and **trusted in myself**. That gave me blind confidence, completely **trusting** myself to push me through it and get it done.

We can also have blind confidence in things we can fail miserably in because we didn't know ourselves and our abilities well enough.

For example, I could say, 'Plastering a room doesn't look hard, I know I can do that, I've watched them do it at least 7 times.' I then realize I don't even know what plaster to buy, how to mix it, measure it, what tools I need, how to apply it, so therefore I'm doomed to fail.

However, if I did an evening course plastering and then maybe worked side by side with an experienced plasterer that would work out better.

If you are going to have complete BLIND confidence, then you need to **know yourself** and your abilities extremely well.

I didn't know how to conduct a full house renovation, but I figured it out. I asked trades, watched videos, read articles and took advice and counsel. I used common sense and I figured things out day by day. I did it because I knew I could do it because **I KNOW MYSELF**!

Where have you had blind confidence? How did it work out?

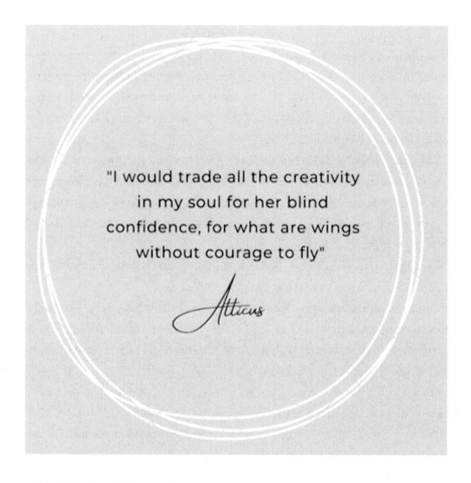

"I would trade all the creativity
in my soul for her blind
confidence, for what are wings
without courage to fly"

Atticus

I had blind confidence when…

_____

_____

_____

We are going to start by exploring confidence first, like confidence in your career, your relationships, in your words and your mindset. Once we explore that, we will get into the equation!

Let's get into it…

What Is Confidence?

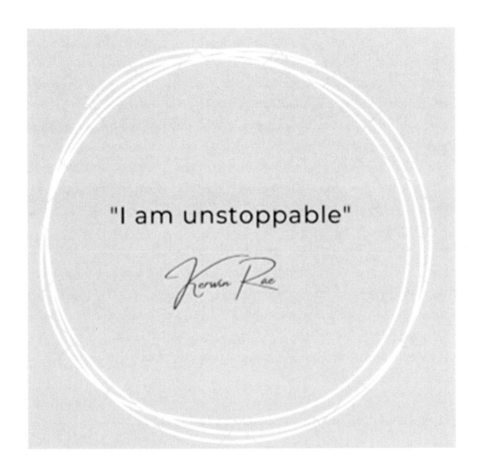

How do we describe confidence?

It can be described in the following way:

'Confidence means feeling sure of yourself and your abilities – not in an arrogant way but in a realistic and secure way. Confidence isn't about feeling superior to others. It's a quiet inner knowledge that you're capable. Confident people know they can rely on their skills and strengths to handle whatever comes.' (Kids' Health, 2021)

So, confidence is about being secure and realistic in your abilities. Have you ever met someone that has had "big talk" about something that they do, only to fail miserably at it and create a disappointing experience? That's because they are confident in their abilities to 'sell / talk'* to others but no confidence to deliver the goods, which means they are unauthentic; therefore, their confidence is only in one area and not throughout their total abilities, does that make sense?

Jocelyne Glei states, 'The clearest definition we got came from a professor at Ohio State University, Dr Richard Petty, who told us that confidence is essentially the stuff that turns our thoughts into action. Basically, it greases the wheels for action. Which I found interesting because that means it's not just an ongoing state of being like, she's confident. It's more action-oriented and doing-oriented. It's really in that cycle of taking action – which includes the willingness to take risks, the willingness to struggle, to fail and to eventually master something that you create confidence. So, it's almost a virtuous circle. Confidence greases the wheels for action, and then the more you engage in that process, the more confidence you build.'

I agree. Your confidence will grow the more you do, so if you push yourself and try new things, your confidence will grow alongside you. It will say, 'Yeah, we did that before and this was the result, so you know what you're doing this time around'. If you are willing to try, confidence will be waiting for you. If you never try new things, people or situations, your confidence will stay the same – so what is it that you want?

How would I describe my confidence currently?

_____

_____

If I had to rate my confidence now, out of 10, it would be:

_____

_____

I want my confidence to grow to be number __ out of 10:

_____

_____

When I reach that number, this is how I will walk, talk, speak, behave, act and think:

_____

_____

What areas do I feel confident in?

_____

_____

What areas do I need to improve in my confidence?

_____

_____

Confidence for me is all about 3 main areas. I believe if you have these 3, you should be unstoppable. These are, knowing yourself, believing in yourself and trusting yourself.

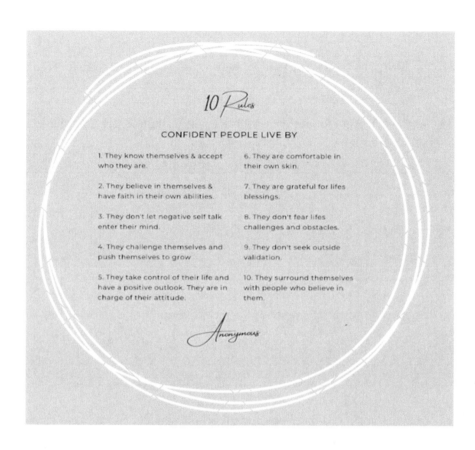

10 *Rules*

CONFIDENT PEOPLE LIVE BY

1. They know themselves & accept who they are.

2. They believe in themselves & have faith in their own abilities.

3. They don't let negative self talk enter their mind.

4. They challenge themselves and push themselves to grow

5. They take control of their life and have a positive outlook. They are in charge of their attitude.

6. They are comfortable in their own skin.

7. They are grateful for lifes blessings.

8. They don't fear lifes challenges and obstacles.

9. They don't seek outside validation.

10. They surround themselves with people who believe in them.

Anonymous

Tony Robbins (2022) states the following:

"Learning how to be confident is important in every part of your life, but there are some instances where it's crucial – especially at times where you feel like giving up. If you are a leader and in a position that requires being convincing and trustworthy, being confident is non-negotiable. No one will follow a leader who appears unsure of themselves. Lack of confidence can seriously impact your ability to put together a winning team and guide them to achieving your shared goals.

Even if you're not in a leadership role, confidence is vital to being a team player in many situations – whether you're in a sales position or need to present a confident face during frequent client interactions. Being confident helps you make instant connections and build relationships that will ensure you and your company succeed.

Knowing how to be confident in yourself is important beyond the workplace, too. Learning how to be more confident can help you attract a partner you can build a healthy relationship with. It can also help you effectively handle conflict and seek out new opportunities that will foster your personal growth."

"Self confidence is a super power. Once you start to believe in yourself magic starts to happen"

Anonymous

Know Yourself + Believe in Yourself + Trust in Yourself = Confidence

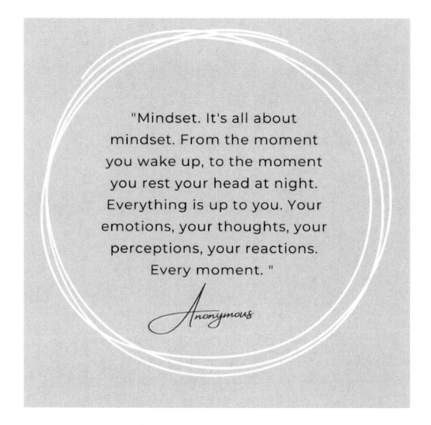

"Mindset. It's all about mindset. From the moment you wake up, to the moment you rest your head at night. Everything is up to you. Your emotions, your thoughts, your perceptions, your reactions. Every moment."

Anonymous

I believe that these 3 are the key ingredient to making confidence a stable skill in your life. It's a mindset and a way of being. Let me say that again, it's a MINDSET and a way of being. A mindset is how you think, behave, act and react. It's a way of being.

An example of this is my mindset – I have a coaching mindset – which means I stay out of judgment, I listen, I remain curious, I see the world from the other person's perspective, I try to avoid assumptions. This is how I choose to "show up" in dealing with others. This is my way of being, my mindset. Of course, I don't always get it right, and I take time to reflect often and think about how I could have done it better / what I need to do differently. This is called self-development. I will always want to be the best version of myself and I'm dedicated to working on that. I'm assuming you are too and this is why you bought this book? This book encourages you at all times to self-reflect – this means thinking about how the situation went, what went well, what didn't go so well, what changes you would make next time and where your accountability was throughout it. Did you play the victim or did you take accountability? I would encourage you to start making a routine of reflecting – it only brings positive personal outcomes. This book will help you do that. I'm not perfect, I work on myself every day. My mindset has come so far – for years I used to judge others. Now I try not to judge anyone else because as far as I'm concerned, until I have lived their life, who am I to judge? But I didn't always think that way… this has taken years of practicing my thinking.

Just a note on staying out of judgment, people judge all the time. It's how we are conditioned as we grow up (fitting the ideal – get married, have 2.4 kids and a career or you are a failure) by our parents, culture, media and friends.

Try not to judge. You aren't perfect and you haven't lived the perfect life, so until you are perfect and you've experienced every situation and scenario in the world, just don't do it. Instead, try this. Just be curious – ask questions that start with "help me understand", avoid assumptions based on your reality and just listen and be present with that person.

I feel sorry for people who judge (and they do it all the time, believe me my followers on Instagram judge without even knowing they are judging). Let me give you two examples of how we judge…

I recently designed my friend's living room and I filmed it for my Instagram stories a few weeks before Christmas. These are some of the messages I received…

First message from a follower, 'There's no Christmas decorations up.'

My friend is currently looking after her dying mum, as well as plan an extension and redecorate the house – there will be no tree this year as she will hardly be at home. Priorities. That comment was unnecessary as there is no value in it, it's not helpful or complimentary. We obviously know there are no Christmas decorations (up as she lives there) and are obviously upset by the fact there are no decorations up, so she took the time to write a message to remind us!!

Next message;

'There's obviously no toddlers in that house!'

She's been trying to get pregnant for 2 years and just recently had 2 miscarriages. The tidy living room was for Instagram, we aren't going to show a messy room, are we? That comment was unnecessary – it didn't add value and was said because they obviously have children and their house is a mess. So their mindset is blinkered, therefore they view the world as they live in it.

These "judgy" comments are judgments without even trying – based on that individual follower's world of what they think something should or shouldn't not look like based on how they live their life…

Just remember, it's not your world they are living in, they live in theirs.

Expand your mindset and learn the skill of curiosity. Ask, ask and ask.

Also, be aware of judgments in your head – your beliefs will become your thoughts, your thoughts become your words…and before you know it, you are judging without even knowing it.

I used to be judgmental – it was a learnt behaviour. Now I'm so the opposite, it's not even funny and I'm appalled by how I used to think. But hey, I now have that experience I can talk about with others, which is all part of our journey right? Not everyone thinks the same way as you! Not everyone believes what you believe! Every single person is different!

> "Your beliefs become your thoughts. Your thoughts become your words. Your words become your actions. Your actions become your habits. Your habits become your values. Your values become your destiny"
>
> *Mahatma Ghandi*

Practice it inside your head, be aware of when you hear a judgmental thought and be aware of it. Try to work around it and play some scenarios through in your head – here's an example – before you message someone on social media with a comment like those above or make a throw away statement to a friend, ask yourself is the comment / thought helpful / useful / supportive / kind?

Consider these…

- Is the other person's behaviour actually your business?
- Is your opinion the truth?
- Is your opinion closer to a hypothesis than the truth?
- Have you experienced what they are going through?
- Are your words, thoughts and actions purposeful or beneficial?
- Do you have empathy?
- Does it matter?

Does it matter is my favourite one – people get caught up in all kinds of nonsense, like scrolling on social media and seeing something YOU don't like and getting all het up about it. Just ask yourself, does it matter? Will it matter in 2 hours or 2 months?

Let me ask you, what's the point of wasting emotional energy on something that's not going to matter in the long term. Just keep scrolling and ask yourself, 'so what?'

If you really think about it, none of it matters. We are on a giant rock spinning through the air…in a universe that is infinite…with a giant ball of energy keeping us all alive. So really…if Bob is planting his petunia bulbs too early, is it worth getting angry and trolling Bob? Sometimes perspective is all that's needed…don't get caught up in it…

Do you argue with strangers on the internet in the comments section? Think about this – do you argue with strangers on the internet? What value does that bring to your life? Ask yourself, why am I arguing with strangers on the internet? What am I trying to prove? (Lots of us do things without thinking. It's now time to start being aware of what we are doing and why).

Just stop and think before judging others until you are perfect you do NOT get the right to judge anyone.

Judging others says more about you than that person…

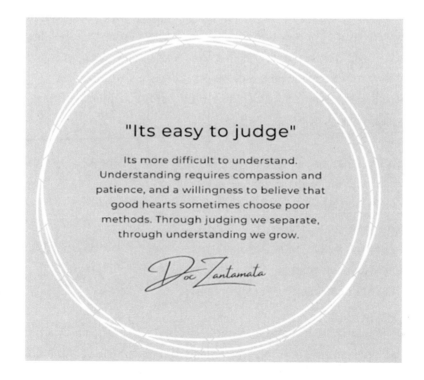

"Its easy to judge"

Its more difficult to understand.
Understanding requires compassion and
patience, and a willingness to believe that
good hearts sometimes choose poor
methods. Through judging we separate,
through understanding we grow.

Doc Zantamata

If you are confident and secure in who you are, you will never want to judge, belittle or ridicule others because you are self-assured. You have enough emotional intelligence to understand when to walk away. You are also aware that you wouldn't waste an hour of your time arguing with strangers on the internet, when you can use that hour to **spend it doing something** you love. Makes sense when you put it like that, doesn't it?

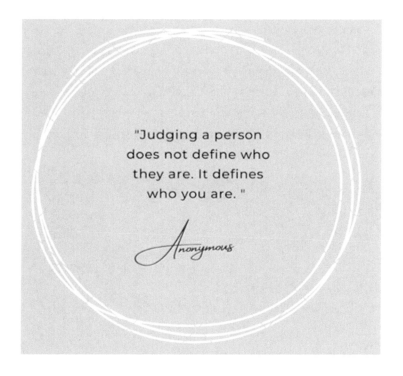

"Judging a person does not define who they are. It defines who you are. "

Anonymous

While we are on the subject of social media, I would like to offer another point of view of which I have first-hand experience in, so I say this with confidence and conviction. All social media is a lie. The most insecure people are the ones who dress up and pose / post the most, facts. They do it because they need the external validation from strangers to make them feel pretty / loved / wanted / confident. Someone who is secure and confident in themselves, does not need validation from followers or strangers on the internet. Let me say that again: **Someone who is secure and confident in themselves does not need validation from strangers on the internet**.

It also goes for the same quote that states, *'You will never be criticized by someone who is doing more than you. You will only be criticized by someone doing less.'* Does this make sense? Think about who trolls who on the internet…it usually fits that statement above.

If you are confident in who you are and what you do, you don't / won't go around criticizing others because you are doing well. This is because you are self-assured and not insecure. If you are not confident, self-assured or secure, you will more than likely criticize others.

Social media is a very interesting place and sometimes not a nice one. I have read stories about young girls who want to be "influencers". One girl went and bought a handbag dog so she could create a page with her and her dog, so She could be "liked" and gain "fame". It worked but what no one realised is that she was abusing the dog, she used the dog literally for photos, never walking it and training it to even go to the toilet, it pooped all over her rented flat (which she didn't keep clean) and eventually went on holiday and left it to die as it starved to death…

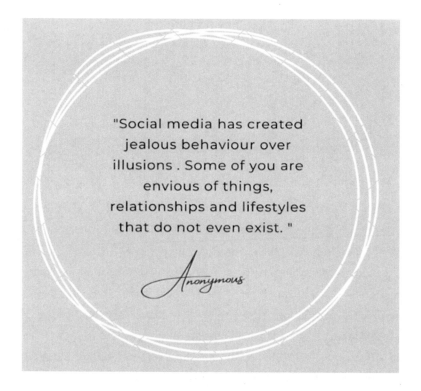

"Social media has created jealous behaviour over illusions . Some of you are envious of things, relationships and lifestyles that do not even exist. "

Anonymous

My point around this is you would have looked at her page and thought this girl was the most popular, confident and happy girl but really it was all a lie and she just wanted likes, fame and influencer deals. She did not actually have the life she was trying so desperately to project to others. Unfortunately believe it or not, this is rife. Almost to the point where girls are literally photoshopping their faces beyond recognition. A celebrity influencer was recently caught on camera saying she takes money for posts but has never tried the product! She endorses it and she HAS NEVER TRIED IT! She was actually mocking the public and it was awful to watch.

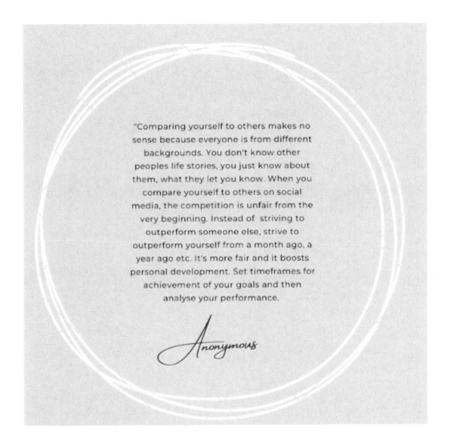

"Comparing yourself to others makes no sense because everyone is from different backgrounds. You don't know other peoples life stories, you just know about them, what they let you know. When you compare yourself to others on social media, the competition is unfair from the very beginning. Instead of striving to outperform someone else, strive to outperform yourself from a month ago, a year ago etc. It's more fair and it boosts personal development. Set timeframes for achievement of your goals and then analyse your performance.

Anonymous

A friend once told me she was at a pool party and some "influencers" arrived. They spent the whole party posing for photos and filming videos for hours on end but didn't actually "enjoy" the party. They were there but they weren't present, they were faking a good time that they never had…it makes me so sad but this is the world we live in now…

To summarize my point here, confidence isn't about seeking external validation – it's about **seeking and acceptance of your own internal validation.**

So, if you want to live a real life, with real confidence and love yourself unconditionally, it means getting to the depths of who you are but more importantly, you want to make that change for yourself and no one else. Do you love yourself? If not, why? I have spent years working on myself, and I know if I don't love myself, I will never be able to love anyone the way that they need.

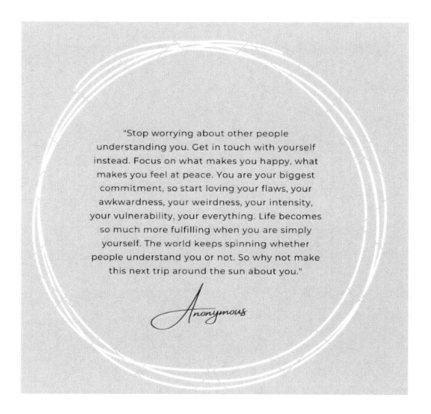

"Stop worrying about other people understanding you. Get in touch with yourself instead. Focus on what makes you happy, what makes you feel at peace. You are your biggest commitment, so start loving your flaws, your awkwardness, your weirdness, your intensity, your vulnerability, your everything. Life becomes so much more fulfilling when you are simply yourself. The world keeps spinning whether people understand you or not. So why not make this next trip around the sun about you."

Anonymous

I also want to add a note about my social media. I started my home Instagram for ideas and ended up with a huge following. (Since I wrote this, my Instagram was hacked, and I have had to start again…) Over the 5 years or so I have had this account, I have had maybe 2 trolls? Most of the energy around my account is positive, filled with love and support. I adore my followers, they are resourceful, supportive, kind and encouraging and I am blessed to have this invisible team behind me. I have nothing but amazing things to say about them all!

Anyway, back to the subject in hand! I am going to ask you to really reach into the depths of your soul and ask you just to be honest with yourself. This takes bravery. You have to want to do this. You have to commit. Be gentle with yourself, take your time and don't pressure yourself. Self-knowledge is the key here.

Without self-knowledge, we are, in general, a liability to be around:

- We don't realize the effect or impact we tend to have on other people: without at all meaning to, we might come across as arrogant or cold or as tending to hog attention or as needlessly shy and hesitant or as getting furious in dangerous ways.
- We may fall prey to unnecessary loneliness: not understanding what we really need and what makes us hard to get to know.
- Difficulties of empathy: not acknowledging the more vulnerable or disturbed parts of yourself; not seeing yourself as" other people in crucial ways. It's hard to understand the deeper bits of others without having explored yourself first. School of life 2022 https://www.theschooloflife.com/thebookoflife/know-yourself/

That's why **knowing yourself, believing in yourself and trusting yourself** is the equation to confidence. You have to feel it and believe it inside yourself – faking it can work sometimes, there is the saying, 'Fake it until you make it,' you have to start somewhere, right? Sometimes faking confidence can actually lead to being confident…its mind over matter.

For example, acting like you are qualified, even if you think you aren't. If I want a promotion, I have to start behaving and acting like I should be in that senior role. I speak to my stakeholders as if I was in that role and ensure my presence reflects my mindset. This is similar to visualization (which I talk about later in the book). I believe this is what is meant by the term 'Fake it until you make it.'

Another way of looking at it, is to keep telling everyone what my dream job is and what that role and what my plans and vision for the area would be. The role doesn't even exist at the minute, but when it does, I know I will be first in line for that discussion. I am speaking it into existence.

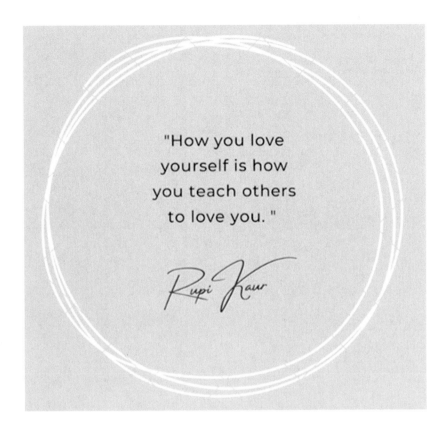

"How you love
yourself is how
you teach others
to love you. "

Rupi Kaur

Working as a coach, one of the main observations around why people lack confidence is that people make assumptions about other people's actions or intent and then create a story around this. We only have access to our own intentions and actions, not anyone else's, so we can only control our own. To go around second guessing everything must be exhausting. We are all adults, if we can't tell someone how we truly feel or tell someone the truth then we are not responsible for second guessing what they might be thinking or feeling. Take what they have said and if they have something else on their mind, trust as an adult they will tell you. It is not your responsibility to second guess anyone's thoughts.

Learn not to take anything personally, it will set you free. Taking things personally is a sign of low self-esteem. When you take things personally, you will be sensitive to the words or actions of others or you choose to interpret things in a negative way. (Key word, choose).

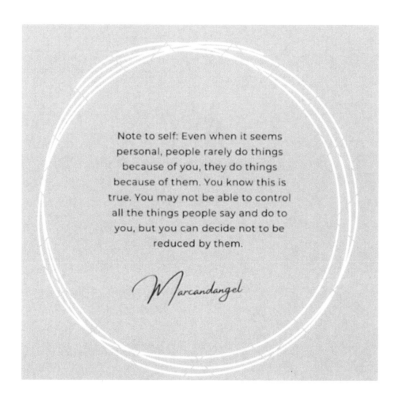

Note to self: Even when it seems personal, people rarely do things because of you, they do things because of them. You know this is true. You may not be able to control all the things people say and do to you, but you can decide not to be reduced by them.

Marcandangel

For example, if you ask a favour from a friend and 2 weeks later, they haven't done it, do you take it personally and start sulking? Or do you pick up the phone and ask if everything is okay? Life is so much easier when you remove assumptions and communicate with curiosity.

When you take things personally, you are trusting someone else to tell you who you are, instead of relying on what you know to be true about yourself; what really defines you as a person without any outside influence. In essence, taking things personally keeps you tied to someone else and, in the extreme, can even make you feel like a victim.

Not taking anything personally and knowing that it's not about you is hugely freeing.

"Don't take things personally"

Nothing others do is because of you.
What others say and do, is a projection of
their own reality, their own dream. When
you are immune to the opinions and
actions of others, you won't be the victim
of needless suffering.

Don Miguel Ruiz

Usually someone else's behaviour is a reflection on them and not you. What I mean by this is if you have had a bad morning for example, say the kids threw up over your work outfit and the dog went to the toilet inside and you had an argument with your partner about whose turn it is to take the kids to the after-school club and your mum is poorly and work is relentless. You may get into work and snap at someone inadvertently. That person may think 'what did I do?' or 'why are they being like towards me?' However, an emotionally intelligent person would think 'I wonder if they are okay, that's not normally like them' and make a mental note to check in on them later that morning and then they go about their day – not holding onto any bad feelings. This person knows that that behaviour was not about them, it was about the other person and what is going on for them. Reframe your thinking!

Here are some tips to help with not taking things personally:

- First of all, start with yourself. Let's hold the mirror up. Were you clear in your communication? Could you have done anything better to help this situation?
- Realize that other people's behaviours or actions are not about you. When someone is rude, it's likely to be a reflection of their own issues. They might be having a bad day, going through a rough period or it might just be their personality. It's important to know that rudeness is not okay and it's not your fault. You deserve to be treated with respect; however, people aren't always nice. While you can't control other people, you can stop taking things personally and instead be kind to yourself.

- You only have access to your own intentions – you can't control others, so let that go.
- Look at what has been said to you – if you choose to view that comment through another lens, what could it mean then?
- You can't please everyone, so stop trying
- Your self-worth depends on you, you can set boundaries, so set them!

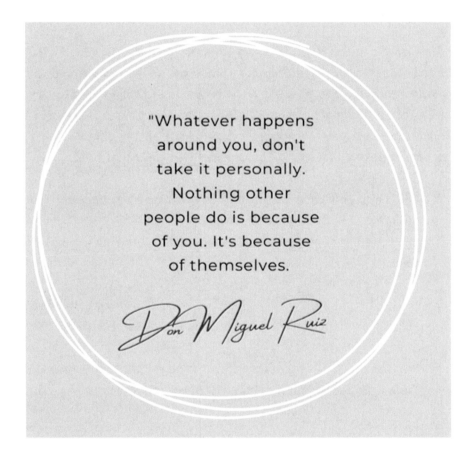

"Whatever happens around you, don't take it personally. Nothing other people do is because of you. It's because of themselves.

Don Miguel Ruiz

I make my boundaries very clear, both at work and at home. For example, let's say I had a partner who wanted to party every night… with my job, that is an impossible scenario for me to even comprehend so I would say 'I don't party Monday–Thursday. My job doesn't allow it. However, if I have the energy I may be up for some events over the weekend. If that person doesn't agree with that or can't work within those boundaries, problems will occur. That is why open conversations around boundaries are so important!

Years ago, I had a friend who mainly declined more or less any social event she was invited to by anyone really. I was feeling bad about this, wondering what I (and my friends) had all done as to why our friend didn't want to come to any of my events, parties etc. I was talking about it with my friends and they suggested that there is something driving my friend's behaviour, as more often than not, people's behaviour is never about you, it's to do with that person. We talked about not taking it personally but more so to find out what was really going on.

Most people often behave in a way towards others that is solely based on them and what is happening in their life – the sooner you learn not to take things personally, the freer you will be. Anyway, back to my friend…we started asking my friend about the situation. It turned out our friend needs lots of alcohol to feel confident (that's the only way she can feel confident) otherwise she doesn't want to be there if she can't get drunk. This creates two main issues:

- She is losing out on making memories, friends and experiences by letting this insecurity and reliance hold her back.
- She can't feel confident unless she is drunk = further issues are at bay here.

When one of my friends, who is closer to her, got the opportunity to speak with her in a safe environment she asked her a few more questions, such as:

- Why don't you feel confident without alcohol?
- What's the main feeling you have when you arrive at a social event and you haven't drunk anything?

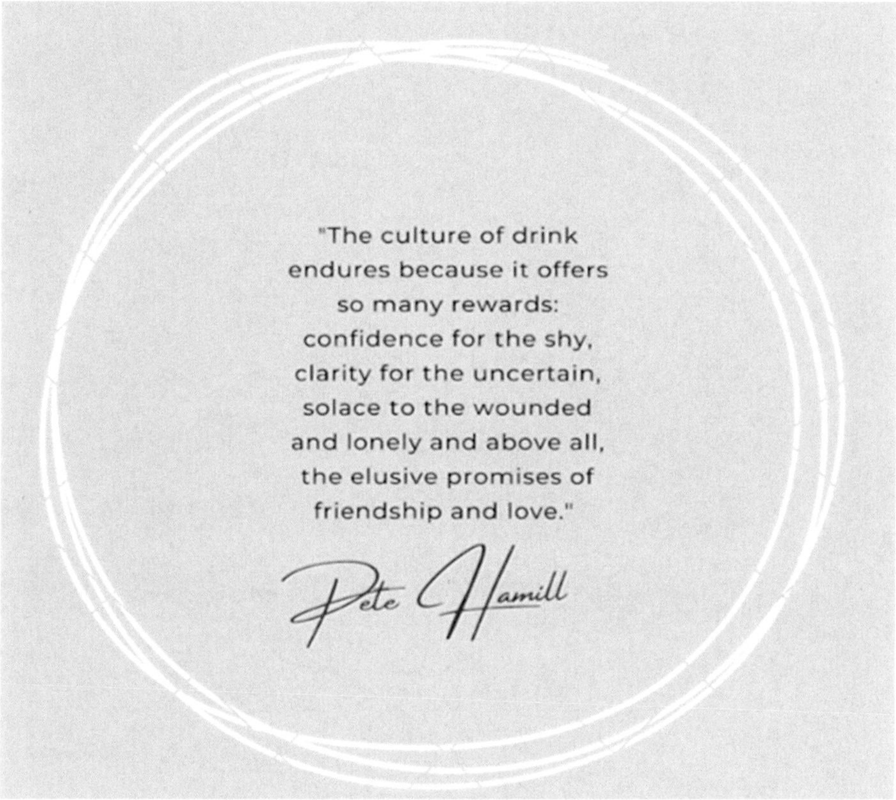

> "The culture of drink
> endures because it offers
> so many rewards:
> confidence for the shy,
> clarity for the uncertain,
> solace to the wounded
> and lonely and above all,
> the elusive promises of
> friendship and love."
>
> *Pete Hamill*

Usually if people have to take something or drink something to feel confident, they are not authentically confident, they are relying on something else to make them feel that. However, that is a dangerous game (having to rely on something to make you feel confident) as it can lead to addiction and even worse patterns. For example, if you drink so you can do your job, then you believe you can't do that job without drinking, it becomes a destructive circle of thinking. You can create a very unhealthy habit very quickly. You start to believe your thoughts when they tell you that you need XYZ to be able to do ABC. The image captures the cycle perfectly:

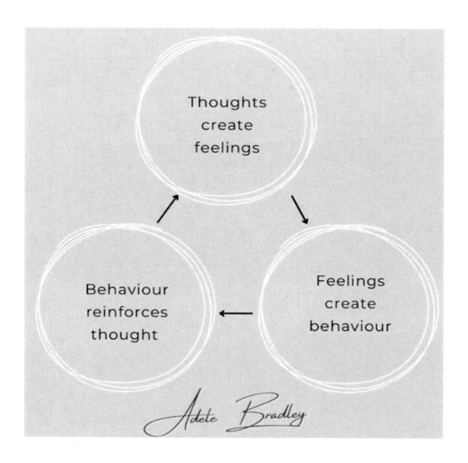

I'm not an expert on addictions but I know how this works. You actually manage to convince yourself you can't do XYZ until you've had just one more drink / just one more pill / just one more line / just one more purchase / just one more smoke / just clean one more thing. It never stops!

You have to find a way to free yourself from this cycle as it is dangerous, reliant and it takes away your power. I believe anyone can change if they really want to, anyone can create a new habit or destroy an old one, it's all about how strongly you want it for yourself or you see the negative impact it has on others around you. You just have to want it more badly than you want your addiction. I will say that again YOU JUST HAVE TO WANT IT MORE BADLY THAN YOU WANT YOUR ADDICTION. (I'm not saying this for all addictions but what I am saying is that mind over matter can be really powerful. I understand some addictions are physical and can't be removed by willpower alone.) And I am not judging either, I completely understand how powerful addictions are…

I would recommend you look internally and understand your addictions, as they come in all shapes and sizes and it's sometimes not just the obvious ones. Look inside and just be honest with yourself as the first step – what do I use to make myself feel confident?

I'm not saying my friend was an alcoholic or an addict but what I am saying is that she found herself with a destructive habit, being reliant on a substance to make her feel a certain way. She may be accepting of this or she may be in denial about it either way, I know she recognizes it. All I can say is that it is down to her to make the change should she want it badly enough.

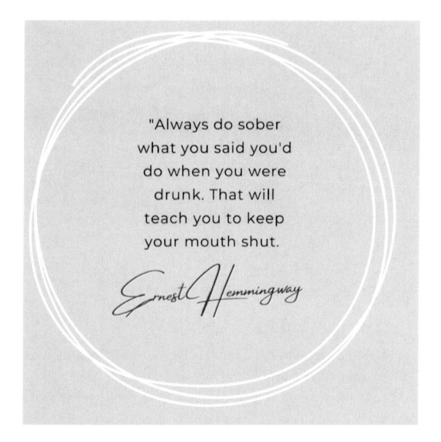

"Always do sober what you said you'd do when you were drunk. That will teach you to keep your mouth shut.

Ernest Hemmingway

So I want to focus on **confidence that comes from within**, that is not fuelled by drugs, alcohol or anything else. I want to focus on the quiet, internal confidence – the one that you can trust and the confidence that no matter what the situation, you can handle anything.

This won't happen overnight. We have a path to walk and all I can ask is that you are truly honest with yourself when you read and complete this book. I know you have an internal voice and compass and even though you can tell yourself all the stories in the world, you and only you know the real truth. If you are in denial (which a lot of people can be and denial is a safe place because no one can get you there) you will know the truth in your heart.

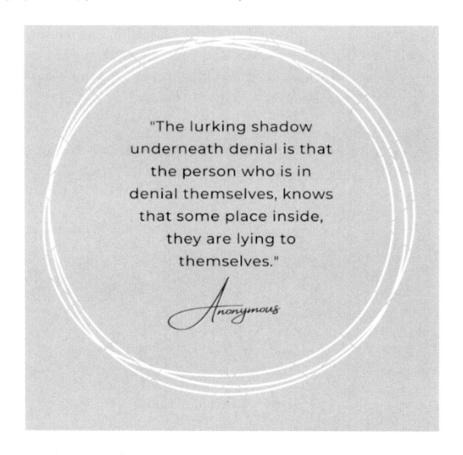

"The lurking shadow underneath denial is that the person who is in denial themselves, knows that some place inside, they are lying to themselves."

Anonymous

One thing I find really useful (and this is also good for anyone stuck in denial) is using the change curve to help me understand why I am feeling what I am feeling and understanding where I am on the curve. Listen, we all go through the change curve, maybe even 10 times a day.

Kubler-Ross Change Curve 2002 (or stages of grief as you may know it)

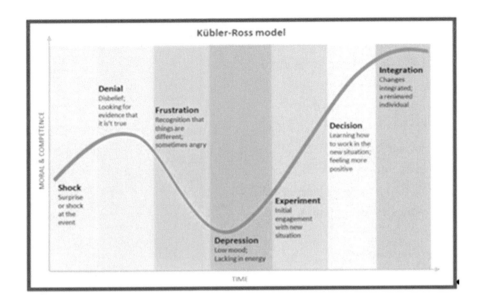

For example, getting to work and realizing you left your mobile at home:

Shock: OMG, where's my phone! OMG is it???

Denial: DO NOT tell me I've forgotten it!

Anger / frustration: OMG, it's on the side I know exactly where I left it, why I am so stupid!

Depression: I miss my phone :(

Reflection / Experiment: Well, I wasn't expecting any important calls anyway!

Integration / Acceptance: Oh, it's okay, I have the work phone if I need it!

That could take about 3 minutes to go through but like any change, it can take 3 seconds, 3 hours, 3 days, 3 months or 3 years!

Knowing the stages of the change curve can really help you get to know yourself. Next time something happens to you, remember this diagram and note your feelings as you move through them. Throw yourself back to a time when a change happened to you. If you look at how you felt, did you see yourself moving through the stages?

Stage 1: Shock

When change is first announced, people start off in shock. You feel numb and unable to react in the first instance. It might be a sudden gasp of 'Oh my god!' or stunned silence.

Stage 2: Denial

It may take time for people to process the news and consider its ramifications. You may refuse to engage with the reality of the situation. It can often be a stressful and difficult stage for all concerned.

Stage 3: Anger / Frustration

When the reality of the situation can no longer be denied, people may become angry. This anger might be directed at yourself, or others. They may lash out and seek to blame other people as a defense mechanism for the discomfort they feel. Of all the change curve emotions, this one has perhaps the greatest potential to cause damage in team relationships.

Stage 4: Depression

This is the lowest emotional point in the change curve. People are likely to be experiencing loss, doubt and confusion as well as fear, regret and even guilt. It may depend on the individual as to how this manifests itself at work but at this stage, you may become withdrawn and disengaged and have difficulty focusing on work.

Stage 5: Experiment / Decision

In the fifth stage, we began to engage with the change but not in a constructive way. People bargain or look for trade-offs. Our might be impractical or unrealistic and are a means of seeking to manage the change so that it does not adversely affect us; in other words, there's still an element of denial in their approach.

Stage 6: Acceptance / Integration

At this stage, people stop focusing on what has been lost. They begin to rationalize and take steps towards adapting to the change. This stage often sees a rise in morale, engagement and performance. These are positive signs but remember that it is possible for us to regress to an earlier stage at any time.

Kubler-Ross

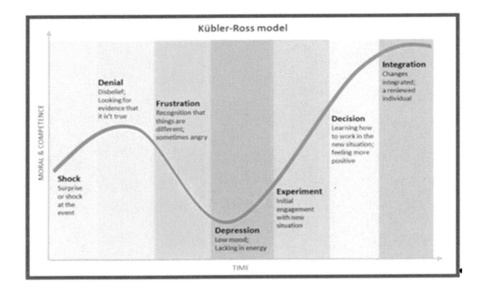

I also like this SARA model too:

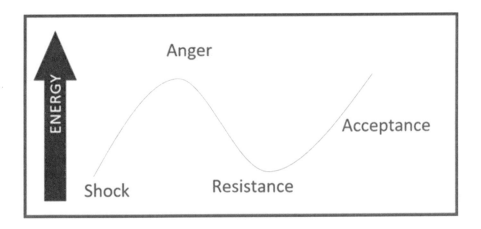

For anyone struggling with relationship break ups, grief, job loss, major change or internal growth – understanding you are progressing through different emotions along the curve at different times is all normal, we all do it.

However, some of us can get stuck in the change curve and never make it to acceptance – from things like knowing you are gay but being in denial about it or constantly being stuck in anger because your child was born sick, eventually those feelings will make you ill or even depressed. It is because you are stuck in the curve and things are left unresolved.

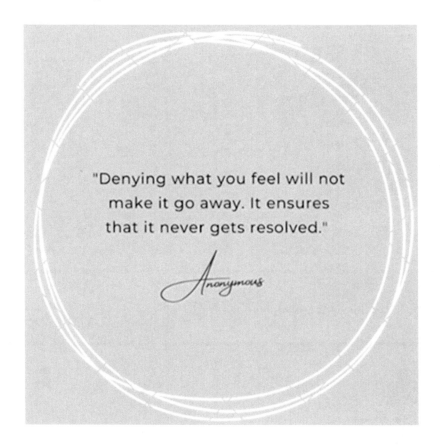

"Denying what you feel will not make it go away. It ensures that it never gets resolved."

Anonymous

If you find this happening to you (or is happening) I have a question that may help you:

What do I need to do to move along the change curve? Or get someone to ask you, what can I do to help you move forward?

Like I said, you have to be honest with yourself and that is scary but you know what's scarier? Never knowing who you are and your full potential because you are letting something hold you back.

Talking about holding onto things, we also need to look into that. If you are holding onto something (and it's weighing you down) if you fundamentally let that stop you from living the life you potentially could, you also have to ask yourself some pretty hard questions.

Why are you holding on to it and by holding on to it, what value or pleasure does it add to your life?

_____

How does holding on to it make you feel?

_____

What would you feel like if you could "let it go" and deal and acknowledge it in different ways?

_____

"They always say time changes things, but you actually have to change them yourself."

Andy Warhol

If you can use the change curve to help, then great. If not, here is a quick, easy and simple way to help:

- Write a list of everything you are worrying about / holding on to
- Cross out everything that is out of your control (and stop thinking about it)
- Do something about what you can control
- Ask for help to do something about them if you need it

- And SUMO what is left (shut up and move on) which is LET GO!

You can only control yourself – you cannot control other people, situations or environments – so if these places or people don't serve you, change your environment, situation or people you surround yourself with. Only you can change, so relinquishing expectations of others is hugely freeing.

Let me say that again – if you have expectations of others in your head, it will be you who is disappointed and let down. Release your expectations of others and take them as they are. No expectations = can't be let down!

Makes sense but it takes some practice! If you read Stephen Covey, 7 Habits of highly effective people, the chapter on reactiveness and circles of influence can really help.

To me, holding onto something makes me visualize me walking around with a huge sack attached to me that I'm dragging everywhere I go. If I let it go, I instantly feel better.

Do me a favour, go and grab a cup or a water bottle…just hold it out in front of you. How does it feel? Probably like nothing and easy to do but what if I asked you to hold it out in front of you now for 5 full minutes.

What would happen? What about holding onto it for 5 hours? The more we hold onto things, the more it hurts us. Learn to let go. It will change your life for the better. I promise.

Letting Go

At some point you just have to let go and move on. It mighe be the hardest thing in the world to do, but you have to summon all the strength you possibly can to finally let go. Some people and things just aren't going to be meant for you, not matter how much you wish they were. Some jobs and situations just won't work out, no matter how much you hoped they would. But know its okay for things not to work out. Nobodys life is a straight line that makes perfect sense. Everybody has twists and turns and has to turn around every now and then. So when you find yourself wishing and hoping things out of your control would change, summon all the strength to let go and start heading in the new direction because it'll lead you closer to your truth path.

When it's not forever 2017 states:

https://www.whenitsknotforever.com/blog/why-you-should-learn-to-let-go

'If you're able to let go and start accepting things as they are instead of how you'd like them to be, you'll find that you'll suffer less from the problems of stress, emotional ties to the past or future, frustration with others, struggles with loss and succumbing to fear. By letting go, you'll set yourself free'

"The root of all of our problems is our inability to let go"

– Lee Babauta

I am learning more every day about my feelings. I recently learned something from my friend who is a qualified yoga teacher. She says it's always best just to feel the feeling and let them run through you. Don't try to hold onto them, just "be" with them. Remember, nothing is permanent in life :)

So PLEASE be honest with yourself as that is where your real growth in yourself, in confidence and in life will occur.

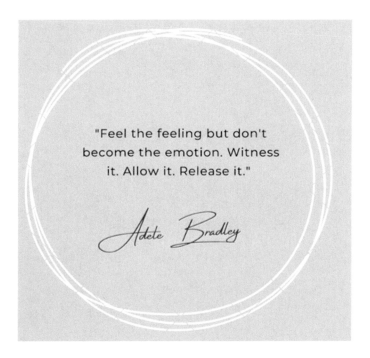

"Feel the feeling but don't become the emotion. Witness it. Allow it. Release it."

Adele Bradley

Just to note – you cannot 'force' anyone to let go of anything – they have to be responsible for that. Even if you have had the same experience and you have let it go, it doesn't mean that others will magically 'let it go' – so telling someone to 'get over it' because that's what you did, is quite frankly abhorrent and unhelpful. And more than likely – you didn't 'get over it' – it probably manifested in your behaviour and what you believe as 'letting it go' was probably you behaving or acting in a toxic way and having no awareness of this at all. Think before you speak and judge others.

Just to note – it's about perspective here – letting go of the fact you were stuck in traffic for 9 hours instead of talking about it for years, maybe you need to understand why you are holding onto that?

As part of our confidence journey, we will look at a few areas and then get into the formula for success, the true equation of confidence. I touch on arrogance, ego and confidence but we also need to see where assertiveness fits in this.

You can be confident but lack assertiveness, which means missed opportunities and missed 'I wish I had said / done that' moments and we all know those right?

You have to be able to find your voice, even when you don't think you can, and make it happen for yourself. You just seize the moment "carpe diem" otherwise you will regret it, play it over in your mind, 'what if I just…'

"Sieze the day or die regretting the time you lost."

Anonymous

Let me put it this way, if you don't ask, someone else will and they will end up with the opportunity. An example of this was one busy day in London, me and my friends were going to a very popular Instagram cafe. As we arrived, there was a queue. (I hate queues, I try to avoid at all costs) which was fairly large and was outside snaking around the building. I asked some people in the queue, 'Do we queue here? What are you queuing for?' They just shrugged and said a table. I decided something wasn't quite right (more on intuition and gut feel later), so I walked past the queue into the cafe and just asked someone, 'Do I need to queue?'

The assistant said, 'Oh, no, not inside seating but outside seating, yes there is a queue for that. Do you want to come in?'

Let me ask you a question, how many of you would have just stayed in that queue? Staying in it for over 30 mins when you could have been sitting inside all warm and toasty? Sometimes you just have to use that assertive confidence and ask!

We've all been that person that "just joined a queue" only to find it was the wrong line or a complete waste of time, so what's wrong with being assertive and asking? A lot of people may internally cringe at this and if that's you, that's fine. But you will never push past into the realms of true confidence if these situations make you squirm, you might actually want to be confident and dream about what it is like but when it comes to it, you prefer your un-squirming comfort zone. It comes down to the fact that if you embrace the uncomfortableness, that is where growth occurs and this is where confidence arises.

Assertiveness

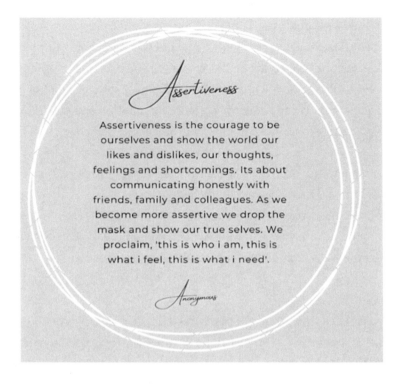

Assertiveness is the courage to be ourselves and show the world our likes and dislikes, our thoughts, feelings and shortcomings. Its about communicating honestly with friends, family and colleagues. As we become more assertive we drop the mask and show our true selves. We proclaim, 'this is who i am, this is what i feel, this is what i need'.

Anonymous

Learn how to be assertive, learn how to ask for what you want and once you see the results, the thought pattern will be positively reinforced.

Here are some hints and tips on assertiveness:

- Learn to say "NO" without over explaining yourself
- Make sure you have your say "your opinions matter"
- Practice saying NO
- Keep control of your emotions
- Speak simply and directly, don't over complicate it
- Set clear boundaries
- Stay calm
- Learn how to be okay with saying NO
- Body language matters
- Create a mantra. Mine is: 'if you don't ask, you don't get'

It's okay to ask but if they say no, also handling rejection with poise and ease is vitally important too. A grateful smile and a thank you will go a long way, and even jokes can help too. If someone says no to me, I usually say, 'well if I didn't ask I wouldn't know' and they usually laugh and agree.

You might want to ask yourself too what scares me about rejection? (This is part of knowing yourself) and then work through any issues you identify. Face your fear and reject negative self-talk.

What holds me back from being assertive?

_____

_____

How can I be more assertive?

_____

_____

Do I fear rejection? If so, why?

_____

_____

Becoming

Be strong. Be kind. Be free. Do things that make you proud of yourself. Surround yourself with people who bring out your best qualities, and distance yourself from people who do the opposite. Be true - true to yourself and true to your morals. Stand up for yourself. Don't let people take advantage of your kindness and soft heart. Don't take shit from anyone and don't put yourself down. Believe in yourself and believe in your journey. Be good to yourself. Be unapologetically you. Embrace your imperfections. Accept the fact that when your grow sometimes you loose people and thats okay. Celebrate your every success and learn from failure. And most importantly, never, ever, let anything stand in the way of the woman you are becoming.

Charlotte Freeman

Boundaries

It's important to note that as you are working on your assertiveness, this is where you can assert your boundaries – and boundaries are important to your confidence journey. If you can't tell people 'no' – how do you define and maintain your own boundaries?

'Boundaries are a way to take care of ourselves. When you understand how to set and maintain healthy boundaries, you can avoid the feelings of resentment, disappointment, and anger that build up when limits have been pushed.' psychcentral.com

Psychcentral also state:

Boundaries can take many forms. They can range from being rigid and strict to appearing almost nonexistent.

If you have more rigid boundaries, you might:

- keep others at a distance
- seem detached, even with intimate partners
- have few close relationships
- not interested in impressing others

If you have more loose or open boundaries, you might:

- get too involved with others' problems
- find it difficult to say "no" to others' requests
- overshare personal information with others
- seek to please others for fear of rejection

Boundaries with Yourself

- Having a bedtime.
- Deciding the maximum amount of time you can dedicate to work every week.
- Setting limits on your screen time.
- Having an amount of times per week you move your body.
- Limit when you drink alcohol or how much.
- Keeping a budget.
- Deciding on vacation days and sticking to them.
- Going to doctor and dentists appointments regularly.
- Paying bills on time.

Amanda. E. White

"In a nutshell, it's knowing how to separate your feelings or 'stuff' from someone else's," says U.K.-based psychologist Dr. Tara Quinn-Cirillo. "As human beings we have our own thoughts, memories, and lived experiences, and sometimes that can become very blurred with someone else's. Boundaries are healthy for helping you identify and keep that space."

Examples of healthy boundaries include:

- Declining anything you don't want to do
- Expressing your feelings
- Removing yourself from situations that don't serve you
- Addressing problems directly with the person involved, rather than with a third party or gossiping
- Making your expectations clear rather than assuming people will figure them out.

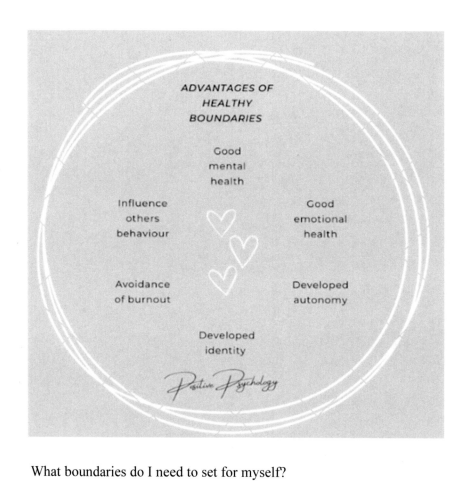

What boundaries do I need to set for myself?

_____

_____

How will these boundaries help me?

_____

_____

Why Is Confidence Sexy?

Confidence creates an aura that draws people in. Because many people lack high self-esteem, they are intrigued by people who have high levels of confidence. They want to learn how these people live their lives with hopes of emulating their energy. (Elite Daily 2022)

Some people say that confidence is the most attractive quality someone can have!! This is because it shows everyone how you feel about yourself, your energy, your body language, your internal thoughts all will shine through in your confidence. It tells a story. It will say, this is a person who has their shit together, shines bright, knows what they want and knows how to get it and I trust them.

Confident people tend to be positive people (no one wants to spend their time with a mood hoover) and because they are positive people they are not easily influenced to join in any negativity, so they keep a good energy around them.

Self-confidence says, 'I accept myself on every level' SEXY.

You know what it's like, we've all been there. At a bar (or office) when someone walks in with a spring in their step and a glow about them, smelling good and looking good. They turned heads and you looked! I mean I do think some people are born with the sexy gene (and believe me, lots of men and women I have met have NONE!) and some are not that blessed. But it's down to confidence, the more things you try and the more encouraging your friends / partners are / is, the more confident you become in your own self and sexiness!

One thing to remember, if you are in bed with your dream partner, they fancy you! That means big bums, bellies, cellulite, whatever, they don't care! If they did, they wouldn't be naked in bed with you, would they? I think getting to know yourself physically is also important, how can you tell your partner what works if you don't know yourself! Spend some time getting to know yourself intimately, it's all part of building confidence in who you are. Being able to express your needs is vital for a healthy relationship.

"No matter what a woman looks like, if shes confident, shes sexy."

Paris Hilton

During some of my external research, I found this quote from a gentleman posted on Quora in 2021 and I just loved it:

A person who exhibits self-confidence is also saying:
I'm a healthy, well-rounded individual and I do not need you to validate or fix me. I have everything I need already, and I'm being healed in areas of my life that have been wounded. I love who I have become and I feel good about my life and the choices I make.

How awesome is that description! That statement to me says everything! Do you feel like that in your soul? Do you love yourself?

This book will help you get there…

I then started reading everyone else's descriptions and I had to share them with you:

'Confidence is usually considered and treated as generally sexy because it is a trait that triggers primitive instincts in people'

'Sexual attraction is very primitive. The females of the charismatic carnivores from humans on down, look for ability to provide and protect as basic skills for a mate. Acting confident is a sign that you are competent to do this. As soon as you screw up big time, you'll have some explaining to do.'

'Confident people seem to know what they want and are not afraid to ask for it or go after it. Nor are they afraid to express themselves. Apparently, this is quite a turn on in the bedroom. They say.'

'A confident person is an indicator for a possibly healthy and potent human being that is not easily shaken by outer forces and influences. A strong person that radiates confidence triggers the need for protection instinct and at the same time inspires and motivates the receptor to behave in similar manners. It is a radiant characteristic that is not easily ignored and that is seriously taken upon consideration by your instinct for possible mating and replication. Evolution works through the survival of the strongest, right?'

'It seems that confident people are noticeable. They stand out. They have a certain air about them that makes you want to get to know them. You want to know what makes them so self-assured. They're intriguing and we're beguiled.'

'Nothing yells sexy more than a truly interesting brain and realistic, existent capabilities. Anyone can be as flamboyant as they want but even seemingly unconfident people hide an attractive mass of interesting traits inside their brain and their spirit.'

'I personally prefer the truly unshakeable type of person that has realised their humanity but does not let life intimidate them in any way. You can spot those sexy beings from miles away. They are usually that calm force presence that stands out in a room full of (possibly lousy) people just by being themselves and shading their energy around space. That's sexy.'

'A confident person is one of the most attractive people in a room, whoever else is in there. Looks (to a surprising degree) go out the window when someone is truly confident in themselves. It's magnetic.'

Let's take a look at the alternative. People who lack confidence are generally insecure. They're often apprehensive and anxious. Many need constant reassurance and attention and take a great deal of energy. How attractive and sexy is that?

Think about it, someone who is confident, happy and secure in themselves is intriguing. It makes a girl wonder what could possibly be so fascinating about this confident guy and makes her want to discover more. A confident person is also easier to approach and talk to.

So people find confidence sexy. If that's not motivation to apply the equation to confidence, I don't know what it is!

Remember, it's the way you walk, talk, hold yourself, the way you laugh, the stories you tell, the eye contact you give and the way you move your hair.

Stand in front of a full-length mirror and strike a few poses – find which one makes you feel the best and embrace it!

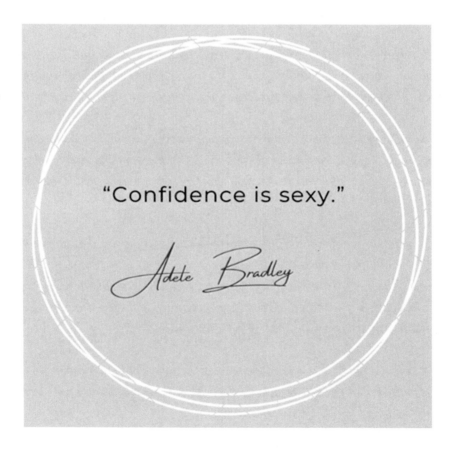

"Confidence is sexy."

Adele Bradley

Meet mindful 2022 gives the following reasons why self-confidence is so sexy, which I wholeheartedly agree with:

Self-confidence is attractive

There have been countless studies done on what attracts us to each other, and while we might not always agree on what that is, one thing's certain: we go where we feel pulled. And people with magnetic energy do the pulling. We're not talking about charm here, necessarily. Self-confidence doesn't need to schmooze or manipulate because it broadcasts a person's full-on acceptance of who they are without trying. Self-confidence says, 'I accept myself on every level' and invites us all to do the same.

Self-confidence is complete

Without needing to explain itself or ask for permission to take up space in a room, self-confidence means you're good enough as you are. My friend Liz (and, let's face it, lots of us) believed she wasn't complete unless she had someone by her side to validate, support and save her. It's what led her to face her life from a limited perspective. Given that mindset, no matter what she did, she believed she'd always be lacking. Fortunately, she gained the confidence that enabled her to unlearn the old story. She realised she was enough, and that she could indeed love, validate and rescue herself.

Self-confidence is powerful

The ability to direct the course of our lives isn't always in our hands, no matter how in-charge we believe ourselves to be. Catastrophe, surprise, drama, the weather and other people's agendas can influence the paths we ultimately take. Having the wherewithal to harness our own inner resourcefulness is a large aspect of self-confidence because it's what informs our response to life as it happens. It reassures us that we're safe, resilient and ready for the world.

Self-Confidence Is Accepting

Even as our relationships may cause us to question our judgment at times, self-confidence reminds us that whatever mistakes we make, no experience or time spent is ever lost. Self-confident people accept themselves for who they are…flaws and all. Self-confidence gives us room enough to rise from the ashes and take the lessons with us into flight. When we accept ourselves as my friend

Liz eventually did, it opens our ability to have compassion for the struggles other people face. It softens our edges, ignites our ability to forgive and unleashes our capacity to love deeply. (Mindful 2020)

Sexy confidence draws you in…you are attracted to it. It is alluring to you and it turns you on…

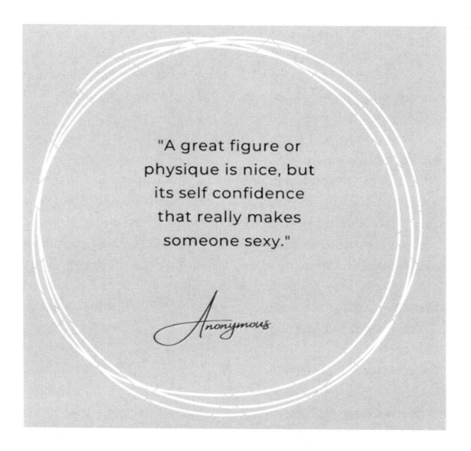

"A great figure or physique is nice, but its self confidence that really makes someone sexy."

Anonymous

There is a theme that isn't there and it starts with you and your mindset.

When somebody has true confidence in themselves, it conditions us to arrive at certain conclusions about their personality and lifestyle. And it's usually associated with positive things.

If you're not that sure of yourself and you see one of these people, you might feel threatened. That's because it's not about the confident person, it's about how you felt inside when you noticed them. Something to think about…

Think of the sexiest person you know…

What do they do differently?

_____

- What makes them sexy?

_____

- How would you describe them? If you want to be like that, visualize it and make it happen!

_____

Here are some tips to help you feel sexier to really enhance your confidence:

- New clothes / shoes / bag, if you feel good you will look it!
- Sexy underwear, freshly shaved and smelling good…
- Always have a good story to tell in your back pocket. Everyone loves a story!
- Have a few jokes up your sleeve
- Practice a sexy dance routine in your new underwear
- Walk around naked, enjoy looking at your body, and admire it. Embrace it! It's the only one you have!
- Wear clothes that make you feel incredible.
- Be inquisitive, show a genuine interest in others around you.
- Complement others
- A hair cut / spray tan / nails, feeling and looking groomed is great for self confidence
- Do dancing lessons, pole / salsa / tango, whatever makes you feel sexy, you won't know unless you try right?
- Practice good body language, stand up straight, walk with purpose.
- Let go of what others may or may not think
- Eliminate negative self-talk
- Do a lap dance
- Smile, relax and enjoy
- Get to know your body
- Experiment with your partner
- HAVE FUN!

"Confidence in bed
is sexy as hell."

Anonymous

Confidence Is an Energy

Einstein said, '**everything is energy and that's all there is to it. Match the frequency of the reality you want and you cannot help but get that reality. It can be no other way.**'

Can I just say…Einstein said that! Einstein! He was a scientist! I believe him. Do you?

"If you want to find the secrets of the universe, think in terms of energy, frequency and vibration."

Nikola Tesla

All matter and psychological processes – thoughts, emotions, beliefs and attitudes are composed of energy. When applied to the human body, every atom, molecule, cell, tissue and body system is composed of energy that when superimposed on each other create what is known as the human energy field (massage magazine 2022)

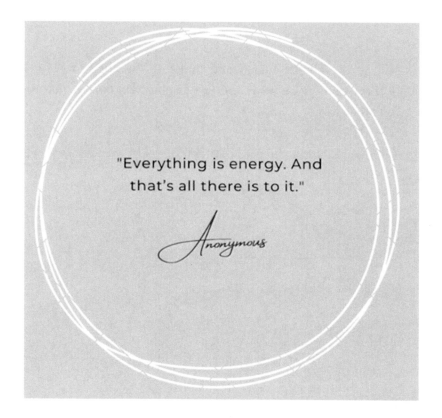

"Everything is energy. And that's all there is to it."

Anonymous

We are all energy. If we could see energy we would be eternally distracted because it is everywhere. Some people can even see energy. They have a gift.

When you feel sad, you radiate sad energy, same when you are happy, sad, confused, scared, turned on, intimidated, confident, angry, calm or worried. You radiate energy all the time. You know when someone is behind you or you look up because you feel something and someone is staring at you. That is you feeling that energy.

Some people are more in tune with how to control their energy than others, I believe that is self-awareness and knowing yourself on a deeper level.

If you can harness your energy and understand it more, you will unleash power you weren't even aware you had.

One of my favourite descriptions of confidence came from Sharon Salzburg, who's a Buddhist expert. She said, 'Confidence is a kind of energy and it has the ability to move toward things wholeheartedly without holding back. I think sometimes we spend too much time judging whether we're ready for something or worrying about it. What if we just assumed that we were ready and started taking action? When you interact with others, you sense and respond to their energies, the same as they respond to yours.'

I would like to recommend you try "The Rice Experiment Love / Hate" (go, google it now!) It's two empty jars, both with a half cup of water in the jar and 3 cups of rice each. Label one hate and one love and every day say into each jar LOVE words and HATE words into the other. (Like, I love you, you are beautiful verses I hate you, you are ugly) The hate jar should go mouldy quicker – try it!! Or watch the experiments on YouTube where they have the metal fillings on a sheet which is hit by a frequency they form a pattern, it's truly incredible!

'Every object has a characteristic frequency or frequencies at which it vibrates most, with the least input of energy. Those vibrations are associated with standing wave patterns called modes. When the Chladni plate, for instance, vibrates in one of its modes, a pattern appears in the sand on the plate.'

(Science Friday 2022)

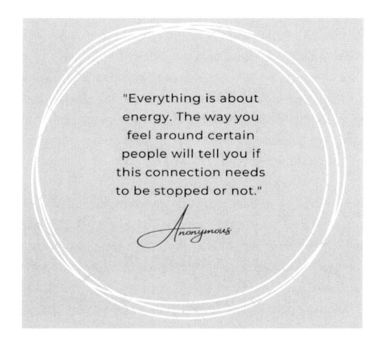

"Everything is about energy. The way you feel around certain people will tell you if this connection needs to be stopped or not."

Anonymous

There are four types of energy: (that we are aware of ... yet)

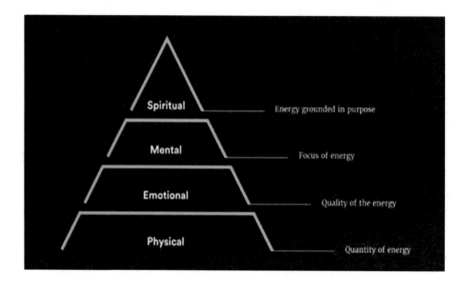

- Physical energy is how tired we feel and the things that directly affect it include exercise, sleep and diet.
- Emotional energy is the time we spend connecting and interacting with others. Positive and negative emotions and your ability to be self-aware is critically important for our relationships at work and home.
- Mental energy includes our mood and our cognitive work and engagement. Mental tasks can drain or energise us but sustained levels of concentration can leave us feeling drained or mentally tired.
- Spiritual energy 'is what we get from doing something meaningful to us, something that speaks to our spirit – it can take the form of wisdom, compassion, integrity, joy, love, creativity or peace [2].' It makes sense that we are increasingly observing leaders seeking workplaces that can support purpose-driven values. (HCLI 2022)

You give out energy all the time – through your thoughts, your behaviours and your moods. We all know a person who has walked into the office and you can tell that their energy is 'off'. We can tell – we comment on it all the time. (She seems off today, wonder what's wrong? / He seems to be in a funny mood)

To be self-aware is to be confident – so I encourage you to observe your energy and how it impacts others around you. (Just like other people's energy affects you).

Which energy are you most in tune with?

_____

Which energy do you use most?

_____

What do you know about your energy? Are you a moody person? A happy person? A sad person?

_____

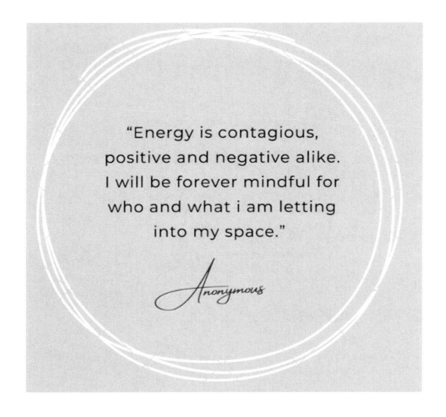

"Energy is contagious,
positive and negative alike.
I will be forever mindful for
who and what i am letting
into my space."

Anonymous

*'Discovering and living your personal brilliant purpose brings energy,
fulfillment and wellbeing into your life.'*

– Dr Jim Loehr

Energy can also be known as presence, making yourself small, large, intimidating, calm, hyper or any other emotions by how your energy radiates from you.

You can stop a room of people talking just by standing and sending out energy. You can hype up a room just by using your energy. There is an art to it and it takes practice. Have you ever seen someone command attention without doing anything? They are simply using their energy.

Your confident energy will radiate from you sometimes without you even knowing. It will show in how you walk, talk, stand and behave. It radiates from the inside out. So, it's important to start tuning into yourself internally, really digging deep to create that energy of feeling confident, which will then seep out of you for others to pick up on. I promise you it's worth it.

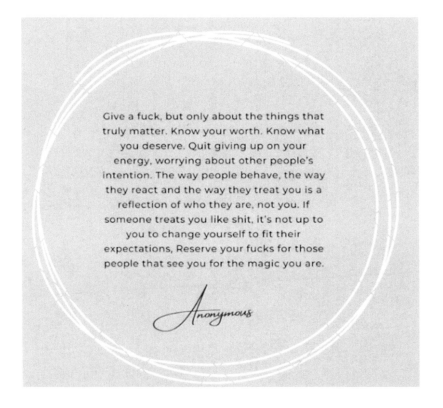

Give a fuck, but only about the things that truly matter. Know your worth. Know what you deserve. Quit giving up on your energy, worrying about other people's intention. The way people behave, the way they react and the way they treat you is a reflection of who they are, not you. If someone treats you like shit, it's not up to you to change yourself to fit their expectations, Reserve your fucks for those people that see you for the magic you are.

Anonymous

Tips for Tuning into Your Energy

- When you're out of balance, drained or have absorbed any negative external energy from your environment, it translates to your aura. Our auric body is composed of particles (just like anything else in this world), and the vibrations of these particles correspond with different meanings and colours.

- Imagine a strand of Christmas lights. They'll be turned off until they're plugged into a power source. When your aura is foggy, it's because there's a lack of energetic flow and your colours aren't as vibrant. They look hazy and give off a static vibration that inhibits you from operating with a clear mind. (Mind Body Green 2022)

For me this translates to eating well, looking after yourself, keeping a good and healthy lifestyle and avoiding toxic environments. If you feel clean, your aura energy will shine brighter.

By doing this, it helps you manipulate your energy. I also love using crystals. I have a huge collection and they are like my babies. I place certain crystals on my chakras for healing and cleansing and I love the thoughts that are from the earth, and radiate positivity! I am also a reiki master practitioner – energy healing – this also helps tune into how and what I'm feeling. I know I wanted to explore the energy concept more, so Reiki seemed like the right place to go.

If you want to learn more about crystals and their properties, start off with a few and study them, get to know them. I can recommend a few books that have helped me:

- The Little Book of Chakras – Elise Wild
- The Power of Crystal Healing – Lucy Knowles.

Whatever makes you feel confident, eh?

To learn more about your own personal energy, you have to practice. Here are a few hints and tips from Gwyneth Paltrow's Brand, Goop to get you started and I recommend you watch Love, Sex & Goop on Netflix, specifically the one on energy!

Helpful Tips in Getting to Know Your Energy System: *(Goop 2022)*

Note: This is a process of becoming aware. You can't do it all at once so embody a spirit of curiosity and be willing to go slow.

- Thoughts are forms of energy. Become aware of your thinking. Start with your first thought of the day and go from there. Make a list. Notice your word choice and where your thinking feels fixed (this is how it is) or flexible (this is how it could be).

- Throughout the course of your day, just stop. Close your eyes. Go inward and feel into where you are. Do you feel present? What is the nature of your breath? Are you holding it? How do you feel in your body? Restricted? Relaxed? Tired and collapsed? Awake and alive?

- Move. Move your body. Different parts at a time. What happens when you move? Notice if any thoughts or feelings come up. Are there certain parts of your body that when energised by movement, stir something up in you? Do you feel you need to contain your energy or do you let yourself move?

- Make a sound. By yourself, or with others, let your voice out. Energise your "yes" and "no." Notice if one is easier than the other. Are you even willing to make noise? Just notice without judgement.

- Where are there forcing currents in your life? Where do you feel a relentless demand of yourself or another? Where are you forcing your will onto people or situations?

- What happens to your energy in the presence of others? Take note of your breath and your body. Do you expand or contract?

- Play with boundaries. Find a friend willing to explore energetic boundaries. Stand a certain distance from each other. As one of you steps towards the other, notice when you begin to feel their energy. See what happens to you as another's energy enters your own energy field. Do you lose yourself at all? Do you feel less grounded? Do you feel you can use your voice and speak up and ask her or him to come closer or back away?

- Make a list of different feelings. Free association with each feeling. What is your relationship to that feeling? What are your beliefs or images about those feelings? Where do you tend to feel those feelings, if at all, in your body?

- Where are you most comfortable meeting the world? Do you lead with reason (thinker), emotion (feeler) or will (doer)? If you lead with one, how do you feel about the others? What parts of your body do you meet the world with? Your head, heart, hands?

- Seek another's experience of your energy and observe the energy of others. How do you feel in their presence? Are you invited in or kept at bay? Do you feel they hold back, hold in, hold up, collapse or scatter their energy? Tune in and feel into it. Don't figure it out, feel it out.

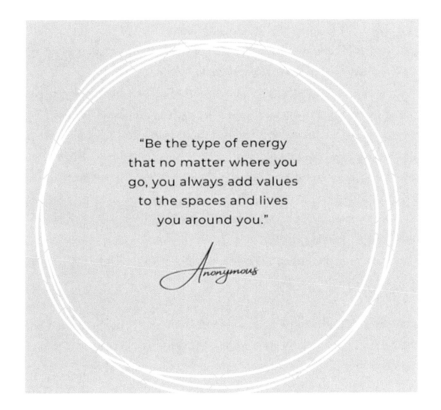

"Be the type of energy that no matter where you go, you always add values to the spaces and lives you around you."

Anonymous

I always find that if my energy is low, a walk in the sunshine with the dog does wonders. I have started to notice myself more and my thoughts more when I'm out walking. I actually feel my energy quite a lot in the palms of my hands when I'm out walking…I'm learning to listen to my body just by noticing how it feels. I sometimes feel like I could shoot fire out of the palms of my hands, like a superhero! I do wonder what us humans are capable of if we have NO distractions. Like millions of years ago. No work, no commute, no mobiles, just thoughts and energy. I wonder what we are able to do with focused attention! I know I'm going to keep experimenting, researching, learning and understanding what I'm capable of. I don't think I will stop learning. There's a LOT of years of research. I mean we could start the debate about the pyramids and how they were built…

I'm in no rush and I look forward to what I'm going to find out. I'm totally open minded to the whole universe!

According to Anthony Meindl (2022) he states:

'Our energetic frequency is naturally joyful and expansive but we rarely hook into that state because we let our habituated way of thinking about things drive our natural frequency down. So, we get stuck at lower levels of energy and forget we're these powerful positive forces of nature.

So, if we begin to see that the causal nature of our reality is generated by where we spend most of our time frequency-wise, we can work on changing that. Smile more. Be nicer. Breathe. Accept. Surrender. Stop beating yourself up. Relax. Enjoy. Laugh. Every time you want to take the Brain Drain Train and obsess for hours over something you did (or didn't) do, what if you just chose to let it go instead.

These acts immediately change our frequency. They move us from energy of resistance and fear and worry to trust and acceptance and love. https://www.anthonymeindl.com/blog/we-all-have-an-inner-einstein-figure-your-frequency-out-first-to-find-it

As part of getting to know yourself, understanding your energy and how you use it to be confident is key. Remember, you control your energy and not the other way around. Learn to harness your energy and see what you are capable of. If you fidget a lot, it's because you haven't channelled your energy correctly, so it's out of control. Learn to sit really still and control your energy. Just being present and still. You could try this through meditation, or even in a work meeting. By being more still, channeling your thoughts and energy can be a game changer. Or you could socialise and meet more people who know how to harness their energy, learn from them!

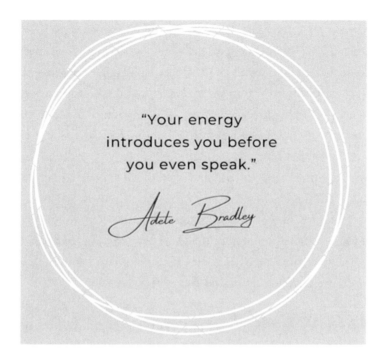

"Your energy introduces you before you even speak."

Adele Bradley

When it comes to energy and the 'life force' within you, Thrive Global 2022 state the following:

There are some effective techniques to practice in order to tap into the positive goodness of Life Force Energy:

- **Practice acceptance.** Following the laws of nature, the law of least effort as nature teaches us, we need to learn how to accept people, situations, circumstances and events as they occur. This kind of acceptance will raise our Life Force Energy. Within the flow of Universal energy lays the wisdom of uncertainty – which allows us freedom from our past, and from the known. By being willing to step into the unknown, we enter the field of all possibilities – a place where we can surrender ourselves to the creative mind that orchestrates the dance of the universe.

- **Practice awareness**. Each level of energy vibration holds your own particular resonance. Some of us create with conscious awareness of this process. But others continue to live life unconsciously. To live a conscious life is to become aware of our own thoughts, actions and deeds.

- **Let go of limiting beliefs**. It is easy to raise our Life Force Energy when we view ourselves as consciousness rather than as separate bodies and minds. If we want to experience the joyful divinity of every present moment, we will need to let go of any beliefs that limit and distort it.

- **Allow happiness.** When we are lost in our emotions, we are unable to experience higher levels of energy. We may refuse to feel any happiness if certain conditions are not fulfilled during life experiences. But we set those conditions ourselves. Many emotions can distance us from our own happiness and we will never find the answer to our experiences solely with logic.

- **See thoughts and words as actions**. The moment you have a thought, you have created an action, the same way that the moment you speak you have created an action. Just as a deed is an action, thoughts and words are creative actions as well. They are all energies at a level of creation.

- **Overcome your feeling of separateness**. Feeling separate from others is an illusion: in fact, we are one spirit, one with all energy, and even one with all matter. But feeling apart from others and from the forces around us causes us to become fearful and develop defence mechanisms that lower our Life Force Energy and seriously obstruct our happiness.

- **Feel the energy, name the emotions and celebrate these milestones.** When someone asks how we are feeling, we often answer vaguely: "bad" or "unhappy", "upset", "disturbed", "negative". It's important to be more specific when describing our emotional state. We also want to feel our energy level. Each time you take a moment to feel your energy and name the emotions accurately that either heighten or lower your energy level, you reach another milestone. Celebrate these milestones by recognising them and slow down to feel what is true for you, instead of simply answering with an automatic, habitual response. Try to feel things fully on emotional, physical and energetic levels.

'Few of us have intimate contact with our Life Force Energy. But the quantity and quality of our energy flow deeply affects all parts of our lives, our emotions, thoughts and reactions. The quality of our relationships, productivity, creativity and health all depend upon our being able to create a high level of harmoniously flowing energy. Our inner harmony is deeply affected by our relationships with

those around us, and the opposite is even truer: our relationships with others will simply mirror our relationships with ourselves. By practising these seven steps, you can become more conscious, of and more connected to, the transforming power of the Life Force Energy within all of us. '(Thrive Global 2022)

I am a firm believer in energy. When you are confident inside and out, you have a "different" aura, it radiates from you. This is pure energy. Notice it, feel it and work with it.

Remember, we all vibrate on different frequencies, so stay with others who have a high vibration that matches yours (you can tell when you just meet someone, it's that instant "click") and your gut usually tells you too. Listen to it! I have learnt to play with my energy, I can dial it up or down instantly depending on the situation. If I'm 121 coaching or facilitating a room full of lively people, I can switch my energy accordingly to get the best out of the situation. Learning how to tune into and use your energy involves you getting to know yourself. To spend quiet time playing and understanding your energy, practising it and exploring and learning about yourself, it's about tuning into who you really are. This in turn will dramatically improve your confidence levels.

I accept that some people might not want to go that deep but if you are going to be truly confident, inside and out, it's something to think about!

Want to know a quick way to test your energy?

Find a nice space with some quiet time. Taps the ends of your fingers together for about 15 seconds, and then rub your palms together and then slowly pull them a few inches apart until you can feel the energy in between them. Like a marshmallow feel. Or light pins and needles. That's the first step. Just being able to feel the energy you can create. (I usually have a crystal in my palm when I do this, whichever you choose is fine, they all have great energy.) Now you can feel that heat, just be aware of it! Stand up and move slowly and with purpose and see how it feels to you. By doing this simple exercise, you are getting to know more about yourself! This will then create a glow of confidence within you because you really are starting to understand yourself better.

You will notice as you read this book that I keep pointing you to the same things over and over again. This is because these areas are the ones that will help you, so find the key messages and themes and make notes throughout, what is a recurring theme?

Become who you are

I was recently reading Daily Laws (day, 29th January) by Robert Greene and I had to share it with you as it really resonated with me:

'Some 2,600 years ago the ancient Greek poet Pindar wrote, 'Become who you are by learning who you are.' What he meant is the following: You are born with a particular makeup and tendencies that mark you as a piece of fate. It is who you are to the core. Some people never become who they are; they stop trusting in themselves; they conform to the tastes of others, and they end up wearing a mask that hides their true nature. If you allow yourself to learn who you really are by paying attention to that voice and force within you, then you can become what you were fated to become. an individual, a Master.'

This is your time to become who you truly are. It's the phrase "own it". Who you are is unique, no one else is you and that is your power! This is self-acceptance. This is self-love. This is a total embrace of you and your soul. YOU ARE YOU for a reason and you can't change your makeup, so we have to learn to love it like we love a cute puppy, enthusiastically and genuinely. We often spend way too much time hating ourselves, or wishing things were different about us – what if we liked ourselves instead and stopped focusing on what we don't like and celebrate who we are!

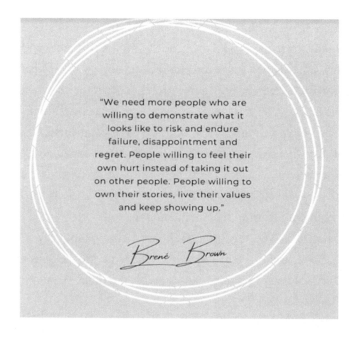

"We need more people who are willing to demonstrate what it looks like to risk and endure failure, disappointment and regret. People willing to feel their own hurt instead of taking it out on other people. People willing to own their stories, live their values and keep showing up."

Brené Brown

There is a certain level of vulnerability that comes with this. What is vulnerability? You are open with others about your truth. You are open and by being open you risk the possibility of attack. The possibility of being hurt – like when we fall in love, we make ourselves vulnerable as often we can put our key to happiness or trust in someone else's hands. And that makes us vulnerable.

"Vulnerability is not winning or losing; it's having the courage to show up and be seen when we have no control over the outcome. Vulnerability is not weakness; it's our greatest measure of courage.'
"People who wade into discomfort and vulnerability and tell the truth about their stories are the real badasses."
Brene Brown 2018

I believe to be vulnerable is to let people see into your soul – and that's OK, you know why? Because nothing in life is guaranteed, so if you do start a relationship and you are worried about it won't work out – you can change your thinking. Instead of thinking that, you can think 'do I trust myself enough to know I can get through this if it doesn't work out?' OR one of the best descriptions I heard of love: 'Giving someone the power to destroy you and trusting they won't use it … or trusting yourself to cope if they do'

Vulnerability comes with having confidence in who you are, what you are about and how you deal with things.

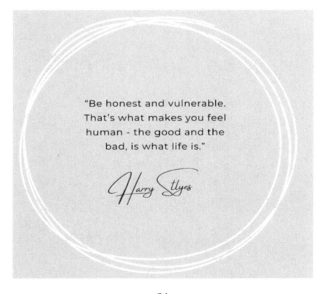

"Be honest and vulnerable.
That's what makes you feel
human - the good and the
bad, is what life is."

Harry Styles

I thought I knew myself properly for a long time, but now, at the grand age of 41, I know exactly who I am and I'm okay, you know! I keep having people tell me on my Instagram and at work that I'm inspirational, that's possibly the best compliment I've ever heard! Now I have proof (even though I have over 3 renovated houses as proof!!) I am really starting to feel it in my soul. I have completely embraced who I am, faults and all. I am proud of who I am and the women I've become. (and still becoming… I am evolving every day) It's been a battle to get here but boy was it worth it! And I'm excited for the future, I can't wait to see what else I can achieve!

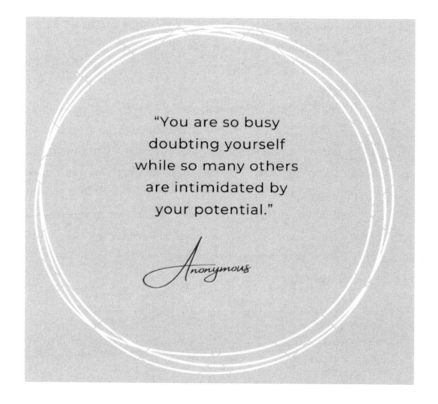

"You are so busy
doubting yourself
while so many others
are intimidated by
your potential."

Anonymous

EMBRACE WHO YOU ARE TODAY

"Don't waste a second of your life thinking that who you are at this moment is not good enough. Because who you are today is the sum of *all the steps* you've taken thus far in your life.

"It is the product of all the experiences you've had, all of the love you have given, all of the growth you've endured. All of the *low and high* moments that gave you a new way of thinking. Who are you today is who you are supposed to be."

"This present moment is all you have, it is what will determine the future, so why waste it thinking that you're not good enough? Instead surrender to this moment and become the *best version of yourself* you can be.

Anonymous

I also loved this quote from Psychology Today:
https://www.psychologytoday.com

'*Perhaps we are all always works in progress. To become who you are does not mean that you reach a height where no more change is needed. Truly, you never arrive at a destination where you can simply be who you are. You must always be in the process of becoming. To be born is to begin dying. To become who you are is to always be in the process of dying to one way of being so that you can become something else.*'

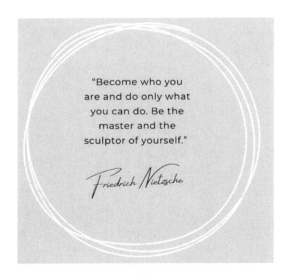

"Become who you are and do only what you can do. Be the master and the sculptor of yourself."

Friedrich Nietzsche

Whether you are introverted or extroverted, bold or shy, direct or indirect, creative or not creative, you will have a quality that is yours and yours only – rather than deny yourself this strength, why not use it, embrace it and be proud of it?

Who do I need to become?

What do you need to 'own'?

TWO VOICES,
ONE WINNER

There are always two voices in our minds, one that comes from a place of SELF DOUBT and one from a place of SELF CONFIDENCE. Some days our self doubt voice clouds and all of the positive words we think to ourselves, and other days our self confident voice overshadows any negative though that runs through out minds.

We may tell ourselves we're not good enough, that it'll never work out, that we'll never get to where we want to be, that we're not worthy and we might ask ourselves, what will others think? Simultaneously, we tell ourselves we are capable, that it will work out, that we're on the right path to achieving our goals, that we don't care what anyone things and that somehow we will get through whatever we're experiencing.

Our minds will always have constrasted voices - it is NECESSARY to experience BOTH SIDES of the SPECTRUM. Without one of the other, we will never be MOTIVATED, INSPIRED or RESILIENT. Be doubtful, but only use it as a TOOL to GROW.

Analyse yout thoughts. Discover the frequency of both sides. Choose to NUTURE the voice that EMPOWERS you and let that voice win.

Ego Vs Arrogance Vs Confidence

Ego comes from self-interest. Arrogance comes from superiority of one's own self-worth. Confidence is an internal and external belief in your strengths and knowing your weaknesses.

They are all vastly different but can get very easily mixed up or blurred.

The ego is a very interesting quality. I have watched a lot of videos and read a lot of articles and the main theme is that ego provides us with awareness and protection. Don't get me wrong, we need our egos, but on the same hand, we need to keep our ego in check.

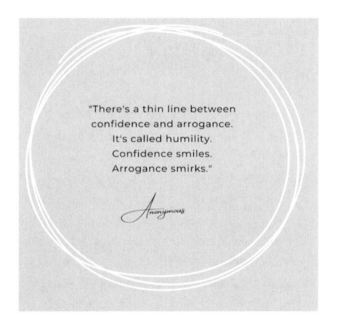

"There's a thin line between confidence and arrogance. It's called humility. Confidence smiles. Arrogance smirks."

Anonymous

Could you imagine being a world-famous pop star and basically everyone you ever meet tells you how incredible you are? Your fans, your staff, your record sales are through the roof and you sell out tours? You have that fed to you

24/7. It's going to shape how you see yourself. That's why certain celebrities are seen as "divas". It's all they are used to!

What you do with your ego is down to you, it can help you but it can take over you. I would highly recommend being self-aware of your ego and the impact it has on you and others around you…

Arrogance is the need to convince yourself and others that you're good at what you do. Of self-worth and self-importance and it looks like superiority.

I have been on dates before where the guy is just telling me how amazing he is. Bragging about this, that and the other… (personally, I just like to show people how good I am at things, rather than telling someone). However, we all know one of these people, those people that insist on telling you how amazing they are, that they have done everything you have done but better, faster or quicker. I always wonder when I'm in these situations why they feel they need to insist on how good they are and why. I mean, if you are really good at something, you shouldn't need to brag about it, as hopefully you've created a reputation where other people are doing it for you! I just find it confusing because when you are getting to know someone, you don't just get to know them overnight, it's a long process, years even. So, if I meet someone for the first time and they are ramming down my throat how good they are, it looks more like insecurity to me, hiding out as arrogance. Does that make sense? Because if you were completely secure in who you were as a person (internal confidence) you wouldn't have to do that because you are totally secure in who you are. I am secure in who I am.

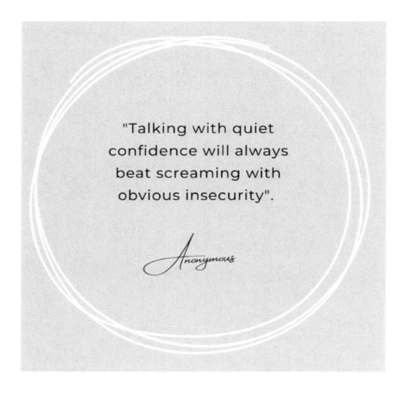

"Talking with quiet confidence will always beat screaming with obvious insecurity".

Anonymous

Questions to ask yourself:

Am I arrogant?

_____

Am I egotistical?

_____

If so, why? What am I insecure about?

_____

Something else to note – you can have too much confidence! I recently met someone who firmly and utterly believed they were really great at something they did – they even convinced me they were. They truly believed they were the 'expert' at what they did. Let me tell you – the reality was not that! They were not good at what they did – yet they believed they were. Delusion springs to mind here – along with that, a few questions popped into my head – have they ever asked for feedback? Were people truthful in providing the feedback? Did they care about feedback?

You have to understand your abilities – and be honest about them. How do you compare to the experts in your market and where are you compared to them? What do you need to do to truly be that expert and not JUST THINK you are.

Types of Confidence

Being confident doesn't mean being loud and bold. Quietly confident people can be the best and let me tell you why. They don't go around bragging about how good they are, they just show you. This is everything because if you are confident and you know you can do it; you don't need to brag right? A saying I love is "let success be your volume". I've met loud people who talk a good game, but when it gets down to it, they don't perform and lack credibility.

Saying that, if you look at some athletes – you'll see them hyping themselves up to perform. Everyone uses confidence differently. Just take a look at a boxer's entrance into the ring!

I'm generally a loud person but I never brag about how good I am at my job, I prefer to show people, my mantra, actions speak louder than words!

Some people are loud with their confidence. Maybe that's their style? I used to be loud when I was younger but that because I lacked self-awareness and I didn't give a f**k. If you are self-aware, you will undoubtedly know you don't have to brag about how good you are at something, however, self-awareness is what a lot of people lack!

"True confidence has no room for jealously and envy. When you know you are great, you have no reason to hate".

Anonymous

Remember: Let success be your volume, you have nothing to prove to anyone if you truly know who you are! And remember this too, the louder your confidence, the more it looks like ego or arrogance ...

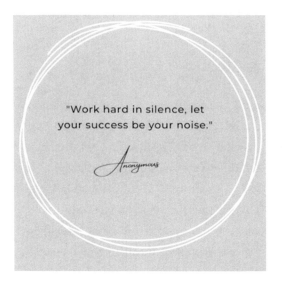

"Work hard in silence, let your success be your noise."

Anonymous

Do I seek validation – if so why?

_____

Is my confidence loud or quiet?

_____

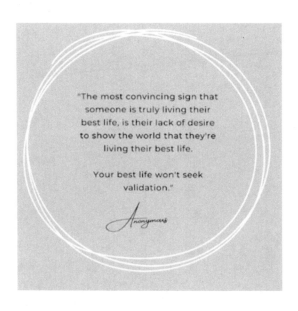

"The most convincing sign that someone is truly living their best life, is their lack of desire to show the world that they're living their best life.

Your best life won't seek validation."

Anonymous

Confident Body Language

"You show confidence and feel confident with the right body language."

Anonymous

How do confident people walk, talk, behave, smell like, act like, behave like? Who do you see that exudes confidence that you would like to be like?

If you walk tall, with purpose and meaning, it is noticed, just like you have noticed others.

So how do you currently hold yourself? If you feel confident within, it should automatically shine through. All us girls (and some men) know that a good fake tan and a pair of eyelashes can transform our confidence. It's because it makes us feel good about ourselves (a tan can do wonders, believe me). For some other girls (and guys) it might be working out makes you feel confident or dressing a certain way. We all want to look good, take care of our appearance, as it creates confidence. You wouldn't go to an important meeting looking scruffy and tired, you would want to make a good impression!

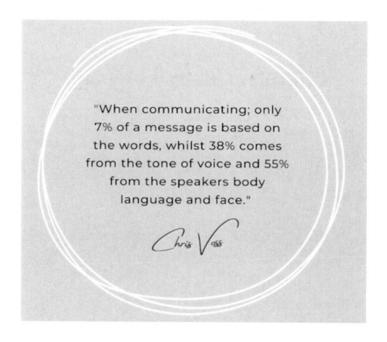

"When communicating; only 7% of a message is based on the words, whilst 38% comes from the tone of voice and 55% from the speakers body language and face."

Chris Voss

By looking at your body language now, you can assess what you need to work on. Do you slouch? Look at the ground when you walk? What have you noticed about your body language? What do others think of your body language?

How do I currently:
- Walk
- Talk
- Sit
- Move
- Listen
- Behave
- Interact

Business trends 2023 state:

'The ability to walk into a room and exude self-confidence that communicates your commitment and trustworthiness is essential in business interactions. Each gesture can say a lot about who you are, how you're feeling, and how much you care about the work you're doing.'

"You are in control of [the message] you are sending out," Barbara Pachter writes in her book *The Essentials of Business Etiquette*. "If you project a confident, credible, composed image, people will respond to you as if you are all those things."

Are your nonverbal cues sending the right message? Do you appear approachable by maintaining eye contact and using gestures that make others feel at ease? Are you leaning forward to listen and engage?

Tips for body confidence

- Keep your chin and your head up
- Stand up straight – no slouching
- No fiddling or fidgeting – stand or sit calm and still
- Breath slowly and steady
- Use eye contact always
- Remove your filler words "ummm" "ummm"
- Think about the position of your feet when standing, do you rock / sway or move your feet nervously? Try planting themes firmly on the ground!
- Use gestures – I could write a whole book on gestures; they are SO important. Here is a brief overview:
- A good handshake is important (ever had a wet lettuce hand shake?)
- Use your gestures meaningfully – we all talk with our hands, so move them with purpose. If you want to highlight something important you are saying, use your hands to do this. Try it in the mirror first so it starts to feel natural and you can see the movement.
- Smile – it unarms people.
- Use the room accordingly.
- Walk with purpose

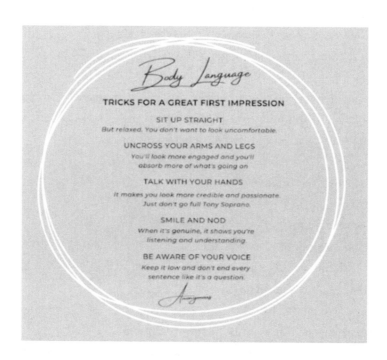

Body Language

TRICKS FOR A GREAT FIRST IMPRESSION

SIT UP STRAIGHT
But relaxed. You don't want to look uncomfortable.

UNCROSS YOUR ARMS AND LEGS
*You'll look more engaged and you'll
absorb more of what's going on*

TALK WITH YOUR HANDS
*It makes you look more credible and passionate.
Just don't go full Tony Soprano.*

SMILE AND NOD
*When it's genuine, it shows you're
listening and understanding.*

BE AWARE OF YOUR VOICE
*Keep it low and don't end every
sentence like it's a question.*

Imagine this, you are walking down the street on your own and you see a group of youths, and you have to pass through them. What happens to your body language? Do you make yourself smaller or bigger or stay the same? What happens to you inside? How does this manifest on the outside?

I always hold my head up high and I say hello as I walk past. It usually unarms them and I get a hello back. Your body language sends out signals all the time. Whatever is usually going on the inside will manifest on the outside – so the term fake it till you make it stems from this, pretending on the outside whilst not really feeling it on the inside.

Make sure you make eye contact with people. Ask yourself, when people don't make contact with you, what do you think and how does it make you feel?

Eye contact shows you are confident! Eye contact is an important nonverbal social cue because it projects confidence, self-esteem and assertiveness.

'Overall, adults only make eye contact 30 to 60 percent of the time when speaking to individuals or groups, communications-analytics company Quantified Analytics tells The Wall Street Journal.'

"Meaningful eye contact has the power to transcend time and space to connect us with others and can be one of the most gracious and important ways to demonstrate attention and respect."

Anonymous

According to a study from the Idiap Research Institute, eye contact shows a person's social hierarchy and dominance in a conversation. The study found that people who are at the top of the pecking order tend to look longer at their subject and they also receive more eye contact in return. (CNBC 2022) https://www.cnbc.com/2017/08/17/how-making-eye-contact-can-help-you-appear-more-confident-at-work.html

Like any other social skill, eye contact gets easier the more you do it. Start by practising with people you feel comfortable around, such as close friends or family members. You can then try making more eye contact with people who intimidate you slightly, such as your boss or senior co-worker.

As you've probably noticed, it's often harder to maintain eye contact with someone who intimidates you. On the other hand, it's usually easy to maintain eye contact with someone when you are in a position of power over them or when you feel "better" than them in some way.

'When we improve our self-esteem and mentally position ourselves on an equal level **to those we come across, it becomes easier to maintain eye contact.**' (Social pro now 2022)

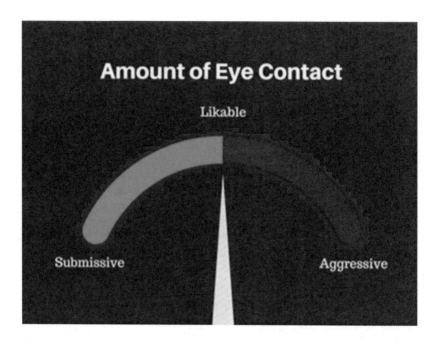

As a coach, it's absolutely essential to maintain eye contact at all times. This shows the other person I am truly listening to and in their moment with them. If I did not maintain eye contact, the relationship would fail. It is vital I demonstrate I am listening and show I am present all the time. This has really helped me with others and maintaining eye contact. I thought it was weird at first to look someone else in the eye for a full 90 minutes but it works! This part of getting out of your comfort zone and being comfortable with being uncomfortable …

Of course, I'm not suggesting you "stare someone out" but what I am saying is that looking someone in the eye whilst talking to them demonstrates true confidence. It shows the other person you have the ability to really see them. It can unnerve some people – people who aren't usually confident!

"Listening is something that happens as much with the eyes as with the ears. Convey your attentiveness and respect for your client by listening with both. The first time you meet a client, be sure to look at him or her clearly and directly, eye to eye. Eye contact is the single most powerful way to communicate care and interest."
https://www.lawtechnologytoday.org

Ask a friend to have a conversation with you. As both of you converse, ask your friend to take three different postures:

- Facing you, looking directly at you;
- With his or her back to you; and
- With his or her side to you, not looking at you.

Notice your emotional reaction to each of the three body postures, what impact do they have on you and why?

This has more to do with behaviour when you are not confident. When people are not confident, they are possibly unsure of what they are conveying, they may be trying to portray something that isn't true or they may be nervous / scared of something. In either case, the person avoids eye contact.

This is largely because maintaining eye contact is intimidating. People often use the phrase "look me in the eye when you say that as" an intimidation tactic. It leaves you vulnerable to judgement and let's read you better.

"The are of eye contact"

Adele Bradley

Let's face it, when we have been out in a bar or a club, I'm sure we have all made eye contact with someone we found attractive, right? It is because we want to catch their eye and strike up a conversation. Eye contact can be very intimate.

When you're the one talking in the group conversation, you want to make sure that everyone feels seen by you.

Why? Because ignoring someone for more than just a few seconds makes them feel like they aren't part of the conversation. When two or more in a group conversation feel slightly left out, the group is soon divided into several parallel conversations. Try to divide your eye contact evenly among the people in the group.

The more you can demonstrate positive, strong, confident body language, the more confident internally you will feel. It's a mindset.

Confidence in Work

Confidence in your work comes from experience, which is learning from your mistakes, learning from what went well and learning what you would change. If you have never done a job before, you won't feel confident as you will be outside your comfort zone.

If you aren't going to have confidence in yourself, why would anyone else? You can't expect people to support you unconditionally if you do not believe in yourself wholeheartedly.

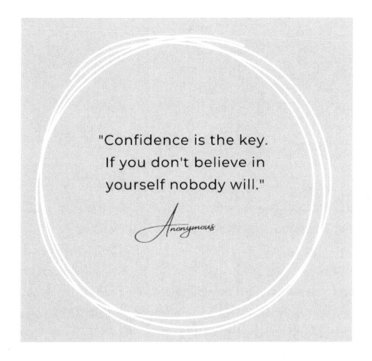

"Confidence is the key. If you don't believe in yourself nobody will."

Anonymous

If you aren't confident in your views and convictions, how can you expect others to listen to what you have to say?

Our work colleagues are not daft, we all have built inbuilt, (or BS detectors in other words) and can smell a fraud a mile away. This will instantly diminish all credibility within your workplace and you will soon get a reputation, so don't try it!

Study your craft, learn your job, learn it well. Understand what good looks like in your job and go for great. Continue to read, create a self-development plan and never stop learning.

"When you are *confident*, people become confident in you."

Anonymous

Everyone respects a person with confidence because with it, you are basically investing your heart and soul into something you feel passionately about. This will raise your own levels of self-esteem. High self-esteem also comes with a skill...the ability to think positively! Think about it, how much time do you waste wishing you were better or moaning about the fact that you don't have more of the things you want in life. Confident people can use this time and brain power in more effective ways. They focus on the positives!

Let me just say something, you can be confident in work based on your technical ability. So, for example, let's take someone in IT, they may be a superuser whizz on a certain IT platform and knows all the answers. People would perceive this person as confident in their abilities, so perceived in work as confident. However, this person may have crippling anxiety and be so shy when it comes to dealing with the opposite sex. Confidence in your job does not mean you are confident everywhere else. Confidence in your job does not mean that you know yourself too...

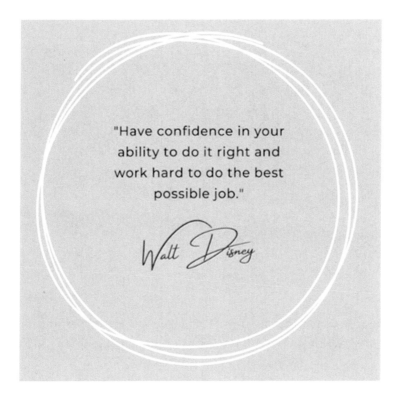

"Have confidence in your ability to do it right and work hard to do the best possible job."

Walt Disney

Being able to reflect and learn from our mistakes made in the workplace (and in life) is KEY to confidence. I have had some major catastrophes in my early career, all of which I have taken as a lesson learned and used these mistakes to help me become better and better at my job. And to be a better person too. A better leader. A better colleague. A better teammate.

It's also okay to not know what you're calling or "job purpose" is – some of us don't really achieve this until later in life or like me, stumbled across a career completely by accident. If you don't know what your calling is yet, keep exploring, keep learning about yourself and all will become clear eventually.

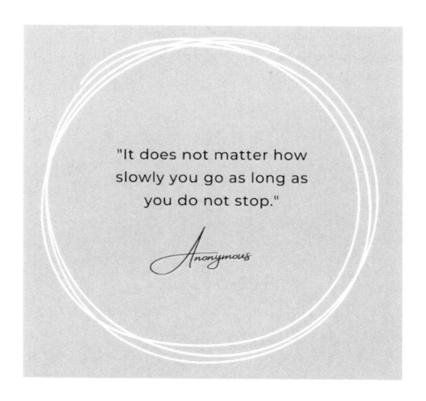

"It does not matter how slowly you go as long as you do not stop."

Anonymous

Experience comes with time, understanding where you performed well and understanding where you didn't – you HAVE to adopt a mindset of growth. If you are not learning about yourself and your performance, what are you doing?

I also believe that no matter what your role or title, we all have the ability to demonstrate leadership skills. Think of confidence as an asset in the workplace – it will shine through in all your relationships, with all colleagues, friends and family.

Confident people encourage positive thinking and demonstrate leadership skills. These are key skills that show how able and adaptable you are in the workplace.

There is no way to even trust someone's ability to lead you if that person isn't confident in his or her own abilities. Leaders must have confidence so that the people looking up to them feel secure, motivated and driven.

Confident people move barriers too with ease. Personally, I don't believe barriers exist – I think we perceive there to be lots of barriers, but that's just it, perception. It's how you choose to view the world. Confident people do not allow these obstacles to distract them from the task at hand, rather they calmly and rationally manage whatever the situation is and move on with whatever it is they are doing. It's the energy.

Some tips to help confidence in the workplace (taken from the website Indeed 2021 with my thoughts):

Tips for Confidence in the Workplace

TIP 1 – Attend professional development training

- What can you study / read / attend a course / get a qualification will all help you feel more confident in your role and craft? I recently read a book and it inspired me to make some changes at work and developed a new intervention for senior leaders. If I think for one second I have reached the dizzy heights of knowing everything, I am wrong. There is so much out there to challenge and push our thinking but you must want to develop yourself, both personally and professionally.

Courses I will enroll for:

_____

Books to read:

_____

Qualifications I want to achieve:

_____

TED talks to watch:

_____

Training for me to attend in the workplace:

_____

Training for me to attend outside of work:

Podcasts / audio books to listen to:

My recommendations of incredible books:

- Simon Sinek – WHY
- Simon Sinek – Infinite mindset
- Nancy Klein – Time to think
- Jay Shetty – Think like a monk
- Atomic Habits – James Clear
- Robert Greene – Daily Laws
- Dr Joe Dizpena – You are the placebo
- Sir John Whitmore – Coaching for Performance V5
- Grit – Angela Duckworth
- Why has nobody told me this before? – Julie Smith

TIP 2 – Acknowledge and develop your personal brand

- What does your brand say about you? What do people say about you when you are not in the room? What kind of leader are you? How you show up at work and how you conduct yourself, how you will be known in your organisation. From your timekeeping, to your consistency, to how you choose to turn up at meetings, it is all noticed. I have recently been working on my brand – both in and outside of work. I have started to use LinkedIn more; I use my network and have lots of meetings with my stakeholders to check in. I always ask for feedback and I'm very clear on my brand, who I am and what I stand for in work.
- Think about you and what you want to be known by, what is your legacy going to be?

- A personal brand statement is a 1-2 sentence that sums up your brand. It explains what you do (value), for whom you do your work (target audience), and how you do it (unique selling proposition).
- Personal Brand statements can look like this:

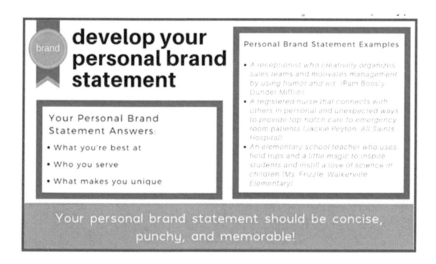

https://workfromhomehappiness.com/personal-brand-statement/

- My personal brand qualities:

_____

_____

- My personal brand statement is:

_____

_____

- My reputation is:

_____

_____

- I want my reputation to be:

_____

_____

- I will ask for feedback from:

_____

_____

TIP 3 – Learn new skills

- What can you learn that will help enhance your career? Similar to developing your current skills, learning entirely new skills or continuing your education can have a lasting impact on your overall confidence. Like a new language or learning to sew or paint.
- Why is learning new skills important? It helps you get new and knowledge-based perspectives on the world around you. It helps you gain new experiences, trains your brain to handle a wide range of challenges, and keeps your neural pathways active. All these factors combine to keep you healthy

- New skills I want to learn…

_____

_____

Tip 4 – Dress for success

- We've all heard of "dress to impress", it's the same. You wouldn't go on a posh night out in your tracksuit, that's why we fake tan, do our hair / make up so we feel confident. It's the same in work, what's your brand? How do you turn up for work? looking good can equal feeling good, so take care and pride in your appearance so you can feel as confident as possible.

- My work wardrobe

_____

_____

- My casual wardrobe

_____

_____

- My going out wardrobe

_____

_____

- My pub wardrobe

_____

_____

Tip 5 – Leave your comfort zone

- Say yes to things that are scary. Try new things. Learn to be the best leader you can be even if that feels different and pushes you outside your comfort zone. If you never push yourself, how do you know what you are capable of?

- I had never stood up in a room full of people and talked. Ever. I had never been asked and it had never come up. Then I got a promotion into a job where I had to do it and not only did I have to do it. I had to remember 3 days' worth of content and teach 15 people over 3 days. Whatttttt! My teacher was a guy called Neil. He was a consultant and he taught me everything I know about facilitation. He was training me and he asked me to stand up and deliver a message. I did it and I was crap! He said, 'Sit down then stand up and do it again' and I did it 5, 6 times and then it clicked and I was off. It was hard work, awkward, difficult but I believed in myself that I could do it and thought I didn't feel good at the time. Through years of practice, I am now one of the best facilitators out there! It takes hard work, determination, resilience and lots of self-confidence!

When did you push yourself outside your comfort zone and what were the results?

_____

_____

Tip 6 – Emulate confident peers.

- Consider the successful people you know or find someone who appears confident and self-assured in their job and observe their mannerisms and how they interact with other people. You can incorporate some strategies you observe confident peers applying in their own careers to help you develop your own confidence. Being able to flex your style and dial up and down behaviours is a key skill. Watch those that are good at it – what do they do?

- I need to work on:

_____

_____

- I have naturally:

_____

_____

Tip 7 – Set goals for yourself

- As I said above, setting goals helps with confidence. Setting short-term and long-term career goals can impact the way you see your strengths and success. Consider setting a goal for yourself to develop a new skill. Vision boards, positive affirmations, however and whatever way you choose to work on your goals, make sure they are achievable. If you have a big goal, break it down into small, bite size chunks. This will help with not feeling overwhelmed. You could go as far as breaking down the goal that you have a small task each day.

How will you achieve your goals?

_____

_____

Tip 8 – Focus on your strengths

- Focusing on your strengths can help you boost your confidence, as it requires you to measure your success and abilities. If you are good at something, demonstrate it. Show others where they can go if they need help from your particular strength.
- Write down your strengths – choose from these words below:

_____

_____

_____

kind, gentle, strong, resilient, caring, assertive, hard-working, reliable, honest, practical, responsible, loyal, mature, creative, consistent, appreciative, capable, quick, sensitive, perceptive, patient, thoughtful, fit, trustworthy intuitive, motivated, versatile, educated, willing, experienced, efficient, open-minded, logical, serious, supportive, resourceful, realistic, funny, punctual, friendly, humane, empathetic, interesting, driven, direct, considered, empathic, quirky, big thinker, fair, fit, sporty, ambitious, flexible, driven, considered, conscientious, responsible, sharp, intelligent, organised by understanding your strengths, you are getting to know yourself!

Tip 9 – Learn from your mistakes

- This is how you grow. Mistakes are usually inevitable when trying new things, so be kind to yourself. The key is to examine your mistakes and learn from them. It's difficult to accept failure, or fear of judgement from others, but failure can influence how you apply your skills in the future.

Write down any recent work mistakes and what you learnt from this, then write how you would approach it differently next time:

_____

_____

_____

Tip 10 – Eliminate negative language

- I use something called "above the line language". This is where I focus on what can be done, rather than looking to blame or make excuses. It's so boring to live in the blame game. Elevate yourself and own your actions, use strong positive language that demonstrates this. Another influencing factor in building confidence is assessing the way you perceive yourself. If you find you are overly critical of yourself or you doubt yourself regularly, you may take steps to change this mindset. You might practice self-affirming techniques such as focusing on all the successes you have had in the past week or journaling what professional skills you admire most about yourself.

What language do you use when you speak?

- Focus on your language at work too. I have read a few books recently where the writer references above the line language but in their own way.

I really like the examples Maria Hatzistefanis used in her book How to live your best life she talks about what she did at work with her language:

'Let's say that someone in my team has done a great job, normally I would say, 'You killed it.' Lately I have come to realise that is a negative word, even though it is used to describe something positive, the subliminal hears negatively. I now say, 'You've done an amazing job, I'm really proud' and that sends positive vibes to both my team and back to myself. Another subtle change is instead of saying, 'I can't wait to see you.' I say, 'I am looking forward to seeing you' leaving out the word can't which sends negative connotations.

I totally agree with Maria's mindset. I have taught a few people over the years above the line language. Here are some examples of negative to positive:

'Sorry for being late' to 'thanks for waiting'

'I can't help you, it's not my department' to 'let me find the right department for you'

And like anything, it comes with practice, practice and practice. It needs to be part of your new confident results focus mindset!

What language do I need to change?

_____

_____

_____

Tip 11 – Ask questions

- Stay and be curious. Always. Avoid assuming anything. Asking questions and being assertive in your self-learning can work to boost your confidence in your career. Consider making a habit of asking at least one question during team meetings, project planning sessions or conferences to help clarify any information that might otherwise be convoluted to you. You will be perceived as confident when you speak up and ask a question, it demonstrates curiosity and listening skills.

What is my plan to ask more questions?

_____

_____

_____

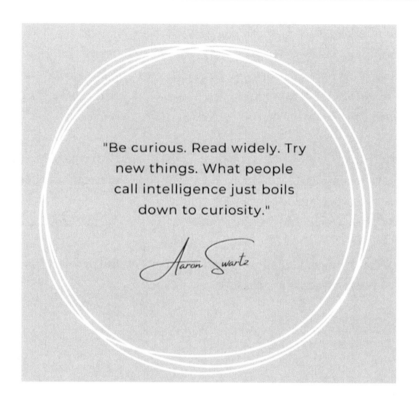

"Be curious. Read widely. Try new things. What people call intelligence just boils down to curiosity."

Aaron Swartz

Planning

I also believe having a plan is key to enabling confidence. This can be a work plan, a career plan, a life plan or a hobby plan. But have some kind of plan. I wish I had a plan years ago. I was drifting for years. Until I learnt something about myself, I needed a purpose. A goal. Something to aim for. I was literally winging my life and don't get me wrong (thanks to manifestation, my positive attitude and my determination!) it turned out okay but if I had planned properly, I could have achieved the goals I didn't even know I had much sooner. I would encourage or even STRONGLY recommend you get a coach. A life coach, a performance work coach, any kind of coach who can help you establish what your life is about and what you want from it. So many of us are just drifting, comparing ourselves to others on social media and not really having a purpose.

That's why I'm now offering purpose coaching to you, so we can help understand and evaluate your life! There is nothing worse not knowing what you are supposed to be doing with your life, what your calling is, you might not even know it exists until later in life. Having a coach provides you the space to think, helps you unravel the messy ball of wool and helps hold you accountable. It's a win-win situation. And why not? What have you got to lose? Contact me over at linkedIn and let's start to understand your strengths and how you can use these for the best life career!

A career coach would ask these questions and help you create a plan, or you can ask yourself these.

A plan might look like this:

'I'm 25, I work in customer services but I think I want to be a mortgage advisor.'

- What age do I want to be a mortgage advisor?
- What do I need to study / what qualifications do I need? And when? How will I pay for these or will I work to assist?
- What is the pay in that role and does that fit in with my expectations?
- What is the career path after being a mortgage advisor?
- What hours will I be expected to work and where?
- Who is in this profession now that I can talk to?
- Are there any openings for new mortgage advisors?
- Who can I connect with on LinkedIn to help me?
- What conferences or extensions can I attend to help me learn more?

You can then create a timeline and a plan, so it may look something like this:

- It takes 2 years to get the right qualifications, and my employer has said they will pay for it if I get the job. So, between now and the next 12 months I'm going to:
- Read 3x books on mortgage advice, 1x on financial advice and 2x on banking.
- Speak to others that have done the qualification and understand the work involved. Then start prepping by studying the areas they said were tricky.

- Practice my interview skills for when a role comes up and ask a colleague to role play with me some tricky questions (and ask for feedback).
- Follow key influencers on LinkedIn, Instagram and Facebook for the latest updates and market trends so I can know what is happening in the market.
- Speak to the head of that area and let them know my interest and my plan. Ask if I can do a secondment or get a week working in that area.

That is a plan and it can be as detailed or as high level as you like. My preference now is for detail, as it holds you accountable. Even if you only make a plan for the next 3 months, it's better than wandering aimlessly through life, we get one shot at it, so let's make some goals and smash them so we have something to be proud of!

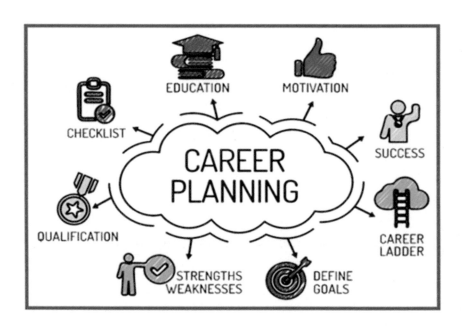

Do You Need to Know Everything?

Let's understand something, it's a work meeting, you are presenting, do you think knowing all the answers to any questions you may get asked is confidence?

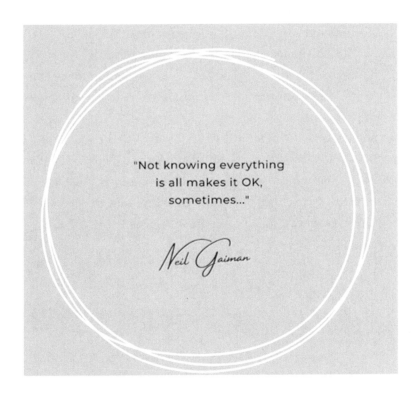

"Not knowing everything
is all makes it OK,
sometimes..."

Neil Gaiman

It's not. You don't have to know the answers to everything and confidence proves this. If you adopt a coaching mindset and you are authentic it's fairly easy. It's okay to say 'what a great question! I want to give this question the time it deserves, I can find out for you, I know who will have the answer!' and be okay with it.

It's ok not to know, it's all in how you deal with it! Let's demonstrate this:

'What a great question, I'd like to debate this one, let's open it up to the floor.' This then creates a discussion and conclusions can be drawn from all the answers within the room.

If it's a direct question to me and I genuinely don't know the answer, I would respond with the following, 'Ohhh, great question. I have been pondering this myself and never actually drew a conclusion, leave it with me whilst I look into it some more. I will come back to you'

Do you see the difference between answering a question you don't know the answer to (which people will see through and could possibly damage your credibility) to being honest about what you actually do know or asking others. That's confidence. And authenticity.

I repeat, YOU DON'T HAVE TO KNOW ALL THE ANSWERS. I genuinely thought I did but you don't. It is called being authentic.

Be okay with not knowing. Remember though, just don't say you don't know, say how and when you will find out, when you will get back to them and if it's okay to park that question for later discussion. That's confidence in your communication abilities.

It's a complete shift in mindset if you adopt the mindset of 'I don't have to know everything' and 'I will turn up and be curious and helpful' and if you want to relate it to the business world, it's a high support-high challenge approach encompassed with a coaching approach. Be okay with not having to know everything! And remember, it helps us remain curious…

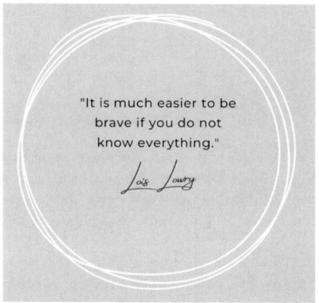

"It is much easier to be brave if you do not know everything."

Lois Lowry

What do I have to work on?

_____

_____

_____

Do I feel I have to know everything?

_____

_____

_____

Confidence in Relationships

Confidence in relationships is an interesting one. It's taken me a few to realise my true self-worth. This came as a massive surprise to me at 41 when one of my relationships ended and I went through a reflective period for many years. As confident as I was, I honestly believed that my self-worth revolved around how flat my stomach was or how skinny my legs were. And because I wasn't the prettiest or the skinniest, I was flattered by attention from men, any men really, I never did get a lot and I never got chatted up on a night out, ever.

I ended up with some good guys, don't get me wrong but I also met some bad ones too and I have to thank both for they both taught me lots about myself, who I am and what I want from relationships. Life is all about learning and if we aren't learning from our experiences, then what are we doing?

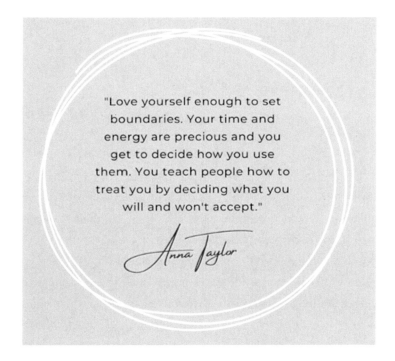

"Love yourself enough to set boundaries. Your time and energy are precious and you get to decide how you use them. You teach people how to treat you by deciding what you will and won't accept."

Anna Taylor

Without knowing ourselves, we can choose the wrong partners, trying to get together with people who don't really suit or compliment us because we don't understand our own needs…we've all been there…when we are "looking" for a partner, the requirements we come up with are often clouded by wishful thinking…we'll say we really want to find someone who is "kind" or "fun to be with", "attractive" or "up for adventure." It isn't that such wants are wrong, they are just nowhere near precise enough! We need to know what we require in order for the relationship to work, and work well or be the formula for a disaster.

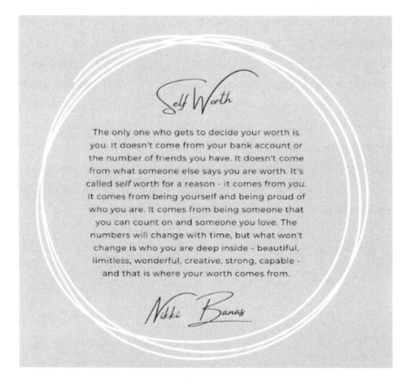

Self Worth

The only one who gets to decide your worth is you. It doesn't come from your bank account or the number of friends you have. It doesn't come from what someone else says you are worth. It's called *self* worth for a reason - it comes from *you*. It comes from being yourself and being proud of who you are. It comes from being someone that you can count on and someone you love. The numbers will change with time, but what won't change is who you are deep inside - beautiful, limitless, wonderful, creative, strong, capable - and that is where your worth comes from.

Nikki Banas

When thinking about your next partner, think about their "mindset", how do they deal with stress? What are they like when they are angry? What are their insecurities? How would they raise children? What are their expectations in a relationship? If you understand how their mindset works, it will help you decide if they are in line with your mindset and values. But you must know yours first!

Let's face it. If you choose to have a family with this person, you're gonna want to know how they raise the kids, their values, tradition, financial savviness, the list goes on…

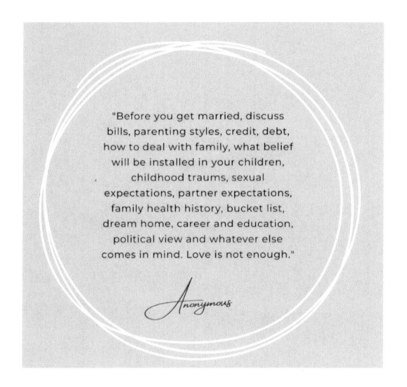

"Before you get married, discuss bills, parenting styles, credit, debt, how to deal with family, what belief will be installed in your children, childhood traums, sexual expectations, partner expectations, family health history, bucket list, dream home, career and education, political view and whatever else comes in mind. Love is not enough."

Anonymous

The above quote is so very important and goes back to my earlier point about similar mindsets and similar thinking. If you are aligned with your partner, you will automatically have more confidence in the relationship because you are a united front. There will be no nagging doubts about how your partner may or may not react over something because you know them so well. It's an important conversation to have and if you don't have it, anything can happen further down the line and nothing is guaranteed. I know for sure that if I was choosing my next life partner, I would want to know we are as aligned in our mindset as we can be, so I would have the conversation, and have it early. I would as always be open to listening but what I know I would do now (from experience) is believe the red flags. The red flags are there for a reason and YOU need to listen to them. I remember fancying my partner so much I ACTIVELY chose to ignore the red flags I saw. (Denial is everything right?) The consequences of this? Mental breakdowns and panic attacks on my side and a relationship I had to unpick and get rid of. It was traumatic. Ignorance is not bliss and the universe will always make sure if you don't learn your lesson the first time around, it will just keep on showing you. I can promise you that.

For true confidence is your relationship and partner, ensure your mindsets are united.

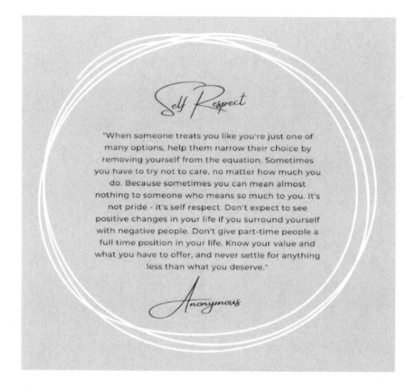

Self Respect

"When someone treats you like you're just one of many options, help them narrow their choice by removing yourself from the equation. Sometimes you have to try not to care, no matter how much you do. Because sometimes almost nothing can mean nothing to someone who means so much to you. It's not pride - it's self respect. Don't expect to see positive changes in your life if you surround yourself with negative people. Don't give part-time people a full time position in your life. Know your value and what you have to offer, and never settle for anything less than what you deserve."

Anonymous

The main thing I have learnt from relationships:

- You need to be treated as you wish and want to be treated, if you are not, get the hell out. By the way, don't expect them to be psychic, if you have set boundaries and clearly explain this, then they know how to treat you. Talk and communicate with them about what you need and why. Anyone who wants to be with you will respect this.

Am I treated right in my relationship?

_____

_____

_____

- You need to be loved the way you need to be loved, if you are not, get the hell out. This means a love that fulfills your soul. I had to leave a partner because he just didn't love me how I needed to. And now I know how I need to be loved; I know myself even better.

How do I need to be loved?

_____
_____
_____

- Your self-worth and value are not based on your dress size, or your face or how big your boobs are…it is based on morals, values, beliefs, acts of kindness, empathy, work ethic, drive, resilience and many many other qualities, your dress size should be last on that list. Maybe write down what your qualities are or ask others to tell you and LISTEN to them.

My self-worth includes:

_____
_____
_____

- You should. never have to beg a man to provide you with affection, love, attention and time, this should be freely given (again if you require more / less, you must communicate this), and if it is not, get the hell out

Am I getting what I need to feel fulfilled?

_____
_____
_____

- You should never have to put up with your partner projecting their insecurities / issues onto you – if they have issues, they need to take responsibility for these first and foremost. Gaslighting, projecting, threatening, ultimatums and manipulation are not acceptable in any relationship.

Have you experienced these behaviours?

_____

_____

_____

- You need to surround yourself with likeminded people, positive attracts positive, so who and what do you want around you? You will be a product of the top 5 people you surround yourself with.

My top 5 people:

_____

_____

_____

- Your partner should be your biggest cheerleader! They should support you and push you to be your absolute best. They should always have your back and want the best for you.

My partner cheerleads for me, by…

_____

_____

_____

- You and your partner ideally should have the same outlook and mindset about life… you will find you will clash if you don't have the same ideals. Finding a hobby or interest you can both do together (like hiking, wild camping, bowling, football, whatever it is) and enjoy spending time together.

Mine and my partner's favourite things to do together:

_____

_____

_____

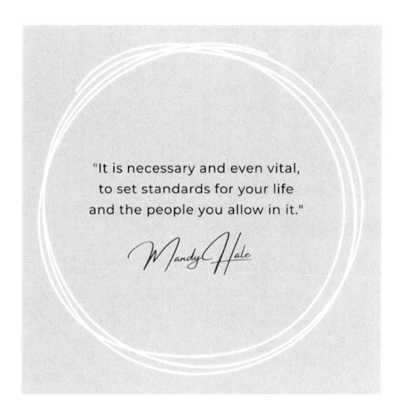

"It is necessary and even vital,
to set standards for your life
and the people you allow in it."

Mandy Hale

What have you learnt from your relationships? What did they teach you? All relationships should teach you something, whether you are in or from breaking up from them.

My main reflective point being what I truly learnt about myself from my last relationship was a game changer – I found my actual self-worth! I always thought I had it with confidence, but now I truly realise I didn't and that was the game changer.

I now know what I bring to the table and I am not afraid to eat alone. What I mean by that, is I know how good I am at my job, I know I am a good, reliable, solid and loyal friend, I know I make an excellent, thoughtful, supportive partner, I know I am sexy as hell, I know how I conduct myself in social situations, I know what I bring to a relationship, and I know the qualities I can bring. (This is not arrogance, this is me purely knowing myself and loving what I see, are you judging me?) So from now on, for me, I will not chase anymore, I will attract the right person at the right time, so I am literally just going to do me and see what happens. This is TRUE self confidence. This is a major lifestyle shift for me, as I have always chased men. Let's see what happens, now I know my self-worth. My new mantra? Men should be queuing up for me and not the other way around. I know my worth. And that is confidence.

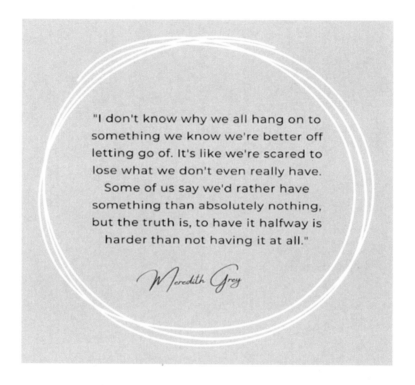

"I don't know why we all hang on to something we know we're better off letting go of. It's like we're scared to lose what we don't even really have. Some of us say we'd rather have something than absolutely nothing, but the truth is, to have it halfway is harder than not having it at all."

Meredith Grey

Learning to love yourself is the new rich. Learn to love all of you, even the bits that you're not keen on. Loving yourself will help solve most of your problems in the mind. It is no one else's responsibility to make you happy, only you have that power. The equation to confidence will help you learn to love yourself.

If you love yourself when the world is telling you not to, you win!

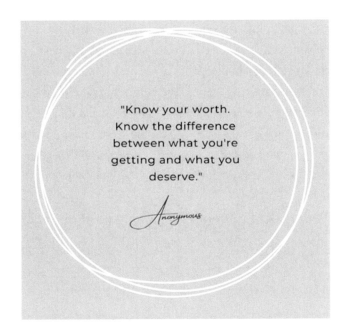

"Know your worth.
Know the difference
between what you're
getting and what you
deserve."

Anonymous

Always communicate what you need and want out of your relationship, be confident and assertive. Your partner is not a mind reader, be open and have the discussions. If they love you and treat you right, they should show understanding and empathy and listen. Remember, if you don't ask, you don't get.

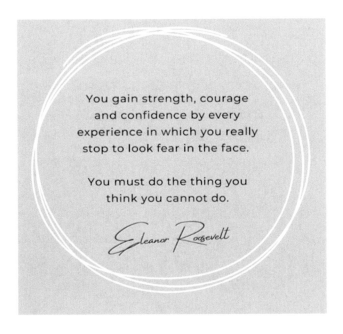

You gain strength, courage
and confidence by every
experience in which you really
stop to look fear in the face.

You must do the thing you
think you cannot do.

Eleanor Roosevelt

Communicate your needs, wants and desires. You only get one shot at this life, don't waste it on being unhappy or just "okay" – ASK!

Having the confidence to communicate your needs and desires are essential. I mean I can tell you some tales of lots of women I know who have never told their partner what they actually want in the bedroom and it blows my mind. They refuse to communicate their wants, desires or needs and then fall out with their partner. This is a recipe for disaster! If you are going to spend the rest of your life with this person, why wouldn't you want to communicate your needs so both of you are happy, fulfilled and get the best out of each other?

What do I need to start communicating with my partner about?

_____

_____

_____

"Respect yourself enough to walk away from anything that no longer serves you, grows you or makes you happy."

Anonymous

I know who I want to be in a relationship, what I stand for and what my boundaries are, and I respect myself way too much now to let anyone ever disrespect me again. That is true inner confidence.

A partner who loves you should want to support you and work in harmony with you – it shouldn't be a partnership of fighting every day.

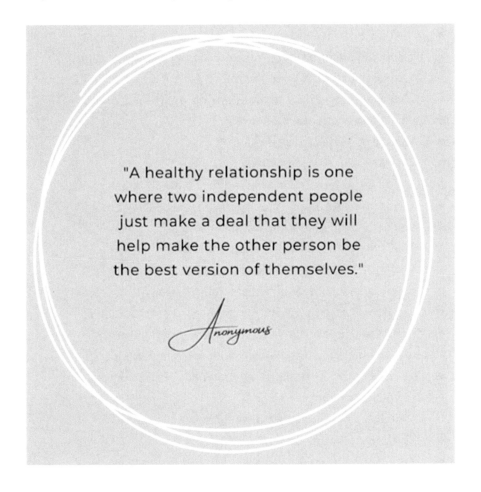

"A healthy relationship is one where two independent people just make a deal that they will help make the other person be the best version of themselves."

Anonymous

Questions to ask your partner:
(You could do one every night?)

- What was the biggest lesson from your worst breakup?
- What are our attachment styles?
- What is our love language?
- What's something you used to believe about relationships but no longer do?

- How does your life compare to how you imagined it growing up?
- What was your dream job when you were a kid?
- What's your definition of romance?
- Do you see yourself having kids? If so, how many?
- If you believe in soul mates, do you think you've met yours?
- Do you believe in God?
- Do you think it's more important to be smart or to be kind?
- Would you rather be loved, respected, or admired?
- What do you think is your best quality?
- What qualities or character traits do you want to work on?
- What's one of my best qualities?
- What do you find sexiest about me?
- What was your first sexual experience like?
- Do you think infidelity is always a deal breaker, no matter what?
- Who is more trusting, you or me?
- Who is more inclined to be jealous, you or me?
- What's the first thing you noticed about me?
- What's the first thing you found attractive about me?
- Is there a personality trait that always ticks you off?
- How do you express anger?
- How do you hide anger when you don't want it to show?
- How do you talk yourself down from anger or frustration?
- Who is more of a risk-taker—you or me?
- Do you have a bucket list?
- If you had a bucket list, what would be on it?
- What's your dream vacation?
- Where would be your ideal place—or places—to live?
- Would you rather own a home you don't love or rent one you love?
- What's something you'd like to try doing but haven't worked up the nerve to yet?
- What superpower do you wish you could have?
- What activity makes you feel the most joyful when you're doing it?
- What would you do with your life if you suddenly became a billionaire?
- Do you think there's such a thing as luck, or do we create our own outcomes?
- Who is more generous, you or me?

- Do you remember your dreams when you wake up?
- Do you have a personal flaw you'd fix, if you could?
- Is there anything you've always wondered about me but have hesitated to?

10 WAYS TO SHOW UP FOR YOURSELF

1. Commit to habits, practices, routines and rituals that are good for your wellbeing - even when you don't want to.
2. Allow yourself to feel a multitude of feelings without labelling it as wrong, bad or negative.
3. Practice listening to your needs and discovering different ways of meeting those needs.
4. Practice self-forgiveness; for not being perfect, for forgetting, for your past, for what you don't know, and for getting "off track" sometimes.
5. Let yourself start again, over and over, as often as needed.
6. Take care of your basic needs: stay hydrated, get enough sleep, move your body, and eat plentifully.
7. Give yourself permission to rest, to take breaks, and to have down time.
8. Spend quality time with yourself: reading, writing, creating and getting to know who you are underneath who you think you should be.
9. Use a lens of curiosity and compassion with yourself as often as possible.
10. Remind yourself that you are as worthy of being shown up for as anyone else in life. Make yourself a priority in your own life.

Anonymous

Authenticity in Confidence

authenticity:

the courage to be yourself.

JANINERIPPER.COM

'*Put simply, authenticity means you're true to your own personality, values, and spirit, regardless of the pressure that you're under to act otherwise. You're honest with yourself and with others, and you take responsibility for your mistakes.' Mindtools 2022*

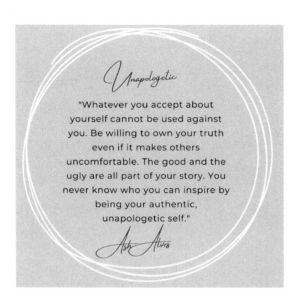

Unapologetic

"Whatever you accept about yourself cannot be used against you. Be willing to own your truth even if it makes others uncomfortable. The good and the ugly are all part of your story. You never know who you can inspire by being your authentic, unapologetic self."

I feel a truly confident person would radiate authenticity, because they are so in tune with who they are.

'To be authentic, we must cultivate the courage to be imperfect and vulnerable. We have to believe that we are fundamentally worthy of love and acceptance, just as we are. I've learned that there is no better way to invite more grace, gratitude and joy into our lives than by mindfully practising authenticity.'
— Brené Brown

Characteristics of an authentic person would be someone who values experiences, both positive and negative because they know they will learn from them. They take time to listen to others and show a genuine interest in what they are saying. They own who they are and because of this they are not afraid to be themselves and express themself. They love who they are and they enjoy loving others. They have a moral compass which helps them steer through life. They trust their intuition and gut feel and make good decisions.

They own their mistakes and acknowledge their faults and they know how to set healthy boundaries.

It's being honest to who you are at all times. To be authentic is to be real. Open minded and curious. You stay out of judgement and practice kindness and patience. Show the world who you are and if you have the equation of confidence, you can stand forth and be proud.

"Be fearlessly authentic.
Bravely be you."

Anonymous

To be authentic is to be true to yourself. Just being YOU. No one else is you and that is your power.

I think an authentic person lives by certain rules or instead creates healthy habits that instill authenticity on a daily basis.

https://www.businessinsider.com2022

Authentic people:

- Self-reflect
- Have integrity
- Focus on all the possibilities / see the good in all situations
- Are in control of their ego
- They have a solid, good character
- A clear vision
- They listen
- They are transparent
- They are consistent
- They are open minded
- They are team orientated
- They use their experience
- They are genuine
- They don't gossip
- Have a sense of humour
- Open to learning from their mistakes
- They mean what they say

This list could go on and on. Maybe it's easier if I show you the opposite of authentic? Someone who is flaky, phoney or false...you know the people I am talking about. I have a few flaky friends and they drive me insane. One of my friends (who I love dearly and I know her so I know her intent so I forgive her) often says, 'Ohhhh, let's have dinner tomorrow night' or 'let's do this and then we can do this' and then when I say to her, 'Are we still on?' She will laugh and make excuses as to why she can't (or even admit she doesn't remember saying it) but I know this about her and I accept it but for those that don't, I would imagine it doesn't do her personal brand very well.

From my point of view, if I make plans with someone, I make plans with them. It's because I want to spend time with them and I don't ever make "throw away" comments about meeting up if I don't mean it. I mean what I say. Let me say that again. **I mean what I say. I say what I mean**.

Other words associated with inauthentic people are: unreliable, spurious, false, apocryphal, disputed, exploded, rejected, counterfeit, **disingenuous,** unfounded, unauthorised, baseless, fabulous, fictitious – do you want to be known as any of these?

To be truly confident, you must get to know yourself, and this includes being authentic. Do you have ulterior motives? Are you manipulative? Do you even WANT to be authentic? What does authenticity mean to you?

Do I want to be authentic and if so why and what will get me there and if I don't, why and what does this mean for me?

RULES FOR SELF LOVE

1. Forgive
2. Let go
3. Speak Love
4. Gratitude
5. Self- Care
6. Connection

7. Patience
8. Live in the now
9. Surround yourself with good
10. Take back your power.

Intent

Our intent is key, why are we motivated to do something, what is our intent? Intent means "intention or purpose" or "determined to do something" but I want to put it in a different way. Someone's intent is what they think or feel during an action or conversation. It's usually the reason or motivation behind the situation. Say for example, you want to give someone some advice. Are you giving them advice to help be the best they can be, or are you giving it to prove a point? Make them feel rubbish? Make you feel good? What is your intent?

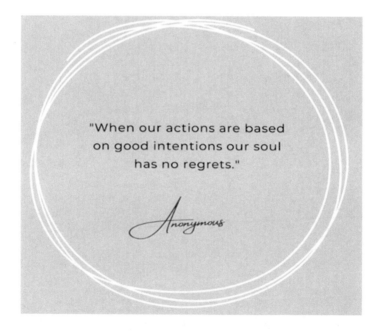

"When our actions are based on good intentions our soul has no regrets."

Anonymous

Revealing your Intent helps build trust and integrity and the following article from HBR 2022 confirm this: https://hbr.org

- *First, talk explicitly about your intentions, what's important to you, the goals you seek, the values and motives that guide your actions and decisions. Talk as well about the sources of your intentions, the experiences that forged them. When you do something or make a choice, explain both the business and personal reasons. Don't assume people will see them. Say them outright. Invite a discussion of them.*

- *The second way to reveal your intentions is through integrity. Walk the talk. Keep your word. Be sure that what you say is consistent with what you do. This will prove your authenticity. If you tell people to be open to new ideas, but you're not, they will doubt what you say. If they don't understand or believe your intentions, how can they trust you to do the right thing?*

- *The third way you reveal your intentions is through consistency. The intentions you speak about and practice should be the same from day to day, from person to person, from situation to situation. If they're not, and there's no reason for the difference, your lack of consistency will lead people to doubt you as well. If there are differences, be sure to explain them. Be sensitive to how others see and interpret your reasons for what you do.*

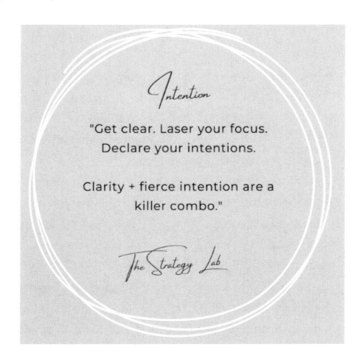

Intention

"Get clear. Laser your focus.
Declare your intentions.

Clarity + fierce intention are a
killer combo."

The Strategy Lab

So, consistency, integrity and communication are the 3 most important things to disclose your true intent. I know it is situational, but if you really reflect on why you are doing something, is it because your intent is pure?

Are my intentions usually pure or do I have some work to do?

_____

What is my usual intention?

_____

Everyday examples of how our intent can be misconstrued from Healthline 2022 are below: https://www.healthline.com/health/intent-vs-impact#common-examples

The idea of intent versus impact shows up more often than you might think in day-to-day life. However – remember, you may have good intent when doing something, but what is the impact of your intent?

Some examples of situations that you might find yourself in:

- Your partner makes a joke that upsets you. You know that they didn't mean any harm, but it still stings. Their intent was light-hearted but the impact is that your feelings are hurt.
- A friend comes to you to talk about an issue they're having at work. You offer them advice, but your friend is defensive and ends the conversation. You later learn that they felt like you were telling them they handled the situation poorly. Your intent was to offer an action plan, but the impact was that they felt judged.
- Your supervisor institutes a new policy at work under the guise of improving the culture, but the staff feels like it's just more work and surveillance, exacerbating the lack of trust in the office. Your supervisor's intent was to add processes for efficiency, but the impact is a decrease in morale.
- Your teen brings home a report card that has grades lower than what's typical of them. You sit them down to have a conversation about the importance of doing their best, and they shut down. Turns out, they feel like your words are coming from a place of disappointment, not love or

encouragement. Your intent was to foster a conversation about the future, but the impact is that your teen feels judged.

I always find, if you state your intent first, it reduces the situation where your intent might be mistaken. A tip on how to state your intent? Tell them!

For example, 'Sarah, is it okay if I give you some advice? I have been in this situation before. I think my advice can help, and I want you to succeed in what you are doing. My advice   comes from a good place.' Try practising your intent from now on, see what happens with it!

The more you practice, the better you will become, the more confident you will feel. Intent is important to authenticity, they are linked. It displays your motivation for why you are doing something...

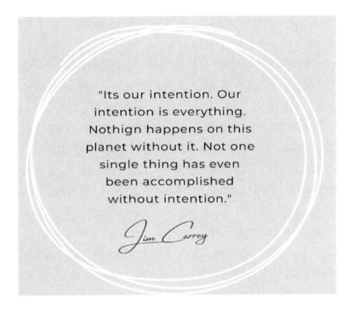

"Its our intention. Our intention is everything. Nothign happens on this planet without it. Not one single thing has even been accomplished without intention."

Jim Carrey

We are overly interested in other people's intentions at the expense of understanding our own...

If you start with yourself first, that is the most important. Learn about yourself and why you do what you do. Learning about yourself is a truly enlightening experience.

Your intent will help your confidence because you will know how you approach a situation, so therefore you will feel more internally confident as you know what your intentions are.

Committing

I was reflecting the other day about when you commit to something. It really does give you focus but you have to maintain that focus, so that means, NO DISTRACTIONS!

When you make a decision to commit to something, you have to invest your energy, time and discipline in this. You have to remain focused. Easier said than done sometimes, so I want to share with you something that I knew I had to commit to, but I was holding myself back.

My main reflection was recently when I decided to put Mia (my dog) through some training. (The training was specialised as she is a rottweiler.) The training involves ignoring her for a whole week, no walks or playtime and only feeding via rewarding good behaviour. (It's a bit more technical than that, but you get the gist) I was really torn at the thought of it, I worried and I procrastinated because even though I knew the training was going to be amazing for her long-term gain, the thought of ignoring her for a whole week with no walks started stressing me out. In my head it sounded awful and I really didn't want to do it. I was putting it off and umming and arrrggging whether or not to do it. Then one night when I got home from work, I decided I was going to start it the next day – I had a window of opportunity where I would be working from home for the week, so I decided to commit. I woke up the next day and just did it and you know what? It wasn't half as bad as what I'd imagined it would be in my head!

Day 1: She had been at mums for 3 days so she was shattered, so all she did was sleep and anytime she chilled near me, she got food. I'm writing this on day 4 and if I'm really honest, I think Mia thinks she's in a spa! No mum bossing her around, getting hand fed when she's good (which is most of the time) and a rest from walking. She was totally chill and NOWHERE as bad as my head painted it was going to be! Plus, what is also weird is I'm GLAD I committed. I'm glad I didn't listen to the thoughts in my head and I'm glad I pushed through because Mia will be a better dog for it. I'm glad I committed!! And that goes for anything, such as deciding to commit to a diet lifestyle, a hobby, exercise or dog training – commit and execute!

Courage is the commitment to begin without any guarantee of success.

That in turn got me thinking about something called the "worst case scenario".

I think I may have subliminally installed this in my brain because it is something I say to others. Again, I don't know if this is a good or bad trait, you tell me?

I always tell others that they should imagine the worst (in certain situations) as then the only way is up, right?

So, for example, I was preparing someone I work with to go into a situation that she hasn't been exposed to before. I told her, 'Prepare for the worst, this was my experience xyz.'

I then said to her, 'I'm preparing you for the worst, so that way you are fully prepared for all eventualities.' I wish someone had prepared me when I went into a situation I wasn't ready for and the worse did happen!

I think we all blow situations up in our own heads…we can go straight to a worst-case scenario when actually the reality can be completely different. Which is what happened with Mia – I blew it up in my head but now I'm in reality, it was okay!!! Don't listen to those thoughts... We have to hold fast onto our confidence!

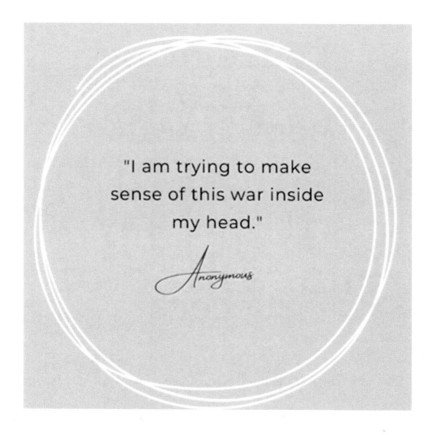

"I am trying to make sense of this war inside my head."

Anonymous

What do I need to start committing to?

_____

_____

_____

If you want to be confident, you have to commit, commit to all the tips, advice and direction in this book. Commit to being a better person, partner, parent, sibling, colleague, friend and lover.

Allan Mallory states, *'A fundamental part of motivation is being firm in our commitments. When we make commitments to ourselves and / or others and end up breaking them, we send a message that we are unreliable and lack perseverance. Sure, breaking a plan or activity on occasion for a legitimately good reason is certainly understandable but getting back up on our feet and resuming where we left off is what sets us apart from the rest. Backing out of*

commitments will suppress our ability to achieve our goals and can also reduce
our credibility and distance us from our allies and supporters.'

If you know yourself, you'll know if you commit to things or if you give up easily. Who are you?

"Be so fucking committed to what's best for your heart that you're willing to sit through the most uncomfortable pain of growth and change, that you refuse to accept anything less then complete love and alignment."

Anonymous

Comparison

"A flower does not think of competing to the flower next to it, it just blooms."

Zen Shin

Comparison is the thief of joy.

When we constantly compare ourselves to others, we waste precious energy focusing on other peoples' lives rather than our own. Comparisons often result in resentment, sadness, envy, bitterness, jealousy or anger.

If you want to be confident, you have to stop comparing yourself to others. You are you and that is your power. I get it. We all do it, how can we not with all the social media that is thrust upon us? I run a home account on Instagram and it's something I do and something I have learnt to switch off. There is ALWAYS going to be someone online who has a better home than me, has spent more money than me, can afford nicer things than me, has more time to do content than me.

Recently my friend got engaged, my other friend is having a baby and my other friend just found out she is pregnant. I am buzzing for all of them because I am secure, confident and happy within myself. I feel nothing but joy for them. (and please note I am single and childless). However, if you aren't feeling like that within yourself, you will start to compare and the possibility of a little jealousy is sneaking in too.

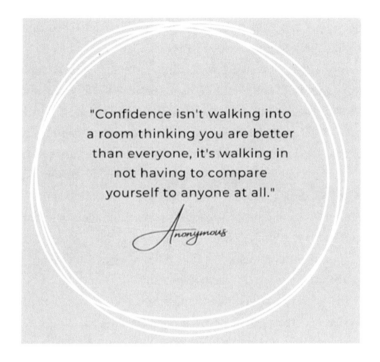

"Confidence isn't walking into a room thinking you are better than everyone, it's walking in not having to compare yourself to anyone at all."

Anonymous

Let me tell you what happened to me after I wrote this book and got the book deal. I noted when I started telling people my good news, there were, on average, 3 reactions to this news. The way I see it, I would be overjoyed for any of my friends, I would probably buy them a card and celebrate with them and I would be first in line to buy it – but if I had never written a book myself before I would be probably thinking in the back of my mind, I should write a book too! But this is me and I am very secure in who I am and I can acknowledge any feelings (negative or positive) that may stir inside me. If a negative reaction comes up, I would look at myself and think 'what needs healing or fixing still inside me to cause that negative thought?' Only by looking inwards when we have a negative / jealous reaction to something can we begin to really understand ourselves.

Anyway, back to the 3 reactions… So the first reaction is one of genuine appreciation and joyful celebration. This is what I would expect from my close friends and family. Interesting to note, not all of them reacted like that. When I told (my now ex) best friend, she couldn't have been more disinterested … that just says so much about her and where her head is at… which brings me to my 2nd reaction – not saying anything or not even acknowledging it. That was interesting when I told some people and they just didn't even say a word. They just changed the subject or went onto reaction number 3… The 3rd reaction is also interesting, when I tell them, they respond with the following 'Oh I'm writing a book too' and then proceed to ignore what I have just told them and just start talking about their own so-called book.

My personal belief is that it just highlights the fact they haven't achieved certain things in their life and therefore feel inadequate, jealous or envious. They instantly compare themselves to you in that moment! They wish they had written a book but never did. They wish they had achieved something they had wanted to do but never did. As I am secure in who I am, I know these reactions are all about that person and nothing to do with me. Please note that some of my close friends and family didn't respond with reaction 1 – which tells me more about them, their mindset and their inner dialogue than anything else ever could. I have removed a lot of these so-called friends from my life now.

It's the same with the houses I renovate too – when I invite people around, instead of celebrating how well I have done and being happy for me, 9 times out of 10 they will instantly start telling me about how they are going to move house, or how they are decorating their house or even tell me the things they DON'T like about my new house. There are limited (if any) compliments and they just continue to talk about themselves – and these are my friends and family!! I have to make the assumption that something is making them feel inadequate to behave like that – and it shows in their behaviour & language.

Are you one of these people? How do you respond to someone's good news (be really honest with yourself here) and how does it show it in your language and behaviours?

Don't get me wrong, it happens to me every now and then and I have to ask myself, what caused that reaction? What is making you feel / think that way? What do I need to do to heal myself?

Sumitha Bhandarkar (Tiny Budda) shares her experiences when she felt like this and how she started to overcome it:

- **Envy is a strong involuntary feeling that you cannot get rid of by just wishing or willing it away**.

Nobody gets up in the morning thinking, "Today I'm going to feel unhappy for my friend's happiness." (At least, I hope not!) And yet, sometimes when we want something bad and find that our friend got it instead, it fills us up with envy. It's not pleasant. It's not welcome. But it's there. Just because you don't like it, you can't wish or will it away.

Research has found that thought suppression is often ineffective, and can actually increase the frequency of the thought being suppressed.

In an experiment, researchers found that subjects asked not to think about a white bear paradoxically couldn't stop thinking about it. Other studies explored this paradox further, and support the finding that trying to suppress a thought only makes it more ingrained.

So first thing, stop trying to get rid of these thoughts. Accept them for what they are—normal feelings that arise in a normal human being.

- **Nail down the source of your envy to let the person who made you envious off the hook.**

At first glance it may seem like the person who made you envious is the source of your envy. However, if you dig a little deeper, you may realise that the reason you feel envious has little to do with the person who brought out the feelings. In my case, the real source of my feelings was that I desperately wanted a baby. Sure, the fact that my friend got what I didn't triggered the feeling of envy, but the source was my want and my fear that my want won't be met.

- **Let this knowledge lead you toward personal growth instead of resentment and bitterness.**

At this point you have a choice. You know that there is something you want but can't have. Will you become resentful of those who can, or will you make peace with the way things are?

I knew there was nothing that my friend could do about my inability to get pregnant. I also realised how illogical it was to expect that nobody in this world would have a baby just because I couldn't.

It didn't mean that I stopped feeling envious instantly; I still desperately wanted to have what my friend had. But separating the source of my feelings from the person made it possible to feel happy for her, in spite of my continued feelings of envy. Ever so slowly, I started to feel excited about her pregnancy and the opportunity to experience the miracle of a baby through her.

- **Focus your attention on addressing the source of your envy, instead of trying to eliminate the feeling.**

Your envy is probably here to stay—for a while anyway. Instead of fighting it, address the source of it.

I knew deep down that four years was a long time to wait to have a baby. But I hated to face it head on. When I realised how easily I fell prey to the green-eyed monster, I knew it was time to take my head out of the sand and deal with the issue.

I started infertility treatment. My friend was right there by my side as my biggest source of support through this emotionally exhausting roller coaster. In turn, I was able to share with her the excitement of her pregnancy. In fact, it was a huge motivation to keep going on rough days when all I wanted to do was give up and curl into a ball.

I finally got lucky. Five months after she delivered her son, my daughter was born. Our friendship had survived the difficult test.

Bad news is:
You cannot make people like, love, understand, validate, accept or be nice to you. You can't control them either.

Good news is:
It doesn't matter.

Anonymous

Tips on How to Stop Comparing Yourself to Others

How do you stop constantly comparing yourself to others? Here are some useful tips that have worked really well – from Josh Becker (Becoming minimalist):

https://www.becomingminimalist.com/compare-less

- **Be aware of its ill effects**. Take notice of the harmful effects of comparing yourself to others, has on your life. What does it do to you? Is it making you bitter, resentful or envious? How does it play out?
- **See your own successes**. Whether you are a writer, musician, doctor, landscaper, mother, brother or student, you have a unique perspective backed by unique experiences and unique gifts. **You have the capacity to love, serve, and contribute.** You have everything you need to accomplish good in your little section of the world. With that opportunity squarely in front of you, become intimately aware of your past successes. And find motivation in them to pursue more.
- **Desire the greater things in life**. Some of the greatest treasures in this world are hidden from sight: love, humility, empathy, selflessness, generosity. Among these higher pursuits, there is no measurement. Desire them above everything else and remove yourself entirely from society' definition of success.
- **Compete less and appreciate more**. There may be times when competition is appropriate, but life is not one of them. We have all been thrown together at this exact moment on this exact planet. And the sooner we stop competing against others to "win,", the faster we can start working together to figure it out. The first and most important step in overcoming the habit of competition is to routinely appreciate and compliment the contribution of others.
- **Practice gratitude**. Gratitude always forces us to recognise the good things we already have in our world.
- **Remind yourself nobody is perfect**. While focusing on the negatives is rarely as helpful as focusing on the positives, there is important space to be found remembering that nobody is perfect and nobody is living a painless life. Triumph requires an obstacle to be overcome. And

everybody is suffering through their own, whether you are close enough to know it or not.

- **Take a walk**. Next time you find yourself comparing yourself to others, get up and change your surroundings. Go for a walk, even if only to the other side of the room. Allow the change in your surroundings to prompt change in your thinking.
- **Find inspiration without comparison**. Comparing our lives with others is foolish. But finding inspiration and learning from others is entirely wise. Work hard to learn the difference. Humbly ask questions of the people you admire or read biographies as inspiration. But if comparison is a consistent tendency in your life, notice which attitudes prompt positive change and which result in negative influence.

We ought to strive to be the best possible versions of ourselves, not only for our own selves but for the benefit and contribution we can offer to others. Work hard to take care of yourself physically, emotionally, and spiritually. Commit to growing a little bit each day. And learn to celebrate the little advancements you are making without comparing them to others.

By learning not to compare yourself to others, it will improve your confidence. It's about that inner dialogue that is safe, secure and confident in who you are. Try and stop comparing yourself to others, we have all been on different journeys, and no one's journey is the same as yours. When we compare, all we are seeing is the output – and the struggle or the pain they have had to endure to get there. You are on your own path – and your confidence will grow in line with that.

Captain of Your Ship

The best way I can summarise this is that you are the captain of your ship – you are in control and steering at all times.

Listen, no one else can breathe for you, eat for you or steer your ship for you. Only you can do that. There is no one else on the ship but you. If you aren't there every day, steering and guiding the ship, it will just drift and be open to the elements. A bit like life.

However, if you have a plan, you can anticipate the elements, if the weather is going to be bad, you can choose to change route, slow down or go faster. You are planning ahead and avoiding disasters. If you don't plan ahead, and don't steer the ship, disasters will happen because you have not anticipated or planned for them, so they will happen to you.

Do you just want to drift through life or plan for the best life ever?

"We can't control the wind, but we can direct the sails..."

Anonymous

You are the ONLY person steering you – learn from your mistakes, get a mentor, read a book, HELP YOURSELF!

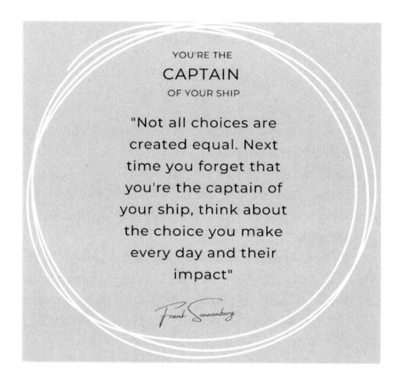

YOU'RE THE

CAPTAIN

OF YOUR SHIP

"Not all choices are created equal. Next time you forget that you're the captain of your ship, think about the choice you make every day and their impact"

Frank Sonnenberg

By Douglas R. Satterfield, April 2, 2021

'Yes, indeed, be the captain of your own ship. If you want to be satisfied with your life and not look back with regret on what you did or did not do, then take the wheel of your ship and steer it. You are accountable for what happens in your life, and you are also responsible for helping others see this unalterable truth.'

Hampus Jakobsson 2017 (Hajak) has created a guide on how to care less about other people's judgement and to become more in control of your own well-being (your-ship):

1. Inner fulfilment is better than external validation

'No man is an island entire of itself; every man is a piece of the continent, a part of the main.'

It is true that you are connected to a whole, now more than ever. Almost everything you eat or enjoy wouldn't be available if you tried to be self-sustainable. But we often let the line blur between ourselves and others.

When do you feel good about yourself or get a kick? Many reasons you rely on other people. If other people make you happy, that might be fine. But, if the absence of external verification gives you worry, doubt or makes you harbour even darker thoughts, you are holding the rule book of the game of life upside down. You should, at least try to, be in the driver's seat.

2. Don't let fear drive your actions and course

You can live in the now, striving towards things, or trying to avoid things. Living life in fear will not make it better, even worse is fearing the fear itself. Fear of something is usually worse than the matter itself. That fear also stretches over a far longer time than the unpleasantness of the possible lousy experience itself.

When you know what you fear, it no longer controls you.

3. You protect your property but not your mind

I bet you have a lock on your door and bike, have insurance, and are gentle around precious objects you own. You wouldn't invite angry strangers to your bedroom.

But you let anyone online get to your mind and create havoc. If something makes you angry, sad, fearful online, do less of it and avoid it. My general rule of thumb is to decide if to Fix, Ignore, or Accept.

I realise I never regretted not doing something or saying No, but more often when I did go, said Yes, or added another thing to my to-do-list or agenda.

Change your Fear of Missing Out to a Joy of Missing Out.

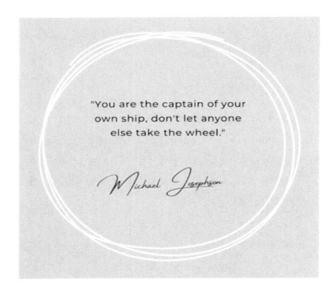

4. Be the great person in the movie

Figuring out who you are, what you think, and what parts of your emotional compass you should trust is something I believe only few can master. And, maybe it is hard to swallow 'What Would Jesus Do', if you are secular.

So, how does one get a NorthStar or guidance?

My favourite trick is to imagine life being a movie, and you are the amazing character. The person who just does the right thing. When in doubt, you just ask yourself "What would Mr Darcy do?" Or whatever your name is in your movie.

Remember, you set the bar.

5. Emulate a single player game

Whenever you are creating things, try to believe that life is a true single player game. Everyone you will interact with are Non-Player characters. Hey, be nice to them, but don't let their opinions kill you.

Write blog posts for yourself. Instagram to remember wonderful moments. Pick up digital garbage, because you want to live in a better world. If someone bashes you online, they are playing another game with other rules and either just accept that or avoid them.

The same applies to buying things.

You don't need any object to make other people like you.

6. Don't pollute

Even if other people don't really exist for you to become happy, you can't treat them badly. Benjamin Franklin had an amazing method to solve this; he wrote angry letters to people he disagreed with. But he never posted them.

Sometimes life truly feels like a mirror; if you send out anger, you will get it back. Same with fear. Same with envy.

Being yourself and the best version of that, means that you will attract people who like the real you.

7. Run a dashboard, not a leader board

It is too easy to compare yourself to the non-Player Characters or even people that are dead. If Mozart did most of the great work at a younger age doesn't mean you won't be worthy of a good life past that age. We tend to pick the best of other people. Dare like Amelia Earhart, invest like Ray Dalio, run like Usain Bolt, love like Mother Theresa, invent like Elon Musk and play chess like Deep Blue. But you have to be all of them, not just their best trait.

Other people are not competitors, combatants, or verification.

Be the best yourself and run the dashboard against yourself.

8. Never be a victim

When someone hurts you, remember Hanlon's razor: "Never attribute to malice that which is adequately explained by stupidity" or "Don't assume bad intentions over neglect and misunderstanding."

A lot of times when people say bad things, or don't invite you, don't credit you, or ignore you, it is not because they want you ill. They might have their ghosts, fears, worries or not just the time to put in the effort to be nice.

Decide who is worthy. If you wouldn't follow someone's advice, why should you be hurt by their critique?

As the stoics say: You can't control what happens to you, only how you react.

9. You are the only one looking after yourself

Your parents, spouse, friends, and everyone else might want you well. But you can't depend on them to make you happy.

As Steve Jobs said, 'Everything around you is made by other people, just like you.' I would say that everything inside you is made by you. It's your choice to get insulted. It's your choice to overreact. As the stoics say:

You can't control what happens to you, only how you react.

"You are the artist of your own life. Don't hand the paintbrush to anyone else.

Anonymous

Ask yourself:

- Who is steering my ship?

- Who around me has a big influence on me?

- Who could possibly start to steer my ship?

- Do I plan ahead and ensure I have looked at what is coming around the corner?

  _____

- How often am I coasting in my ship?

  _____

- Am I the captain?

  _____

- Habits I will create to help me be the best version of myself:

  - _____
  - _____
  - _____
  - _____
  - _____
  - _____
  - _____
  - _____
  - _____
  - _____
  - _____

Positive Mindset

I believe to my soul that having a positive mindset is literally life changing. I believe positive people are confident and vice versa. The two are linked, the happier you are, the more confident   you will be and the more confident   you are, the happier you will be. The two are intrinsically linked.

    I believe that positive people with a generally happy disposition live a longer and more fulfilling life. I believe they also are very rarely ill and can bounce back from setbacks quickly. If you haven't read Nancy Klien's *Time to Think* she had cancer and how she overcame it, you must.

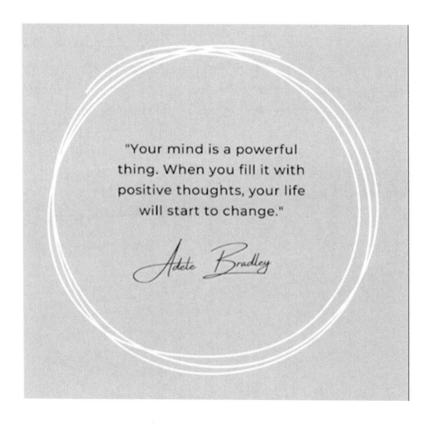

"Your mind is a powerful thing. When you fill it with positive thoughts, your life will start to change."

Adele Bradley

WebMD states, *'Positive thinking, or an optimistic attitude, is the practice of focusing on the good in any given situation. It can have a big impact on your physical and mental health.*

That doesn't mean you ignore reality or make light of problems. It simply means you approach the good and the bad in life with the expectation that things will go well.'

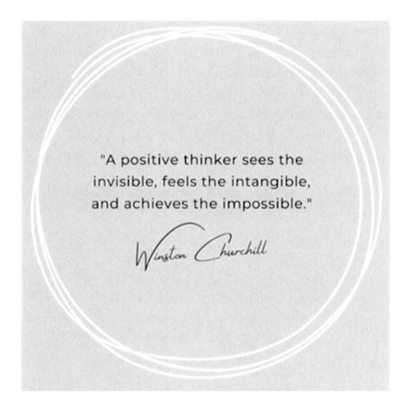

"A positive thinker sees the invisible, feels the intangible, and achieves the impossible."

Winston Churchill

Some others called it "PMA" – positive mental attitude. Wikipedia defines that as *'Positive mental attitude is that philosophy which asserts that having an optimistic disposition in every situation in one's life attracts positive changes and increases achievement. Adherents employ a state of mind that continues to seek, find and execute ways to win, or find a desirable outcome, regardless of the circumstances.'*

I first learnt about PMA when I was about 19 years old and I knew I had it just in me. I bounced back easy, I had a forward moving attitude, I was happy and positive, just very directionless!

I have reflected on what my "positive attitude" is and how I could describe it – and it got me thinking. There are a few things that define it, so let me see if I can put it into words (I'm describing my mindset...)

One thing I NEVER see are barriers, I only ever see opportunities. Nothing stands in my way, ever. **I don't believe barriers exist,** I don't know why but I have never believed it and continue to do so. If a barrier is put in my way, I go over, under, around or I blow it up. It's that simple. As far as I'm concerned, I will keep **moving forward** and I will overcome anything. There are no other options and it's always been like that. If you look at the bigger picture, find the positive in the situation and trust the process, it will happen.

I am optimistic to the core. I always want to see and believe good things are happening and opportunities are everywhere just waiting for you to make them happen. I believe optimism is also intrinsically linked to a positive attitude. This then creates confidence!

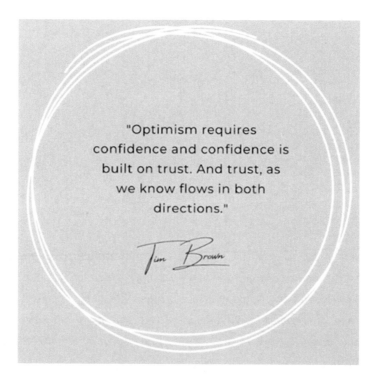

"Optimism requires confidence and confidence is built on trust. And trust, as we know flows in both directions."

Tim Brown

How do we describe optimism? Wikipedia states, '*Optimism is an attitude reflecting a belief or hope that the outcome of some specific endeavour, or outcomes in general, will be positive, favourable, and desirable. A common idiom used to illustrate optimism versus pessimism is a glass filled with water to the halfway point: an optimist is said to see the glass as half full, while a pessimist sees the glass as half empty.'*

My glass is always half full, always. And the statement is correct – it is all about "ATTITUDE".

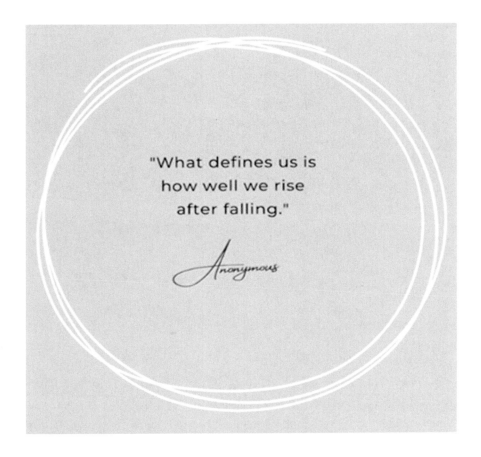

"What defines us is how well we rise after falling."

Anonymous

If I'm honest, I can't stand negativity and negative people. I would rather someone say, 'I have seen a few challenges and this is how we might overcome them' rather than 'this is the problem' and then spend all the time talking about what is wrong. I feel people focus their energy sometimes on things that aren't productive, like worrying, moaning, complaining, focusing on problems, getting caught up in the details, bitching and gossiping, micromanaging and fault finding. I think to myself, imagine if they used that energy on productive and positive things? Imagine what they could achieve!

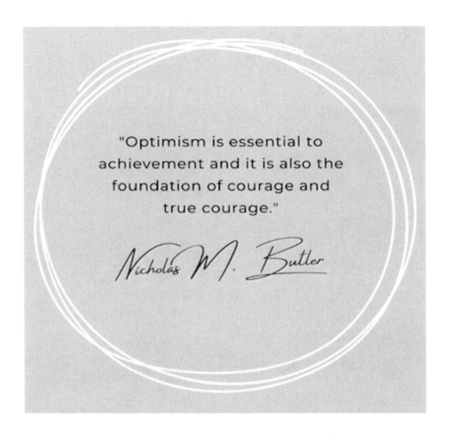

"Optimism is essential to achievement and it is also the foundation of courage and true courage."

Nicholas M. Butler

Another way I work is that I refuse, point blank, to spend any time with any people who are negative, toxic, draining, problem-oriented or drama queens. **You can't have a positive life if you hang out with negative people.** Facts. Surround yourself with likeminded people who want the best for you, you will have a beautiful support system which is genuine and authentic. This isn't easy – you may have long standing friendships, or it might even be your family that isn't so good for your mindset. You have to make a decision, by being honest with yourself, about what is best for you. I have removed a few friends from my inner circle recently and it wasn't easy at all. I got caught up in my own head about how best to do it, but that nagging inner voice wouldn't give up. Loyalty, the amount of time I had known them, our memories together, I really did struggle. I took counsel with a few close friends on how best to go about it – and then I did it. I don't miss them now which speaks volumes. Only you can navigate this situation and you will benefit in the long run. Remember, you are the captain of your ship!

I try to stay away from drama – I don't enjoy it and I can't be arsed with it! It's like arguing. No one is listening in on an argument, just two shouting how upset they are at each other. It's pointless. Yes, don't get me wrong. I've had few explosive arguments in my time but I know why. It's been down to two things – lack of communication from the other person or when the other person presses your hot button so hard, you explode and react (not respond) and hey presto "boom" argument starts.

I try to over communicate in relationships now, I **often tell my partner how much I adore them** and why I love them. Lots of compliments, honesty, trust and intimacy is key.

Another part of my positive mindset – believing. **I believe I can do anything** and nothing is impossible for me. I don't know what it is but I've always had it. Nothing phases me, I feel like if I put my mind to it, knuckled down, it gets done. I've proved this a few times…

Don't use lack of time as an excuse. If you are making excuses for yourself, only you will know why…if you really wanted to, you would.

My friend often complains about how he does not have any time and she's only studying! I don't really have empathy for people who say they don't have time, that is an excuse. We all make the time for things we want to do and that is fact. I will say that again. WE all MAKE time for things WE want to do.

So, we can all do anything if we REALLY want to do it…

If you know yourself, you will know if you are a motivated person or a lazy person…you will know deep inside what your levels of determination are if you truly want something. You will KNOW yourself.

Another example of my positive mindset:

Like I said before, I don't see barriers, so that helps with my positive mindset. I moved house in July 2020 (During COVID) and the renovations started in October 2020, so I was working from home whilst this was all happening (yes in the same house!) And at the same time, I was doing a difficult qualification and had recently got a promotion – however I saw none of this as an issue, I just cracked on. None of this is permanent and every day is a step closer to my goals and I will get through it. I had a few sayings like, 'embrace the chaos' 'short term pain for long term gain' 'trust the process' and even when things go wrong, it's always fixable… there is a solution to every problem! I remember being in a meeting once (virtual) and the builders were working directly above me, installing the bathroom. By the end of the meeting, I was covered in crap that had been falling on from the ceiling throughout the call! I laughed; it was funny!

To be honest, because I know myself, I know I like spinning LOTS of plates at once. I love having multiple projects on the go and being busy. I enjoy it. However, at the time of writing this book, I have had some down time which I haven't had in a few years. The renovation is complete and the house is 100% done. I am single and I often WFH, so I have free time that's why I cracked on with this book!

I am extremely resilient, like hardcore resilient. I am good at letting go, bouncing back and moving forward. I think I adapted quickly as a child and now it's just ingrained within me. I let stuff go and often, things I hold onto do me no good. I obsess over it and it becomes all consuming. This is because I know myself.

If a situation happens, I usually do a quick assessment of it in my brain – why am I doing this? Is it serving me in the best possible way?

Resilience

You never know when you are minutes away from a breakthrough. You never know when you are one project away from the promotion. You never know when you are one hour of studying away from passing the exam. You never know when you are one song away from landing the record deal...That is why you keep going; that is why you keep trying. That is why when you fall down, you stand back up. Because the truth is too many people quit before even giving themselves a real chance. They stop because it isn't happening fast enough or how they thought is would work out...My beautiful friend, remember that all good things take time. Be patient, your time will come too.

Nikki Banas

My positive attitude is because of this. I don't dwell on the past and I don't let it weigh me down or hold me back. I understand how to process situations, my emotions and what level of self-care I need to provide for myself. I know how to look after myself and I know what my heart, body, mind and soul need and I ensure I take care of them. (I might not always do it, but I know!) I have learnt to cancel plans to stay in and do nothing for self-care, where it was needed the most. I learnt to say no to people in my life, situations I didn't want to be in and relationships that didn't fulfill me. I set boundaries. I respect myself. I know what I need to do for myself to be the best version of her.

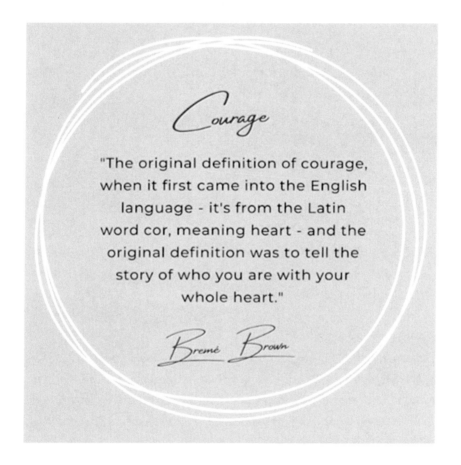

Courage

"The original definition of courage, when it first came into the English language - it's from the Latin word cor, meaning heart - and the original definition was to tell the story of who you are with your whole heart."

Breme Brown

Courage and bravery are also my mindset. I'm not afraid to be brave or have courage when it is needed. The dictionary defines courage as:

The ability to do something that frightens one; bravery. 'She called on all her courage to face the ordeal.'
Strength in the face of pain or grief. 'He fought his illness with great courage.'

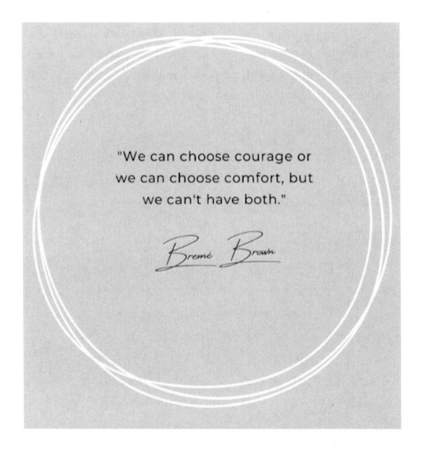

Better Up state*: 'Courage doesn't necessarily come with an absence of fear. In fact, being courageous normally involves taking action in spite of fear. It's knowing full well that something will be dangerous or hard but doing it anyway.*

Bravery tends to be more spontaneous, whereas courage comes with a high degree of choice and forethought.'

https://www.betterup.com/blog/bravery-vs-courage

You have to be brave if you want to be confident – this involves courage and self-belief. The other option is the opposite of this is cowardly… it all depends on who you want to be?

Steps I will take to work on being brave:

Step 1

_____

Step 2

_____

Step 3

_____

Step 4

_____

Step 5

_____

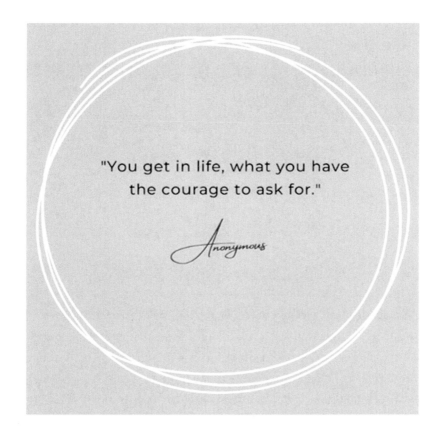

"You get in life, what you have the courage to ask for."

Anonymous

Acceptance

A Part of having a positive mindset is something called acceptance – things don't always turn out the way you thought they would and that's okay! Life isn't perfect, no one ever said it was and things don't always go right, it's okay!

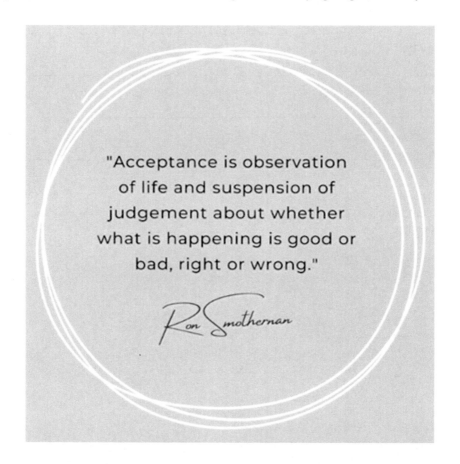

"Acceptance is observation of life and suspension of judgement about whether what is happening is good or bad, right or wrong."

Ron Smotherman

If you can learn to accept what is, learn from it and grow from it, that is the right thing to do for your mindset. If you remember the change curve we discussed earlier in the book, gaining acceptance is part of processing and accepting what is. Without acceptance, we will be stuck in other negative feelings which can have a detrimental impact on you. It's part of the change curve – getting to acceptance can be 3 seconds or 3 years – it all depends how quickly you move through the cycle.

"Acceptance is the road to all change."

Bryant McGill

Megan Brueanu of MindbodyGreen state these are the 5 things everyone should know about acceptance:

- **Acceptance does not mean liking, wanting, choosing, or supporting.**

No one is suggesting you like, want or support whatever it is that you're accepting. But by struggling against the pain by resisting and rejecting it we create undue suffering. It doesn't mean that you've chosen or endorse what you're accepting. It doesn't mean you like your anxiety, want your chronic pain, would choose your body, or support an injustice that's happened to you or someone else.

Rather, you're choosing to allow it to be there when you can't change it at moment. To make space for it. To give yourself permission to be as you are, feel what you feel, or have experienced what you've experienced without creating unproductive shame or anxiety. The pain might still be there, but some of the suffering will be alleviated.

- **Acceptance is an active process. It must be practised.**

Remember that accept is a verb. It's an active process, one that must be practised consciously. It's rare that we one day choose to accept our emotional or physical pain, our bodies, our difficult relationships, or our pasts, and never think about it again.

It can require effort at times (or most of the time, at least initially). It can be frustrating at times. But, like creating a clearing in a grass field by walking the same path many times, every time you practice acceptance toward something, you create and strengthen neural pathways in your brain, facilitating ease in the future.

It's natural to vacillate back and forth between feelings of acceptance and feelings of resistance. Make space for the spectrum of experience and notice your internal critic get quieter.

- **Acceptance doesn't mean that you can't work on changing things.**

Many people believe that acceptance is a sign of apathy. Passivity. Giving up. Relinquishing agency. However, this doesn't have to be the case. Practising acceptance does not necessarily mean you won't be able to make a change. You can accept your body and still change it, accept your emotions and acknowledge their impermanence, and accept your behaviour one day when you might change it tomorrow.

- **Acceptance doesn't mean you're accepting it's going to be that way forever.**

Try to focus your acceptance on the present, alongside an open and realistic gaze at the future. Focusing too much on the present can be counterproductive, as a large part of acceptance involves letting go of the desire that things will change, detaching from hope that, in some cases, creates suffering.

But sometimes imagining practising acceptance forever can seem daunting, overwhelming, or impossible, so try to find that sweet spot where you're accepting the current moment but not under the pretence that things will change in the future.

- **We can practice acceptance toward our experience, people, appearance, emotions,** ideas, and more

We can practice acceptance toward our experience, people, appearance, emotions, ideas, and more. Acceptance can be practised in all areas of your life: You can exercise it toward your current experience or reality, others' beliefs or ideas, your appearance, your emotions, your health, your past, your thoughts or other individuals.

Again, this doesn't mean you necessarily endorse whatever it is that you're accepting in these realms; rather, you recognise that you can't change the current nature of this exact moment and accepting manages anxiety and helps calm.

I encourage you to consider how acceptance has benefited your life in the past, and how you can practice it more in the present.

It's like the quote says:

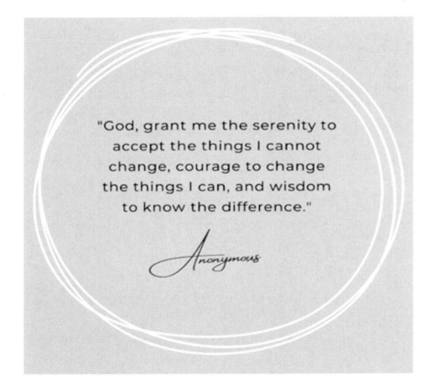

"God, grant me the serenity to accept the things I cannot change, courage to change the things I can, and wisdom to know the difference."

Anonymous

By learning to be positive, looking for the positive in a negative situation and having a positive outlook can literally change your life. It will make you more confident because you see the possibility in every situation. You will know how to overcome barriers because you apply your thinking through a positive lens, rather than the opposite. Being positive is a mindset that takes practice, dedication and commitment.

Ask yourself these questions:

_____

- Am I a positive person?

_____

- Am I a negative person?

_____

- How does this playout in my life?

_____

- What changes do I need to make to embrace a more positive mindset?

_____

- What do I need to learn to accept?

_____

- Do I have courage?

_____

- Do I have resilience?

_____

Chatting S**T

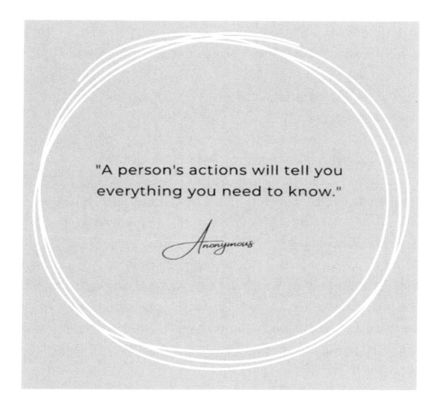

"A person's actions will tell you everything you need to know."

Anonymous

If you chat s**t, people are not going to like you, it's that simple. I describe chatting s**t as the following: '*Someone who says they will do someone, have big plans to do something or talk a good game but literally have no intention of doing anything, they are just chatting s**t*'

I call it 'action speak louder than words' and if you say you are going to do something but your actions don't match, essentially, you are just chatting sh*t. This gets you a reputation. And it's not a good one. I have a friend who does this all the time… her intention might be that one day she will actually do the stuff she is saying she is going to do – but after knowing her 20 years, I know she is has no intention and that she is just "chatting sh*t". She often says, 'oh, I am going to do this' and then it never happens. If you do it often enough, you will create a reputation for yourself. So now, when she says something is going to happen, I don't hear it because I know it's not true. In her version of her reality, it is, but deep down we all know it's just insecurity manifesting.

Chatting s**t will not give people confidence in you and that's something to think about. I recently gave a friend of mine an opportunity to collaborate with me on an Instagram project. It didn't go well, in fact, it was one of the worst experiences I've ever had. I have never known someone to chat shit so bad! These were the actual words he used;

'You have my word it will be done by the end of this week' 'I promise I won't let you down'

'I'll get straight on it now and get it sorted for you' Did any of these statements come true??

After 6 months of hearing this, I actually LOST my shit at him! It was all just talk and nothing got done or sorted, and I ended up telling him I didn't want to be friends anymore. It was a nightmare.

It also taught me about my core values (be meaningful with your words and be reliable) and solidified that I could never end up in any relationship with anyone whose words were empty. Reliability is a no1 Value to me.

You will also give yourself a reputation if you chat sh**t about others, people will think, if they are saying that about them, what are they saying about me? If you talk badly about others behind their backs, it says more about you than it does about them. People will view you as a harmful gossip and this in turn creates a (not so great) reputation for you.

Ask yourself honestly:

- Do I say things I don't really mean?
- Do I actually believe the things I am saying?
- How often do I say things and then never do them?

Make sure you have good intentions and avoid chatting s**t about yourself or others. All it will do is damage your reputation or give you a bad reputation. What do you want others to say about you when you are not in the room? What would you do if your friends were slagging you off behind your back?

"People who talk shit to you, usually talk shit about you."

Anonymous

If you are truly confident in who you are, your own abilities and limitations, you won't need to chat shit. Your actions will be done with purpose because you are confident in who you are and what you are about.

Be mindful of false promises, wishy washy gestures and false words. They will return to you and have a not-so-great impact. Say what you mean, mean what you say.

Be Impeccable With Your Word. Speak with integrity. Say only what you mean. Avoid using the word to speak against yourself or to gossip about others. Use the power of your word in the direction of truth and love.

So now we have covered some of the main areas of confidence – we are going to DIVE into the EQUATION to Confidence.

Remember – this next section of the book is a journey – you won't just read it overnight and be cured – it takes years of work. And the first place to start is here. This equation will work if you commit and like any commitment as discussed earlier, it needs focus and dedication. I know you can do it – let's go!

Equation part 1: KY (Know Yourself)

Confidence consists of three things; well this is my assessment after years and years of thinking about the question. That and constantly being asked about my own confidence (have you always been with confident / why are you so confident / where does your confidence come from) so after giving it some reflection and lots of thought over a long period of time, I have now come to the conclusion that confidence is made up of three key areas and I wanted to share with you what I think makes the **ultimate equation to confidence**.

Knowing yourself

Self growth

Self development is a continuous journey of trial and error. The process will test your strengths, reveal your weaknesses, and empower you to put yourself (finally) first. Keep going, no matter what. Dive deep into answering the questions that you refuse to, no matter how much the answer hurts. Be honest, be open, and be less critical of yourself. You deserve respect and understanding in the process of self discovery.

Today, I hope this reminder serves you well- to help you know that we are all in this together, on a journey of self-discovery and growth.

@tmoule_t | Tiffany Moule

What do I mean by knowing yourself? Do you know who you are? What you believe in, what you stand up for, what your moral compass is, your value set and your interests and dislikes? What scares you? What makes you happy?

I'm not talking about the surface level stuff either (favourite colour, music, car etc.) I'm talking about what makes you, you. Knowing yourself will bring you face to face with an extreme vulnerability of your deepest fears, self-doubt, vulnerabilities and insecurities. It is true soul searching.

Knowing yourself means you are self-aware. You know how you are (and by that, I mean act, think, behave, treat people) in all situations or could possibly be in all situations. You are aware of yourself in every last detail, you know what happens when you are faced with conflict, emergency, silence, praise and complex situations.

You are aware of how you react to things, you're aware of your emotions, you're emotionally intelligent, you understand yourself how you behave. You know your own mindset you may have a few blind spots but generally once you know who you are and you know yourself well then there is no stopping you. You are aware of your energy and the impact you have on people.

Knowing yourself also means owning yourself. What do I mean by owning yourself? When somebody says the word 'own it', it means embracing who you are, you are aware of your strengths, your faults, your toxic traits, your positive traits and how you interact with people. For example, I'm assertive, others call it bossy. Whatever you want to call it, I'm forthright, direct and I will say what is on my mind. That's me. I'm not a quiet wallflower, I will always have something to say. But I'm not ashamed, upset or worried about it because I own it, it's me! I know this quality about myself (note I refer to it as a quality) and it's who I am, I can't be "like" somebody else because I AM ME! It's how I choose to conduct myself knowing that is who I am. So even though I am assertive, I recognise and understand boundaries, when to cross the line, when to play with the line and when to stay behind it. I understand situations where I have to dial my assertiveness up and down depending on the situation. I'm not bossy, I don't shout and I'm not rude. I'm clear in my direction and I use inclusive language. I use my personal abilities to influence and it works every time. My way of being assertive works for me and I'm confident with it, so I own it. I trust myself and I believe in myself.

'Knowing yourself means respecting (but not attaching to) your strengths and weaknesses, your passions and fears, your desires and dreams, your thoughts and feelings, your likes and dislikes, your tolerances and limitations' (Habits for wellbeing 2022)

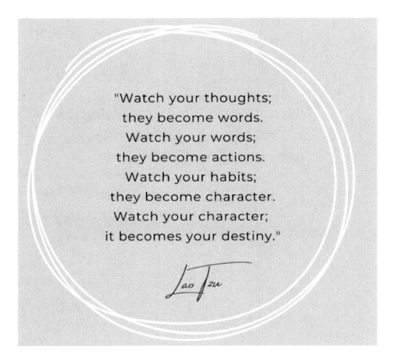

"Watch your thoughts;
they become words.
Watch your words;
they become actions.
Watch your habits;
they become character.
Watch your character;
it becomes your destiny."

Lao Tzu

Knowing yourself means you know exactly how you behave after 1 glass of wine or after 4 glasses of wine and by knowing yourself that well means you may choose to make a different option or choice. You are socially aware. You're aware of the impact you have on people and you're aware of yourself. Knowing yourself is about your experiences, as well how you grew up, what your childhood traditions / traumas were, your childhood school, childhood experience, your school friends, your tolerance and limitations. All these experiences: your first job offer, your first kiss, your first drink. Whatever it is, makes you know and understand yourself. I don't mean you will wake up one day and PING you know everything about yourself (I wish). It's ongoing and it always will be. It's a journey (as cliché as that sounds) of self-learning.

This is why this book is "the only book you will need" as throughout your journey, you can come back and complete some of the answers you didn't know, when you discover what they are. This could take a day, a week or years. This book is designed to be 'your bible' and the book that starts out blank and you complete all the answers.

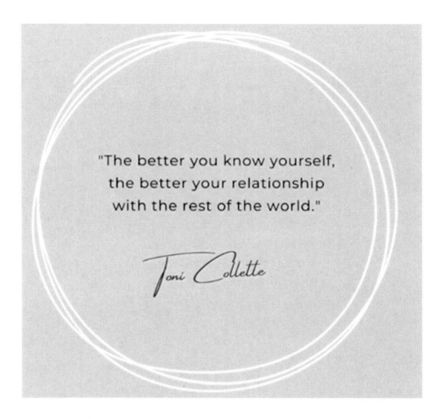

"The better you know yourself, the better your relationship with the rest of the world."

Toni Collette

How to 'know yourself'

First things first: Have a go at describing yourself:

_____

_____

_____

Ask others for feedback – questions such as:

- What is my worst trait?
- What is my best trait?
- What is one thing I could change about myself to make me a better person?
- What is my blind spot? (Something you do that others are aware of, but you are not)

Remember – if you ask for feedback, be prepared to hear things you might not like or agree with – you don't always have to accept it, but listening to it and being open to it, is important.

Keep a diary of how you "flare up" in difficult situations, where does your mind go? Do you react in the moment or take time to digest before responding?

- What do you think about yourself?

- When you are speaking, how do others react?

- Do you listen or do you wait for your turn to speak?

- Do you like to show off? Why? Who are you trying to impress?

- Do you impress yourself?

- Would you date yourself?

- How patient are you?

- How empathic are you?

- How do you operate under stress?

- How do you know when you are stressed?

- Do you always finish a job or leave it "kind of done" or "not done at all?"

- What's your relationship like with your family? What impact does that have on you?

- Do you know what you want out of life?

- Do you judge others? If so, why?

- What is holding you back? (and you can't blame others)

- What are your insecurities?

- What bias do you carry around, either conscious or subconscious?

- What happened in your childhood that you carry through in adulthood?

- Is your heart pure?

- Are you a good listener or do you just wait for your turn to speak?

- Do you approach every situation with good intent?

- What are your strengths?

- What are your areas for development?

- What kind of person do you want to be?

- Do you have hidden agendas?

- What is your purpose?

- Are you reliable? Conscious? Responsible? Assertive? Honest?

- Are you a rebel? And if so, why?

- Are you a good person?

- Are you a bad person?

- Do you feel guilty about things? Why?

- How do you have fun?

- How do you relax?

If you know the answers to all these questions – you know yourself! And if you don't, I would encourage you to reflect on a question a day and learn more about yourself. Take one question per day to really think about.

Take some time to answer these questions and start getting to know who you truly are. Time to start getting comfortable with the uncomfortable!

The Benefits of Knowing Yourself

Maybe it's obvious, but here are a few reasons why you might want to get to know yourself:

Happiness

You will be happier when you can express and fully embrace who you are. Expressing your desires will make it more likely that you get what you want. Knowing what makes you happy is super important… How can anyone make you happy if you don't know yourself? It's no one's responsibility to make you happy, only your own. Do you know what makes you happy?

Happiness is a state of mind, knowing yourself and what makes you happy will help you live a more fulfilling and satisfying life.

There are lots of books on happiness, my belief is that it comes from within, your life is what you make it, no excuses. If you think happy positive thoughts most days, you feel it and it will radiate through you, it's an energy. If you think negative thoughts most days, you will be unhappy and more than likely this will show in your life. (Read Solve for Happy by Mo Gawdat)

No one day on this earth is promised, so why spend it being unhappy? Find out what makes you happy and do it – do it as much as you can.

At the time of writing this, I'm truly the happiest I've ever been. Happiness is not a destination, it's an ongoing experience within your life. it can be found in your daily routine, from enjoying walking your dog, to cooking your favorite food, you can find happiness in every day, rather than waiting for an end destination. That's a lot of years to live waiting to be 'happy'!

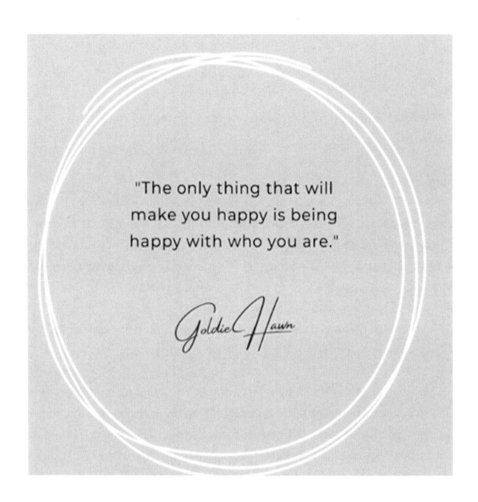

"The only thing that will make you happy is being happy with who you are."

Goldie Hawn

Less inner conflict

When your outside actions are online with your inside feelings and values, you will experience less inner conflict. This applies in relationships too. If you align your values with others that have the same values and standards, it will help you feel at peace.

If you understand how your thinking works, you might find you have internal clashes with beliefs or values. If you can understand these, it will help you understand yourself, and therefore, bring more peace.

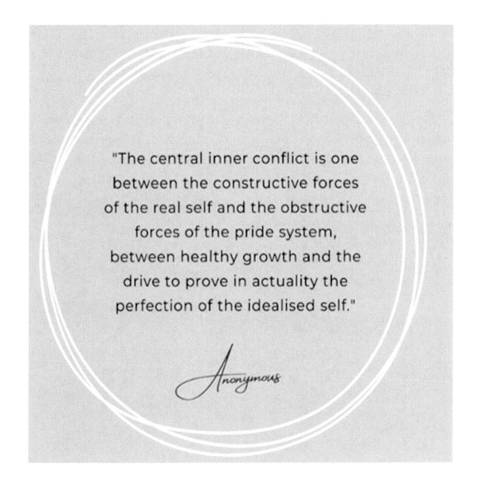

"The central inner conflict is one between the constructive forces of the real self and the obstructive forces of the pride system, between healthy growth and the drive to prove in actuality the perfection of the idealised self."

Anonymous

Better decision-making

When you know yourself, you are able to make better choices about everything, from small decisions like which jeans you'll buy to big decisions like which partner you'll spend your life with. You'll have experience to apply to solve life's crazy and dramatic problems. Overthinking is a killer of dreams. Getting caught up in your head and going around and around is frustrating and unproductive.

When I'm renovating houses, I need to make about 20 decisions a day – and I can't procrastinate. I have learnt some key questions to ask using my coaching experience and now I have the experience of what decisions will need to be made, my coaching experience in asking the right questions and I have true confidence in my decision-making abilities. I didn't have the experience in the first reno to ask the right questions, but I very quickly learnt. Looking back on the last renovation, which was x 2 extensions and total house re-map, there is only one decision I regret. But I used the mistake to create something different and creative and then I let it go. Procrastinating about past mistakes achieves nothing, as it can't be undone. We need to use it as a lesson learned and take the new learning into the future.

I know lots of people who get caught up in overthinking everything and these people struggle to move forward – analysis paralysis… If you want to change this and become rock solid inside, it takes a reframing of your thoughts on a daily basis.

If you know yourself, you will know what your decision-making skills are like and where you need to sharpen them.

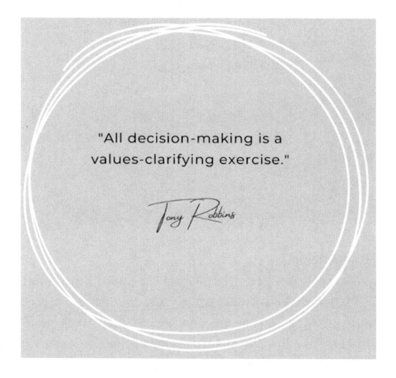

"All decision-making is a values-clarifying exercise."

Tony Robbins

Self-Control

When you know yourself, you understand what motivates you to resist bad habits and develop good ones. You'll have the insight to know which values and goals activate your willpower. For example, if you have a big presentation on Monday morning and you say "no" to a drinking session on Sunday evening…

I talk about addiction and bad habits in this book. I recently gave up smoking after years of doing it on and off. I just decided one day, it was no good for my business reputation and that I needed to knock it on the head. So far it's been 8 months and I'm doing well. I stay away from the smokers and I'm slowly saying no to cigarettes offered to me on a night out. Self-control is something I have but it's not as strong as it was when I was 21. The older I get the more it wanes but I just really have to talk myself into it (and I know this because I know myself). What are your levels of self-control like? Are you easily influenced into doing something? How is your discipline?

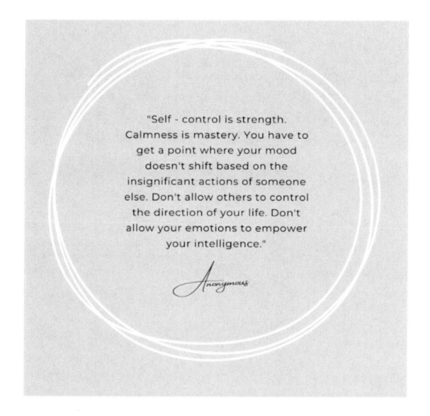

"Self - control is strength. Calmness is mastery. You have to get a point where your mood doesn't shift based on the insignificant actions of someone else. Don't allow others to control the direction of your life. Don't allow your emotions to empower your intelligence."

Anonymous

Resistance to social pressure.

When you are grounded in your values and preferences, you are less likely to say "yes" when you want to say "no."

We've all been there.

When I split up with my partner this year, everyone seemed to want to take me out and get me drunk. My friends rallied around and I was booked for festivals, weddings, bridesmaid duties, parties and nights out. It was the opposite of what I wanted to do. I wanted to crawl into my sofa and just feel numb. It gave me anxiety about the thought of drinking and how hard the next day would be.

So, I had to let a few people down and say no. Yes, I definitely had to do the wedding and bridesmaid duties, but some of the other events, no matter how big or fancy, I just didn't want to go to. So, I said no, and I'm continuing to do so. I say yes far too much, I know I'm a social butterfly but sometimes, now for my own peace, I just say no.

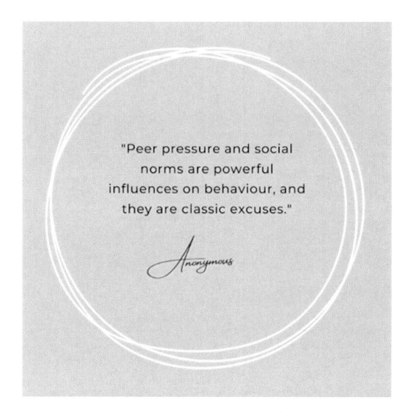

"Peer pressure and social norms are powerful influences on behaviour, and they are classic excuses."

Anonymous

Tolerance and understanding of others.

Self-awareness of your own issues can help you empathise with others. Knowing what you have been through, how you coped and how you felt, with help you connect with others. No one's life is a fairy-tale, everyone goes through relationship issues, work drama and friend problems. However, trusting your own experiences, you can be open to all situations and even if you haven't experienced it, you can still demonstrate genuine empathy. Stay open minded. Don't judge. Just empathy and love. Remember until you have walked a mile in their shoes, you don't get to judge.

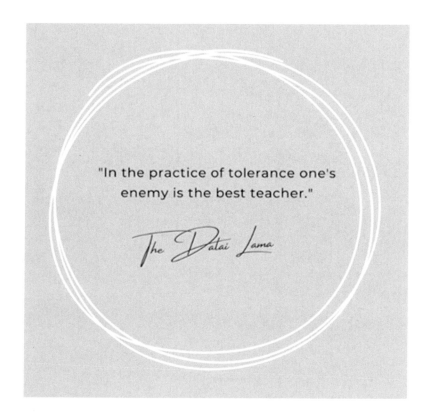

"In the practice of tolerance one's enemy is the best teacher."

The Dalai Lama

In the Moment

Being who you truly are helps you feel more alive and makes your experience of life richer, larger, and more exciting. If you are out on a walk, what do you think about? Do you think about the past, mistakes and regrets? Or do you think about the future, what's coming and what's happening at work etc.? Or are you in the moment, feeling the breeze on your skin, the sun in your hair, the smells around you, the noise the trees make…just being there, mind body and soul? Often, we can lose ourselves in our heads, which pulls us out of being in the moment. Start to recognise when you lose yourself out of the moment and try and pull yourself back, observe what your body language and mindset does.

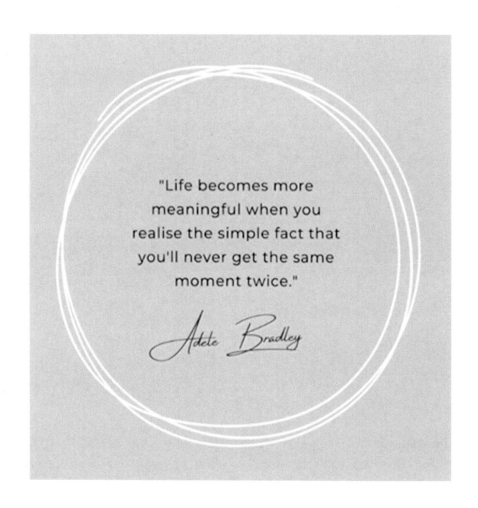

"Life becomes more
meaningful when you
realise the simple fact that
you'll never get the same
moment twice."

Adele Bradley

Being Alone

How do you like being alone? Do you get "lonely" or do you enjoy the time? Some people are naturally happy alone. But for others, being solo is a challenge.

Being alone can really be a good thing. It can really help you to get to know yourself. It all depends on how you choose to view the situation.

"Before I used to be afraid of being alone. Now, I'm afraid of having the wrong people as company."

Anonymous

It's important to understand that being alone doesn't have to mean you're lonely. Yes, you can be alone and feel lonely, but the two don't always have to go hand in hand.

The more time you spend on your own, the more you understand yourself. You know what you are like when your alarm goes off, your first waking thoughts and you know what you are like when it comes to going to bed...how you wash up, how you are around the house, how you keep your home, your thinking, your habits and your routines. This is all part of getting to know yourself.

So many people bounce from relationship to relationship so they don't have to be alone. This is so they don't have to deal with the pain or healing they need to do. Lots of people live in a safe space called denial. This can eventually create toxic behaviours.

Ask yourself: 'What do you know now that will be apparent in 6 or 12 months' (You know you are in denial about something – how will this show itself) Being on your own or doing anything on your own, like travelling alone, going on holiday alone, living alone – it is all worth experiencing. Naturally as humans we are social creatures, and it's not healthy to spend any long periods alone. However, being comfortable with being alone is where your confidence will lie.

I am more than happy to spend a weekend on my own. Just walking the dog and having no plans. I don't do it often, but I'm totally comfortable with it. Now I'm single I spend most evenings on my own and I don't mind in the slightest.

My advice to you? If you've never had a period of time on your own, create one. I 100% recommend travelling when you have finished school / college / Uni or even taking yourself away as an adult for new experiences, maybe volunteering abroad for a while.

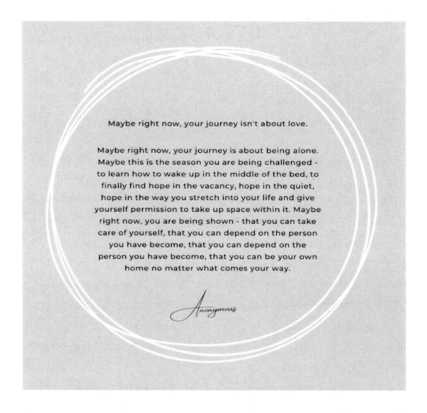

Maybe right now, your journey isn't about love.

Maybe right now, your journey is about being alone. Maybe this is the season you are being challenged - to learn how to wake up in the middle of the bed, to finally find hope in the vacancy, hope in the quiet, hope in the way you stretch into your life and give yourself permission to take up space within it. Maybe right now, you are being shown - that you can take care of yourself, that you can depend on the person you have become, that you can depend on the person you have become, that you can be your own home no matter what comes your way.

Anonymous

It will teach you so much and it will teach you things YOU will NEVER learn in a classroom. And if you didn't do it when you were younger, do it now. Life isn't guaranteed, avoid regrets by at least giving something a go, even a short break away!

More importantly, the point of this is that we need to be okay with who we are and spending time alone can help us with that. Learning to heal and giving yourself time after relationship breakdowns is so important. Grieving loved ones is vital for self-healing. Any trauma that happens to you needs to be dealt with – talk about it, get help. We all go through so much, throughout our lives, all of us. Some of us deal with things better than others – why is that? I believe it's down to our mindset and the stories we tell ourselves.

What story do you tell yourself?

I tell myself that 'I won't be alone forever and that I will meet the right person at the right time. I have goals I need to achieve; men are a distraction so stay focused and place your trust in the universe, it has your back. Everything will work out the way it's supposed to.' And I believe myself when I say it, because I trust myself. And I trust the universe too but that's a whole other book…!

Whatever you tell yourself. It's true! So, tell yourself positive, helpful, encouraging stories!

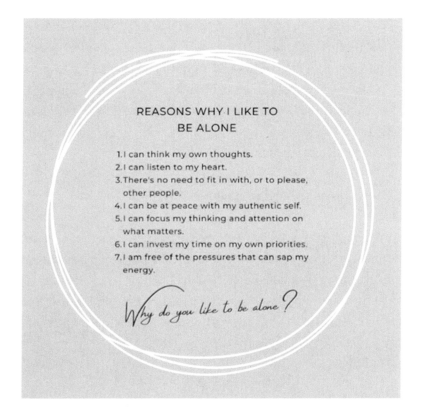

REASONS WHY I LIKE TO BE ALONE

1. I can think my own thoughts.
2. I can listen to my heart.
3. There's no need to fit in with, or to please, other people.
4. I can be at peace with my authentic self.
5. I can focus my thinking and attention on what matters.
6. I can invest my time on my own priorities.
7. I am free of the pressures that can sap my energy.

Why do you like to be alone?

Get to Know You

Things that can help us get to know ourselves:

- **Remove social media / social media detox**

Social media isn't necessarily bad or problematic but if scrolling through your feeds makes you like you are comparing, left out or feeling stressed, take a few steps back. That timeline doesn't tell the whole story. Not by a long shot. You have no idea if those people are truly happy or just giving the impression that they are. Either way, it's no reflection on you. So, take a deep breath and put it in perspective. Unfollow accounts you don't like. Hide stories you don't want to see. Follow accounts that benefit your mental health! Follow accounts that help grow your confidence – not the other way around!

Perform a test run and ban yourself from social media for 48 hours. If that makes a difference, try giving yourself a daily limit of 10 to 15 minutes and stick to it. Lots of phones have the tech to enable you to do it, so do it!

Unfollow all those accounts that don't make you feel good and fill your timeline with inspirational, motivational and empowering content!

Once you have worked out whether it was you feeling 'bad' or if social media made you feel 'bad' – you will start to see the differences. Take it away and see if you feel or behave differently. It's all part of getting to know yourself.

- **Take a break from your phone**

Going on a walk? Leave your phone at home. Just go be in the moment and enjoy being present. It will transform your walk. Or even take a camera and do a photoshoot on the walk, enjoy the little things. I like to enjoy the sounds of the birds, the wind in my hair and smell nature. Sometimes I might even go for a drink solo too on-route!

- **Meditate**

There are so many guided meditations online (YouTube), find one that you like. Try and make it a daily habit, even if it's just 5 mins per day. Meditation helps you get into a state of deep relaxation. This will help you tune into who you are. Can you meditate? Do you have the attention span? Or can you meditate for hours?

I like to meditate on my dog walks, it's great for resetting yourself. I also do affirmations on my walks too.

- **Let Your Mind Wander**

It's okay to switch off and just let your thoughts be. Good things come from having down. Just be. Watch where your thoughts wander to – understand yourself.

If my mind wanders, I've either won the lottery, married a film star or a zombie apocalypse has broken out. I find my imagination is WILD and it never stops. It is lots of fun getting lost in my own head sometimes!

- **Take Yourself on a Date**

I do this all the time and I love it. I highly recommend it. I work away loads, so I'm forever eating by myself. I enjoy the time to be honest, I can catch up on emails / texts or read a book. There's no drama, great eh! If you can take yourself out for dinner, you can do anything!

- **Take yourself on a weekend break / holiday**

Take yourself away for a few nights. I booked a chalet recently over NYE and met up with some family along the way but it was 3 nights on my own with the dog in a cabin. I loved it! Long walks on the beach, making nice food, thinking time. What's love? I've just booked another one and I can't wait!

More recently, I took myself to a retrcat in Portugal – a total detox for 6 days, with no caffeine, sugar, salt, meat, dairy, phones and alcohol allowed and with complete strangers and it was one of the best times of my life. I highly recommend it!

- **Exercise**

  Yoga, Pilates, running, walking, climbing, self-defence classes, whatever takes your fancy. Just try something new, then you can find if you are really good at something, that's you getting to know yourself!

- **Get out into nature**

  I love being outdoors. I love walking. I love the smells, the openness, the feeling you get after (let's face it, it's never a bad feeling). Watching sunrises and sunsets are incredible. I actually love taking myself on adventures, I like being with others though camping in nature, it makes it more fun! The thinking time and self-reflection time are all designed to help you understand yourself. If you don't like being outdoors, what do you like?

- **Walk naked around your house**

  If you love alone, why not? I love my body, I am not ashamed of it and it's the only one I have, so why would I spend my life hating it? (because society told me to?) Learning to love yourself is so important. If you don't like being naked, ask yourself why? This all helps in getting to know yourself.

- **Volunteer**

  If you like to serve and give back, volunteer to help out with something you care deeply about. It will make a difference, I promise you. I used to foster dogs and walk them at the shelter. I loved that I made a small difference in their lives, even if it was just for an hour that day. If you don't want to volunteer, what is holding you back?

- **Practice Gratitude**

  What are you grateful for in your life? I do this every day, I set my alarm on my phone at 4.30pm, and I say I am grateful for. This will help you understand what's important to you, all part of self-discovery. Take time to be grateful for the wonderful little things in our lives, like healthy family and friends, a roof over our heads and access to clean water and a safe bed to sleep in.

- **Create a new recipe / meal**

  Experiment! Nothing ventured, nothing gained!! I decided a long time ago that I didn't like certain things, and now from trying new things, I've learned that I like lentils!!

- **Be creative**

  Do you like to paint? Arts and crafts? Designing things? Where can you spend your time being creative? Have you ever not tried something new? You could go to a painting class or even photography, dance lessons, literally the world is your oyster.

- **Make lots of plans with family and friends**

  Having something in the diary to look forward to always makes a difference! Picnics, walks, cooking Sunday dinner, weekends away, concerts, museum tours, holidays and parties…why not!

My plan to get to know myself is:

_____

_____

_____

_____

_____

_____

Confidence and Emotional Intelligence

Emotional intelligence (otherwise known as emotional quotient or EQ) is the ability to understand, use and manage your own emotions in positive ways to relieve stress, communicate effectively, empathise with others, social awareness, overcome challenges and defuse conflict...

'Emotionally intelligent people are also more at peace with who they really are, focusing more on meeting their own standards than the standards set by others. Self-awareness and high emotional intelligence are also correlated with greater levels of success. For example, recent psychological studies indicate that many top business leaders have both of these traits, and that plays a key role in their continued achievements.' (Google, 2021)

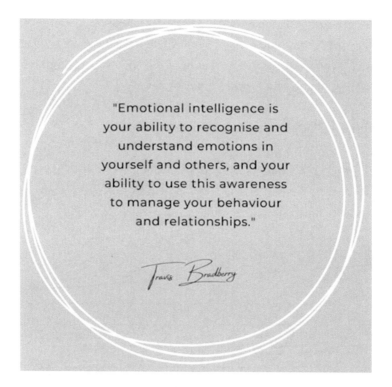

"Emotional intelligence is your ability to recognise and understand emotions in yourself and others, and your ability to use this awareness to manage your behaviour and relationships."

Travis Bradberry

There are lots of key exercises to find via google if you want to see how emotionally intelligent you are, however the best way is to really ask yourself as many questions as you can, reflect and learn from situations and experiences. Some examples of EI questions are:

- If you started a company today, what would its top values be?
- If a fight started in a bar, what would you do?
- How could you create more balance in your life?
- What makes you angry?
- How do you have fun?
- How good are you at asking for help?
- How did you deal with a bad day?
- How do you react to criticism?
- Can you read a room through subtle body language?
- Can you name the emotions you are feeling and understand what caused them?
- Can you see when you might be projecting your emotions onto others?
- What do you do to avoid taking out a bad mood on somebody?
- How good are you at your job, really?
- Do you respond or do you react in the moment?

I asked earlier to have a go at describing yourself … let's really start to work on that now – try this for starters. 'How would you describe yourself?'

Did you answer:
'A loyal husband who dotes on his family, love Liverpool FC and enjoys listening to music'
Or
'Driven, strong, dramatic, fun, loyal, enthusiastic, caring'
Or
'Good at my job, likes dogs, likes cars, enjoys helping people'

Try going deeper with your descriptions, really THINK about WHO YOU ARE… something like this:

'I'm a firefighter, I chose this career as I realised I had a love for all things outdoorsy, from rock climbing, orienteering, surfing, cave diving. One day a fire happened on my campsite and I just knew what to do, so I joined the firefighters. I get to combine my love and passion with my role. I realised I really like helping people and this gives me great satisfaction. Outside of work, I'm fairly peaceful, I like simple things and my life isn't complicated. I like to meditate and eat well.

I'm fairly balanced when it comes to my emotions, and work did some training with us too that helped. I'm not selfish or greedy, I like to share and give back. I play football every week too and I'm thinking of starting a 5 a side at work as a social aspect. I don't often get angry but when I do I blow up, so I try and go for a walk if I feel this happening because those words are said in the moment you can never get back. People have described me as boring before but I'm okay with that. If being outside and being with nature is boring, then I feel sorry for them! I would describe myself as alpha as I'm 6'6" and strong as I lead a team of guys, but outside of work, I'm much more chilled.'

Now how would you describe yourself?

_____

_____

_____

"We are dangerous when we are not conscious of our responsibility for how we behave, think and feel."

Marshall B. Rosenberg

Part of being confident is Emotional Intelligence. Emotional intelligence is vital within any place, be it the home, the office or with friends. I didn't have much EI when I was younger, and I really wish I had. But it is what it is. I had no idea of my impact on people around me. I was a walking disaster – completely oblivious! I have it now and that's the importance of this.

Daniel Goleman's 1995 book Emotional Intelligence, Goleman suggested *'emotional intelligence', a term developed by Salovey and Mayer (1989), is twice as important as cognitive intelligence for predicting career success and there was currently far too much emphasis on traditional predictors of employee performance. He suggested high levels of emotional intelligence improve working relationships, help to develop problem solving skills, increase efficiency and effectiveness and catalyse the development of new strategies. Rather than influencing exam scores or report writing, emotional intelligence influences how we control our own emotions and deal with relationships. Goleman defines it as 'the ability to identify, assess and control one's own emotions, the emotion of others and that of groups.'*

1. Self-awareness

Individuals with high levels of emotional intelligence are comfortable with and understand their own thoughts and emotions and they know how they impact on others. Understanding and accepting the way you feel is often the first step to overcoming it.

Emotions can affect your team at work, for example:

- A manager in a bad mood, with no self-awareness, makes bad and biased choices.
- A manager, in a bad mood, with heightened self-awareness realises and isolates negativity, refocusing on the task at hand.

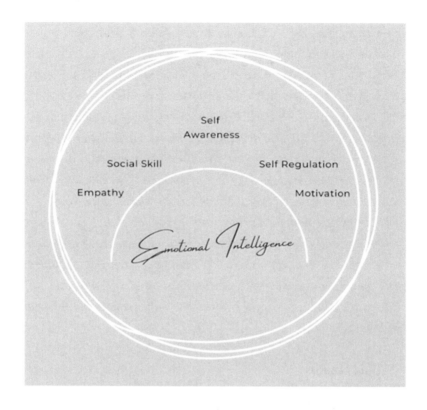

If you're self-aware, you know and feel comfortable with yourself.

We can have internal self-awareness. This is an awareness of our own values, passions, inspirations, reactions, thoughts and feelings.

If you are known to have mood swings and you don't control these in front of others, it means you aren't really aware (or don't care) about the impact that this has on others.

Maybe you are a parent and you were brought up a certain way and knowing that this parenting style wasn't the best for you, you have made a decision to parent differently. This is self-awareness as you are aware of the impact that certain parenting style has.

I am aware that I am "different" from the norm and I am also aware of the potential impact that this can have on others if I am not in control of myself. I can get very hyped very quickly, to the point it almost becomes uncontrollable – so I just make sure I don't allow myself to get into that space unless the situation dictates it.

Self-awareness is so important, if you don't know yourself, how can others? What do I need to do to raise my self-awareness?

_____

_____

Emotion   *Possible Meaning*

DEPRESSION   ········>   Hidden anger you don't feel
                                          justified having

ANXIETY   ········>   Wake up to your needs!

JEALOUSY   ········>   What you want

RESENTMENT   ········>   Violated boundaries

BITTERNESS   ········>   Withholding forgiveness

ANGER   ········>   It's time to make change

SHAME   ········>   Letting others define who you should be

GUILT   ········>   Letting others define how you should act

SADNESS   ········>   What you love and care about

DISAPPOINTMENT ····>   Shows you actually tried

IMSOMNIA   ········>   Two of your core beliefs
                                          are conflicting

2. Self-regulation

It is also important to be able to control and manage your impulses and emotions. Acting in the moment or without caution can lead to mistakes being made and can often damage relationships with clients, friends, colleagues and family. You have to be able to respond and NOT react. A response is considered, reacting is in the moment based on your emotional state. How many relationships have you hindered by just doing and saying exactly what you want in the moment – only never to be able to fix it because what you said or did was just too much?

My favourite tool for self-regulation is model called E+R=O

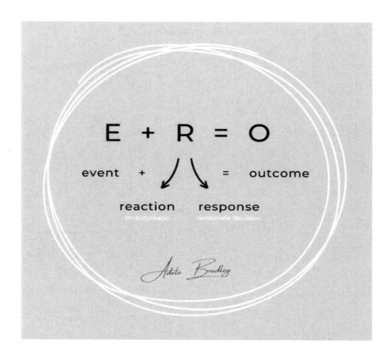

Sean Spurgin, Learning Director at Ele8v, talks about the following:

'Just by starting to think differently, you will begin to respond and behave differently and ultimately start to achieve differently. Food for thought as we enter the weekend, to spend the time with the people we love! This weekend, will you choose to argue or slow down to have a conversation? Will you flip your lid without seeking to understand? Will you bite at your partner's inane questions? And so on. What response will you choose?

If we want to change the results we get, we must change how we respond to events in our lives. If we show up with the right mindset and respond to events that happen to us in the right way, we are much more likely to have successful relationships whether that be at work or home.

We get stuck in conditioned responses to our family, to our work colleagues, to our customers and to the world at large. If we gain control of our thoughts, our mindset and our behaviour we are likely to get better outcomes. If we don't like the outcomes we are getting, we need to look at our mindset and how we respond to events.

Regardless of what unfolds in life's events (and sometimes this can be very hard), you get to choose how you are going to respond. We are in the driver's seat. We have the freedom to choose. We write our own story.

Jack Canfield, a business coach, created a formula to explain this concept. 'The Event (E) can be anything; a feeling, a friend's comment to you, a misunderstood email, your partner's behaviour, anything. In other words, anything and everything that is outside of your control to change.

Following an event, we naturally Respond (R). The response we give directly impacts the Outcome (O) we achieve. When people don't like the outcomes they are experiencing, most choose to blame the event (E) for their lack of results (O). The reality is we don't control Events and we don't control Outcomes. The only thing we can control is how we choose to Respond.

No doubt we have all experienced events that we blame on the economy, the weather, lack of money, family, our boss's attitude, how our customers speak to us and so on. This is what most people do.

It's true that these factors exist and that they impact us. However, if they were the deciding factors in whether someone succeeded or not, nobody would ever succeed.

For every reason it's not possible, there are hundreds of people who have faced the same circumstances and succeeded. The deciding factor in achieving successful outcomes is not the external conditions and circumstances. It's how we choose to respond (R). Or the mindset we decide to adopt before we respond.'

(Sean Spurgin, LinkedIn 2022)

E + R = O

"I do not control events. I do control my response."

Anonymous

'In my experience, successful people take a different approach to events. They simply change their responses (R) to the events (E) until they get the outcomes (O) they want.' (Source: Jack Canfield)

This is my favourite tool because I used to react very 'in the moment' depending on who had pressed my hot button (hot button = something that triggers you, like bad manners, road rage, bad time keeping, people blaming you, someone questioning your values etc.) Your siblings and you know this very well, as kids you knew exactly which button to press to get a reaction and I would gladly say things that I can never take back. I would destroy relationships with my mean words. I just let rip based on how they made me feel with their words, unintentional or not. I didn't know how to respond...

The first thing I had to do to change it was understood what my hot buttons were (all part of getting to know yourself) and write these down. Hot buttons are behaviours in others that can upset or irritate you when you encounter them. It's important to be aware of what triggers your emotions so that you don't get caught off guard. We're able to remind ourselves, "They're likely not doing this intentionally; it's just a hot button for me."

I invite you now to do the same:

Things that trigger me or push my "hot button":

1. _____
2. _____
3. _____
4. _____
5. _____
6. _____
7. _____
8. _____
9. _____
10. _____

Once you are aware of what these are, you will know when they are being pressed. That way you can course correct before you react.

- Know your HOT BUTTONS.
- Be aware of your CONFLICT ATTITUDE.
- Recognize your FRAME OF MIND.

How I will work on controlling my reactions:

_____

_____

_____

_____

The next thing to consider is, when an event happens, this is the point when you ask yourself, 'What is the outcome I need here?'

Then you can respond accordingly. This in turn will give you more confidence. Why? Because you will know you have control over yourself and your emotions if you find yourself in a situation where you want to react. This should provide a quiet confidence like the ability of knowing you have your shit together.

How and when do I need to regulate myself?

_____

_____

_____

3. Internal Motivation

Being driven by only money or material rewards is not a beneficial characteristic, according to Goleman. A passion for what you do is far better for your emotional intelligence. This leads to sustained motivation, clear decision making and a better understanding of the organisation's aims.

Allam Mallory 2022 states the following

https://alanmallory.com/2018/02/emotional-intelligence-self-motivation/

'Self-motivation isn't just our ability to get out of bed each day, tidy our homes or show up to work. It involves our personal reasons for doing something; it's a combination of our drive, initiative, commitment, optimism, and

persistence to accomplish something beyond money or recognition. In mountaineering, for example, someone may be initially motivated simply for the recognition or "bragging rights" of having accomplished such a difficult feat, but that level of motivation wouldn't last long once the reality of the task sets in. There has to be a deeper meaning involved, and a commitment to yourself and others on your journey that make it all worthwhile. This is where the emotional intelligence piece fits in. Although there are certainly people who are highly motivated, it doesn't necessarily mean that they are able to exhibit or understand the other components of emotional intelligence such as empathy and self-awareness. These people are usually not driven to accomplish things for reasons other than personal or financial gain.'

What makes you get out of bed every day? What is your purpose? What is your motivation? I know my purpose, but it took me a long time to find it. It was mid late 30's when I finally figured it out. I'm here to make a difference. I want to make a difference every day, a difference to the way someone thinks, a mindset shift, a new thought process. I work with incredible people and I am honoured that they trust me enough to let me challenge their thinking. I want to demonstrate these behaviours on my Instagram with my followers, with my friends and family. I enjoy inspiring others to think differently. I have so many other things I want to achieve and it's all designed around helping, inspiring and motivating others.

What motivates me?

_____

_____

_____

What is my purpose?

_____

_____

_____

4. Empathy

Not only must you understand your own emotions but understanding and reacting to the emotions of others is also important. Identifying a certain mood or emotion and reacting to it can go a long way in developing any relationship.

Empathy is the ability to emotionally understand what other people feel, see things from their point of view, and imagine yourself in their place. Essentially, it is putting yourself in someone else's position and feeling what they must be feeling.

When you see another person suffering, you might be able to instantly envision yourself in the other person's place and feel sympathy for what they are going through.

Very well mind state:

There are some signs that show that you tend to be an empathetic person:

You are good at really listening to what others have to say.

- People often tell you about their problems.
- You are good at picking up on how other people are feeling.
- You often think about how other people feel.
- Other people come to you for advice.
- You often feel overwhelmed by tragic events.
- You try to help others who are suffering.
- You are good at telling when people aren't being honest.
- You sometimes feel drained or overwhelmed in social situations.
- You care deeply about other people.
- You find it difficult to set boundaries in your relationships with other people.

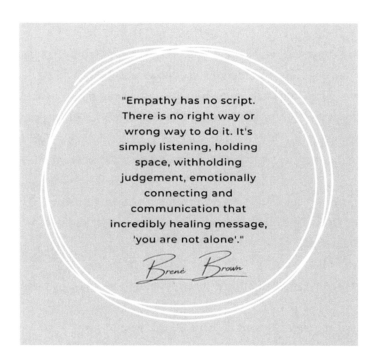

"Empathy has no script. There is no right way or wrong way to do it. It's simply listening, holding space, withholding judgement, emotionally connecting and communication that incredibly healing message, 'you are not alone'."

Brené Brown

There are different types of empathy that a person may experience:

Affective empathy involves the ability to understand another person's emotions and respond appropriately. Such emotional understanding may lead to someone feeling concerned for another person's well-being, or it may lead to feelings of personal distress.

Somatic empathy involves having a sort of physical reaction in response to what someone else is experiencing. People sometimes physically experience what another person is feeling. When you see someone else feeling embarrassed, for example, you might start to blush or have an upset stomach.

Cognitive empathy involves being able to understand another person's mental state and what they might be thinking in response to the situation. This is related to what psychologists refer to as theory of mind, or thinking about what other people are thinking.

Fortunately, empathy is a skill that you can learn and strengthen. If you would like to build your empathy skills, there are a few things that you can do:

a. When someone tells you something heavy, and you haven't experienced anything like that personally, just say, 'I can't imagine what you must be going through right now, I'm so glad you told me.'

b. Work on listening to people without interrupting, just be with them in their moment and just listen. Hear what they're saying. Use facial expressions to show you are listening and to demonstrate empathy.

c. Try to understand people, even when you don't agree with them. It's okay to have a different point of view, just acknowledge that.

d. Don't interrupt them or try to give them advice. Just listen.

e. Ask people questions to learn more about them and their lives. And listen to their responses!

f. Don't judge – that means not making it about you and your experiences!!

g. Imagine yourself in another person's shoes – put yourself in that situation.

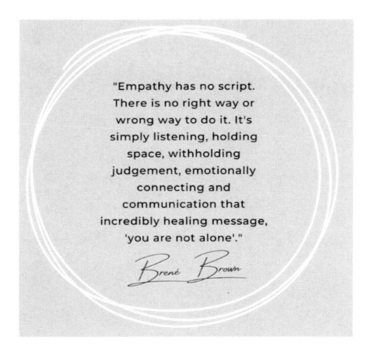

"Empathy has no script. There is no right way or wrong way to do it. It's simply listening, holding space, withholding judgement, emotionally connecting and communication that incredibly healing message, 'you are not alone'."

Brené Brown

5. Social Skills

Social skills are more than just being friendly. Goleman describes them as "friendliness with a purpose", meaning everyone is treated politely and with respect, yet healthy relationships are then also used for personal and organisational benefit.

Social skills include communication, influence, conflict management, leadership, embracing change and building relationships.

Luckily for me, not only did my times in my career teach multiple social skills, I happen to be an extrovert who loves people.

I am very good at spotting a fight brewing, intervening and breaking up fights. I am good at communication, though I am self-aware and sometimes I need to use more words because my written communication is always brief. I am very good at influencing, both in the short term and long term. My ability to be confident, charming and interested creates a way forward to influence. I love change and I will always be a change agent, always looking for ways to improve something or try new things. As you can imagine, building relationships comes naturally to me, people fascinate me and I am always observing them where I can.

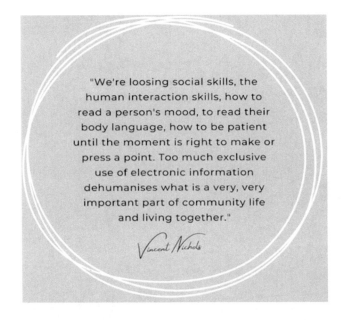

"We're loosing social skills, the human interaction skills, how to read a person's mood, to read their body language, how to be patient until the moment is right to make or press a point. Too much exclusive use of electronic information dehumanises what is a very, very important part of community life and living together."

Vincent Nichols

You can learn so much just from watching. What is my style of?

- Communication

_____

- Influence

_____

- Conflict management

- Leadership

- Embracing change

- Building relationships

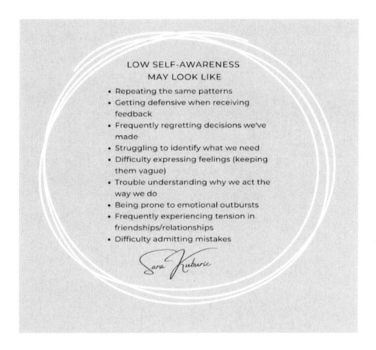

LOW SELF-AWARENESS
MAY LOOK LIKE
- Repeating the same patterns
- Getting defensive when receiving feedback
- Frequently regretting decisions we've made
- Struggling to identify what we need
- Difficulty expressing feelings (keeping them vague)
- Trouble understanding why we act the way we do
- Being prone to emotional outbursts
- Frequently experiencing tension in friendships/relationships
- Difficulty admitting mistakes

Sara Kuburic

What do I need change to be better at:

- Communication

- Influence

- Conflict management

- Leadership

- Embracing change

- Building relationships

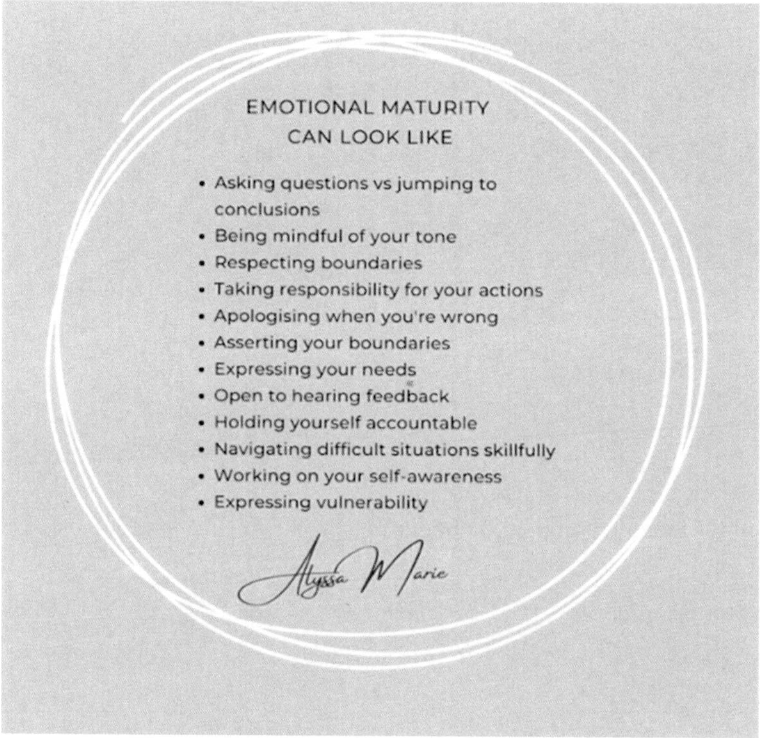

EMOTIONAL MATURITY
CAN LOOK LIKE

- Asking questions vs jumping to conclusions
- Being mindful of your tone
- Respecting boundaries
- Taking responsibility for your actions
- Apologising when you're wrong
- Asserting your boundaries
- Expressing your needs
- Open to hearing feedback
- Holding yourself accountable
- Navigating difficult situations skillfully
- Working on your self-awareness
- Expressing vulnerability

Alyssa Marie

My actions I will take to be better at:

- Communication

- Influence

- Conflict management

- Leadership

- Embracing change

- Building relationships

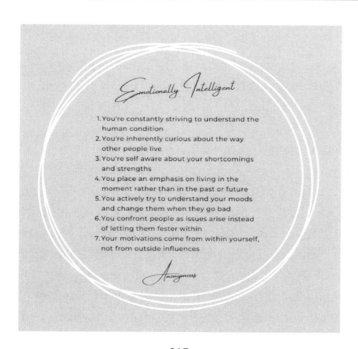

Emotionally Intelligent

1. You're constantly striving to understand the human condition
2. You're inherently curious about the way other people live
3. You're self aware about your shortcomings and strengths
4. You place an emphasis on living in the moment rather than in the past or future
5. You actively try to understand your moods and change them when they go bad
6. You confront people as issues arise instead of letting them fester within
7. Your motivations come from within yourself, not from outside influences

Anonymous

Values:

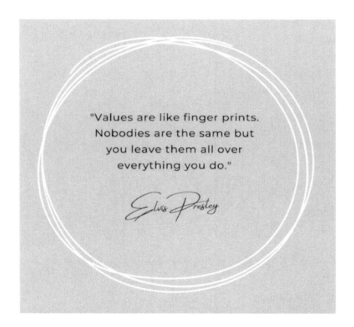

"Values are like finger prints.
Nobodies are the same but
you leave them all over
everything you do."

Elvis Presley

Values are basic and fundamental beliefs that guide or motivate attitudes or actions. They help us to determine what is important to us. Values describe the personal qualities we choose to embody to guide our actions; the sort of person we want to be; the manner in which we treat ourselves and others, and our interaction with the world around us. They provide the general guidelines for conduct.

Value sets can range from bad manners, timekeeping, how you love others, integrity and how others treat animals… your values will be your moral compass that guides you through life …

Core Values: (underline those that apply to you)

/ / Achievement / / Ambition / / Caring / / Charity / / Collaboration / / Creativity / / Curiosity / / conscious / / Community / / Dependability / / Empathy / / Encouragement / / Enthusiasm / / Ethics / / Excellence / / Fairness / / Family / / Friendships / / Flexibility / / Freedom / / Fun / Gratitude / / Generosity / / Growth / / Happiness / / Health / / Honesty / / Humour / / Individuality / / Innovation / / Intelligence / / Intuition / / Integrity / / involved / / Joy / / Kindness / / Knowledge / / Leadership / / Learning / / Love / / Loyalty / / Making a difference / /

Motivation / / Optimism / / Open-mindedness / / Passion / / Perfection / / Performance / / Personal development / / Popularity / / Purposeful / / Power / / Professionalism / / Punctuality / / Quality / / Recognition / / Relationships / / Reliability / / Resilience Respect / / Risk-taking / / Responsibility / / Safety / / Security / / Self-control / / Service / / Spirituality / / Stability / / Success / / Thankfulness / / Traditionalism / / Timekeeping / / Understanding / / Wealth / / Well-being / / Wisdom / /

Is there a theme coming through? What have you noticed about the words that you have selected?

_____
_____
_____

The benefits of identifying your values:

1. **Finding your purpose:** Knowing your values helps you figure out what you want out of your life.
2. **Guiding your behaviour:** They help you behave in a way that matches who you want to be.
3. **Helping you make decisions:** When you're facing a decision, you can ask yourself what someone who values the things you do would choose.
4. **Helping you choose a career:** When you know what matters to you, it's easier to choose the right career path.
5. **Increasing your confidence:** Identifying your values brings a sense of safety and stability into your life because you know what you want and what's important to you.

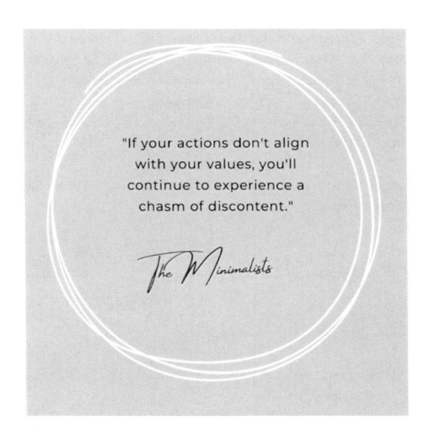

"If your actions don't align with your values, you'll continue to experience a chasm of discontent."

The Minimalists

The best way to get to know yourself? Start to write it down – a great way of understanding is to have some time to think, a pen and this table:

Write down your likes and dislikes – do these in line with your VALUE set	
LIKES	DISLIKES

To go even deeper, you could repeat this exercise with the following:

- How do I react when someone gives me critiqued feedback?

- How do I behave under stress and pressure?

- What do I like about myself?

- What don't I like about myself?

- What are my top 5 strengths / weaknesses?

- What am I all about?

- Who do you most admire and why?

If you know yourself, you are powerful. This means you can walk into any room and not have to prove anything to anyone, because you are actually aware of who you are, your self-worth and what you bring to the table. It's very freeing, very powerful and creates peace within your soul.

"Who am I, you ask?
I am made from
all the people I've encountered
and all the things I have experienced.
Inside I hold the laughter of my
friends,
the arguments with my parents,
the chattering of young children
and the warmth from kind strangers.
Inside there are stitchings from
cracked hearts,
bitter words from heated arguments,
music that gets me through,
and emotions I cannot convey.
I am made from all these people and moments.
That is who I am."

Ming Di Liu

Here are some more questions to think about:

- What are the two biggest lessons you have learnt in life?
- What would be your absolute perfect day?
- What did you learn a little too late?
- What gross or unhygienic things that other people do bother you?
- What habit do you have that you think not many people have?
- What are you too hard on yourself about?
- What habits do you have that annoy other people?
- How do you know when you have reached burnout?
- What is something you should probably do, but never will?
- What do you believe is the biggest sign of weakness in a person?
- What do most people overestimate or underestimate about you?
- What makes you nervous?

- What makes you angry?
- What is one thing that you have always wanted to do, but never did?
- What's the best mistake you ever made?

By being emotionally intelligent – it will increase your confidence. You will know yourself better, understanding how you behave, react, respond, love, fight, bond with others and so much more. It is only through self awareness that you will find true inner confidence. I would encourage you to continually work on your emotional intelligence – do your emotions help or hinder you?

Insecurity – the Opposite of Confidence

One thing we do have to talk about is the opposite of confidence – which is insecurity.

Insecurity is a feeling of inadequacy (not being good enough) and uncertainty. It produces anxiety about your goals, relationships, and ability to handle certain situations.

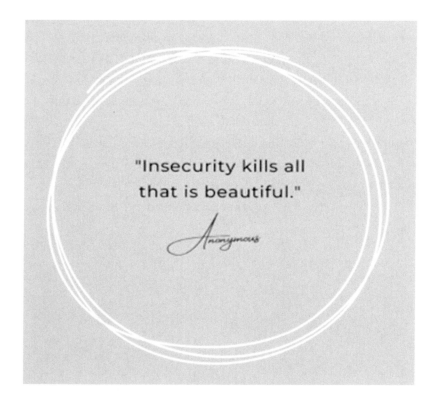

"Insecurity kills all that is beautiful."

Anonymous

Insecurity is the root of all evil in relationships and it usually stems from trust being broken in a past relationship of some kind / past trauma. Insecurities can show themselves in all sorts of ways and it's usually ugly. I had a partner and we were very happy, but sadly his insecurities split us up. I was completely confident and trusting in our relationship and sadly he was the opposite. He would project his insecurities onto me and it was exhausting!! They were usually around cheating… Once I was accused of cheating on him because I sneezed…that was how bad it got. It was the little comments and digs and I always got given a hard time, especially when I had to work away. It became too exhausting to maintain and my mental health took a real hit. No matter what I did or where I went, I was always 'trying to cheat' and it just got too much. They were his issues, not mine. I conducted myself perfectly but having a partner who constantly wants to 'try and catch you out' is not my idea of trusting, harmonious relationship. Until he fixed his own past issues, we could never have a real relationship. Unfortunately, he was in denial and did not want to be self-aware around this, so there was nothing I could do. I had the confidence to walk away as I knew it wasn't working…it was a hard decision but I believed in myself, trusted myself and I knew I could do it… even though he told me the whole time I couldn't do anything without him… I knew not to listen and stay focused on what I knew the truth was. It was hard but it worked. He tried to manipulate me, gaslight me, threaten me, intimidate me and play mind games with me. I dread to think how a less strong woman would have dealt with it because I know how strong I am and I really did take a massive hit…to my own confidence, self-worth and self-love. I Aam lucky as I have good friends around me and they reminded me who I am and that was all I needed to hear. A reminder. What I stand for and what I am about. I trusted myself that this was the right thing to do, and it was. However, he taught me a massive lesson about my worth and I know I will never let anyone ever treat me like that again, ever. For me, in a partner now, it all starts with mindset.

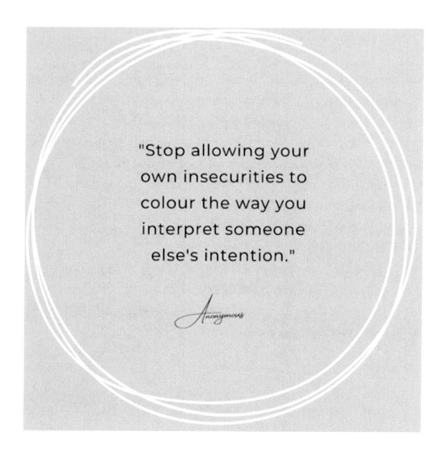

"Stop allowing your own insecurities to colour the way you interpret someone else's intention."

— Anonymous

So, make sure, when you are dating or choosing a potential partner, that they have the same mindset as you and that you are both aligned in your values and morals. It makes for a much more harmonious, non-toxic, drama free environment, I promise. You ask your partner or potential partner some of these questions if you every fancy creating more intimacy and getting to know them on a deeper level:

- Are you more likely to avoid conflict or engage in it, and why?
- Are you proud of what you do for a living?
- As a kid, what was your idea of fun?
- Can you think of a couple you know that have a great relationship? What characteristics of their relationship would you like to see in yours?
- Describe your first childhood crush
- Do you feel you have had closure from your previous relationship(s)?
- What is your favourite thing about me?

- What do you admire in me?
- What is your favourite pastime?

Insecurities come in all forms, like imposter syndrome, anxiety, procrastination, jealousy and feeling open to danger. If you are self-aware of where your insecurities lay, you can actively work on them.

'Insecurity involves an overall sense of uncertainty or anxiety about your worth, abilities, skills, and value as a person, conveying the message that you're at risk or in danger of something or someone. The negative impacts of insecurity could be physical, mental, or emotional.'
https://www.choosingtherapy.com/insecurity/

Everybody deals with insecurity from time to time. It can appear in all areas of life and come from a variety of causes. It might stem from a traumatic event, patterns of previous experience, social conditioning (learning rules by observing others), or local environments such as school, work, or home.

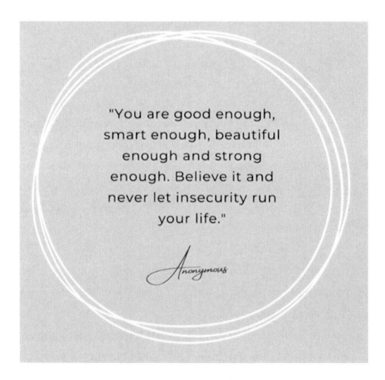

"You are good enough, smart enough, beautiful enough and strong enough. Believe it and never let insecurity run your life."

Anonymous

Only you know your insecurities, whether it be your looks, weight, hair, shoe size, nose, boobs, penis, job, car, partner, the way you dress, your breath, it could be anything, just remember, if you know what they are, you can start working on them. If you leave them, they will grow larger and you will look for evidence that isn't there and it will become toxic. Learning to accept yourself – flaws and all will SET YOU FREE.

My insecurities are:

- _____
- _____
- _____
- _____
- _____
- _____

How will I work on these?

- _____
- _____
- _____
- _____
- _____
- _____

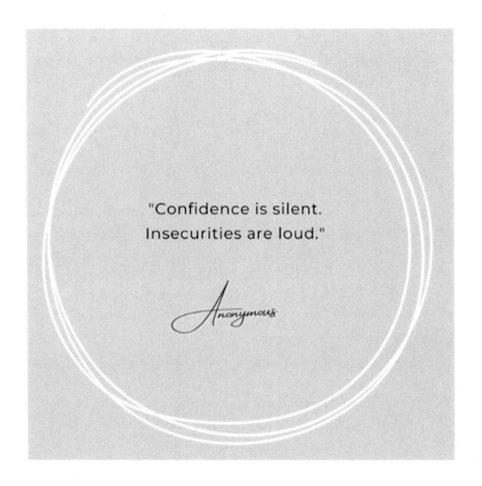

"Confidence is silent.
Insecurities are loud."

Anonymous

Self-acceptance

Self-acceptance is when you vibrate at your highest. We all use the word "vibe". It is just short for vibration; it's a "vibe" you give out. Confidence is naturally associated with this.

'Self-acceptance is defined as 'an individual's acceptance of all of their attributes, positive or negative.' When we're self-accepting, we embrace every part of ourselves, not just the "positive" things! To be self-accepting is to feel satisfied with who you are, despite flaws and regardless of past choices.

Self-acceptance is KEY. Self-acceptance is exactly what its name suggests: the state of complete acceptance of oneself. True self-acceptance is embracing who you are, without any qualifications, conditions or exceptions'
(Seltzer, 2008).

Do you accept yourself, flaws and all? Self-acceptance can be a difficult one, especially when society makes us spend most of our time hating ourselves.

'You accept that, as a fallible human being, you are less than perfect. You will often perform well, but you will also err at times...you always and unconditionally accept yourself without judgement'
(Grieger, 2013).

When you practice unconditional self-acceptance, you can begin to love yourself, embrace your authentic self, and work on improving your less-than-desirable traits and qualities.

Following the plans in this book will help you find the answers to raising your self-acceptance. However, when you start learning about yourself, remember that none of us are perfect, we all have our own unique flaws and qualities. I want you to understand that this is about acceptance of who you are, good, bad and ugly. You can choose to work on the things you really don't like about yourself, or you can choose to stay the same. Whichever it is, own it.

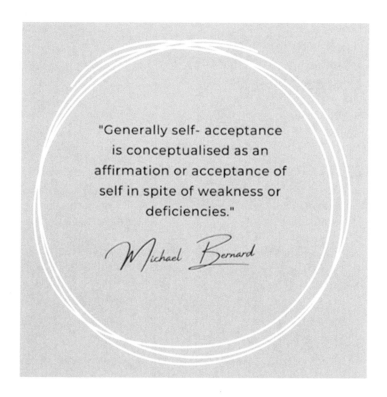

"Generally self- acceptance is conceptualised as an affirmation or acceptance of self in spite of weakness or deficiencies."

Michael Bernard

Another example of being self-aware … I am like a bull in a China shop. I know full well I rush into things and mess them up (like painting, DIY, washing up and many more things) and that I make more work for myself as a result of this. I have accepted this about myself and now I own it, if a job like that needs doing, I call someone else! If I paint, I get more over me and the floor than the walls. I don't like cooking meals that mean using loads of pans and need 50 different things. I like to cook quickly and in one I can. I have to force myself to clean and I can never be bothered to do ironing. I react to emotion rather than responding properly. When I have PMT (or PMDD in my case) I could actually kill someone. PMDD is crazy, because I am me and then it is like the devil takes over. For a few days I feel like evil personified, it's so weird. I know I need to not be around people when I am like that!! Knowing yourself is key. It means you can communicate with partners, colleagues, family and friends clearly and concisely. It can change relationships for the better.

Acceptance

- Knows the situation is temporary
- Is honest and realistic
- Acknowledge unfulfilled dreams with loving kindness
- Lets go of past feelings
- Genuinely listens
- Feels safe even amid uncertainty
- Is connected and humble enough to ask for help

Resistance

- Sees the situations as permanent. It will 'always' be this way
- Avoids feelings and unavoidable facts because they seem to big
- Clings to the past or what "should" be happening
- Feels resigned and hopeless feels jilted that life is not fair
- Seeks to avoid feeling vulnerability and shame

None of us are perfect. I know and accept my flaws but it doesn't mean I can't keep working on them but I understand that some of them are just "me" and that's okay. I accept it, I have fun with it and I can learn how to manage it.

If I killed someone every time I had PMDD. I think I would be in a tiny bit of trouble, so learning to manage that and finding another outlet (meditation / yoga) works wonders.

Keep exploring your mind – keep trying new things, keep curious and open minded. Sometimes we tell ourselves something when we are younger and we carry it around, whether it's a belief and disliking a particular food. If 20 years go by, try it again, who knows what might have changed?

Questions to think about:

- Do I accept myself?
- If I don't accept myself, why?
- Am I accepting of situations?
- What do I resist and why?
- How quickly do I move to acceptance?

Another way to get to know yourself better is to do a SWOT analysis. Taking the strengths you selected earlier in the book – place them now into a personal SWOT analysis.

What Is a Personal SWOT Analysis?

A Personal SWOT analysis is an exercise in self-introspection to help you understand yourself and prepare for growth. Basically said – what do you need to focus on?

What Does SWOT Stand For?

SWOT stands for **Strengths, Weaknesses, Opportunities and Threats**. It is a way to review and analyse yourself using a tool.

First, we need to review some qualities! You have spent some time already throughout this book looking inwardly, so hopefully this exercise should be a bit easier for you...

The biggest benefit to doing your own personal SWOT analysis is the structure it gives your self-evaluation. You might think about what you're good at or what's getting in the way of your personal growth. To understand yourself and be honest with yourself is a great way to really acknowledge who you are.

Secondly, the SWOT focuses on both positive and negative aspects. If you only focus on the good things, then you won't have a clear direction of what to improve or what needs to change. However, if you only focus on your weaknesses and threats, you might get overwhelmed and disinherited before you make it to your action plan.

Thirdly, the SWOT analysis focuses on internal characteristics and factors that affect your opportunities. You'll always have much more control over internal factors compared to external ones. (Note: I don't like the word weakness – I prefer the word 'development' – sounds kinder!)

Strengths:

- What have been your biggest successes?
  (think school, sports, work, group project, passing driving test)
- What characteristics made those accomplishments possible?
- What do you do best?
- What are your positive qualities?
- What qualifications do you have?
  (certifications, degrees, education, training, internships, etc.)
- What projects have you worked on and completed?
  (whether in school, at work, or in your personal life)
- What values do you have that others might not have?
- What knowledge-based skills do you have?
  (languages, digital skills, software knowledge, and other technical skills)
- What soft-skills do you have?
  (teamwork, leadership, dependable, hardworking)
- What positive personality traits do you have?
  (friendly, funny, empathetic, enthusiastic, honest, patient)
- What do other people in your life say are your strengths?
  (friends, parents, co-workers, bosses, teachers)
- What is your passion?

'I know I am an excellent driver. I also have a huge interest in helping others and I'm very patient. Because of this I made it a career and I absolutely love it.'

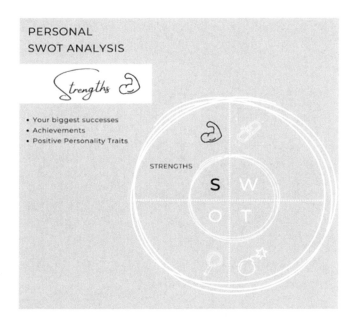

https://slidemodel.com/personal-swot-analysis-quick-guide/

Weaknesses

- What times have you "messed up"? (school, work, relationships, with your family, etc.) What about you or what did you do to cause that issue?
- What tasks do you avoid doing because of a lack of confidence?
- Are you missing any technical qualifications from your education or professional experience?
- What disadvantages do you have?
- What situations and tasks do you usually avoid? Why? What does this say about you as a person?
- What bad habits do you have?
- Have people ever complained about you? (Keep in mind that not all complaints are true reflections of a person) What have been the valid complaints?
- What fears do you have that may be holding you back?
- Think about things that aren't necessarily weaknesses, but things that you could improve.
- What would others say you could improve?

"I need to improve my self-control, especially when it comes to doing things that are necessary like budgeting or cleaning up after myself. I can be impatient and moody. My family says I'm messy."

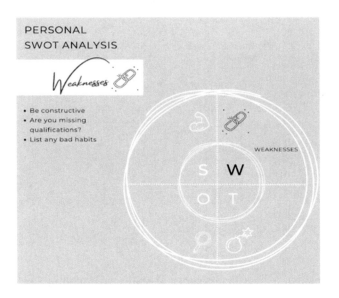

Opportunities:

- How can you turn your strengths into opportunities?
- How can you turn your weaknesses into opportunities?
- What activities or hobbies could you start doing or learn to do?
- Are there any groups you can join?
- What could you achieve in your personal life if you improved on some of your weaknesses?
- Is there a need in your department that no one is meeting?
- What could you do today that isn't being done?
- How is your field changing? How can you take advantage of those changes?
- What new technology may help you meet your goals?
- Do you have contacts that could help you?
- Who in your network could help and support you?
- What books could you read?
- What could you study?

'I have been told if I work on my organisation skills, I could get a promotion in my job. It also means I can organise more girls' holidays!'

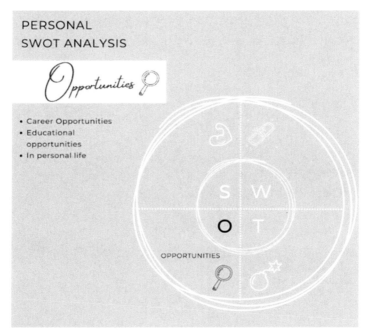

Threats

- Is there someone in your life holding you back?
- Think about your weaknesses: Does anyone in your life exacerbate these weaknesses or encourage them?
- Are there any new trends, technologies, or processes that you can't or haven't gotten involved in that are keeping you from advancing?
- Are there certain tasks, errands, or projects that bog you down and keep you from advancing?
- Is your job, education, or personal life getting in the way of advancing in one of the other areas?
- Do any of your personal traits of weaknesses directly lead to a threat to your success?
- Think about things that, if they were different, would help you move closer to achieving your goals. What are they?
- What obstacles do you face?
- Could any of your weaknesses prevent you from succeeding?
- Do any of your strengths hold you back?

- Is your job (life, health, etc.) changing?
- Do you have any obligations (work or otherwise) that may limit your development?
- Are you competing with others for what you want?
- Are there changes in your field or in technology that could threaten your success?

'I know if I don't sort out my timekeeping, I'm going to get fired from work.'

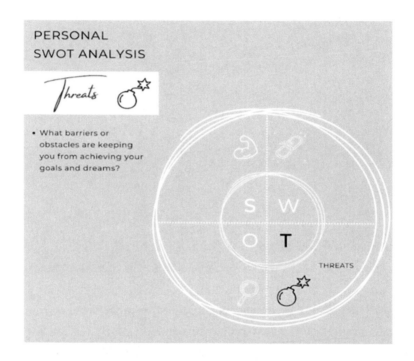

Once you have done your SWOT and had time to breathe, you should ask yourself a few questions:

- Do you notice the theme throughout all of your answers?
- What is the theme?
- What are you going to tackle first?
- How will you prioritise what you will do and when?
- What goals will you set for yourself?

'The biggest difference between successful people and unsuccessful ones (in health, in business, and in life) is that successful people are determined to make the situation work for them rather than playing the role of the victim and searching for reasons why a situation won't work'

https://jamesclear.com/nothing-will-work-if-you-dont-believe-in-it 2008

Work SWOT

We can also repeat this exercise from a work-based point of view – how can we use our professional skills to understand where we want to develop, what opportunities this may produce for us and what might stand in our way.

Strengths

- What advantages do you have that others don't have (for example, skills, certifications, education, or connections)?
- What do you do better than anyone else?
- What personal resources can you access?
- What do other people (and your boss, in particular) see as your strengths?

- Which of your achievements are you most proud of?
- What values do you believe in that others fail to exhibit?
- Are you part of a network that no one else is involved in? If so, what connections do you have with influential people?

Weaknesses

- What tasks do you usually avoid because you don't feel confident doing them?
- What will the people around you see as your weaknesses?
- Are you completely confident in your education and skills training? If not, where are you the weakest?
- What are your negative work habits (for example, are you often late, are you disorganised, do you have a short temper, or are you poor at handling stress)?
- Do you have personality traits that hold you back in your field? For instance, if you have to conduct meetings on a regular basis, a fear of public speaking would be a major weakness.

Opportunities

- What new technology can help you? Or can you get help from others or from people via the internet?
- Is your industry growing? If so, how can you take advantage of the current market?
- Do you have a network of strategic contacts to help you, or offer good advice?
- What trends (management or otherwise) do you see in your company, and how can you take advantage of them?
- Are any of your competitors failing to do something important? If so, can you take advantage of their mistakes?
- Is there a need in your company or industry that no one is filling?
- Are there any networking events, educational classes, or conferences you can attend?
- A colleague going on an extended leave. Could you take on some of this person's projects to gain experience?

- A new role or project that forces you to learn new skills, like public speaking or international relations.
- A company expansion or acquisition. Do you have specific skills (like a second language) that could help with the process?

Threats

- What obstacles do you currently face at work?
- Are any of your colleagues competing with you for projects or roles?
- Is your job (or the demand for the things you do) changing?
- Does changing technology threaten your position?
- Could any of your weaknesses lead to threats?

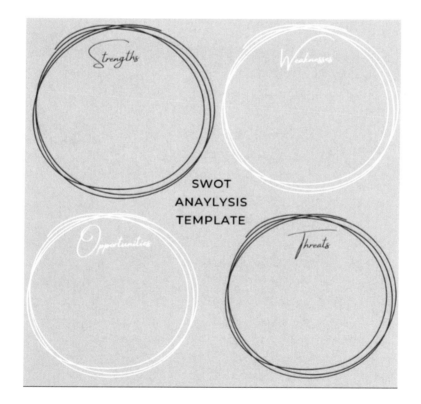

Knowing yourself as well as you can is key to confidence – remember though, that at 41 I am still learning things about myself I never knew – and for me it's a delight when that little light bulb moment happens. It's like, 'Oh yes, I get it now!'

Limiting Beliefs

If you know yourself, you are aware of that negative voice in your head. The one that tells you can't do things because of xyz. The one that stops you. I call that voice 'fear'. It's looking out for you, because it doesn't want you to get hurt. Then because you listen to the voice, and you don't do it (whatever it was), you wonder, what if? Then you torture yourself, then regret kicks in.

Sometimes, these thoughts can manifest when we are young. For example, I know someone who believed she couldn't look after herself (in her very early twenties) and married a man "to look after her" and she held onto that thought for 20 years. She knows full well that now she can look after herself, but it has taken 20 years to get to that place.

What beliefs do you hold on to and why? What stories do you tell yourself to avoid really facing the truth? Do you have regrets? If so, why?

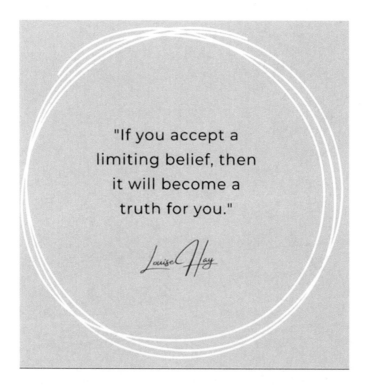

"If you accept a limiting belief, then it will become a truth for you."

Louise Hay

I learnt in my early 20's that regret was NOT going to have a place in my life. I realised quickly how bitter and toxic regret was and how it could have a very negative impact on my life. So, I turned regret into experiences, and I turned experiences into lessons learnt.

If I did something and it didn't go to plan, I didn't regret it, I just chalked it down to experience and learnt from it. After all, my core belief is that the meaning of life is experiences. Some regrets will always be regrets, like over plucking our eyebrows in the 90's – I mean that's a humdinger, right? Hehe.

Like I said at the beginning of this book, your mindset will define your life – and the quality of life. If you can turn negative thoughts, experiences and situations into positive lessons learned life experiences, you will live a better life. You are learning to let go and learn – after all, did anything good come of holding onto the past?

This will all help you to get to know yourself better, which is where the key to confidence lies.

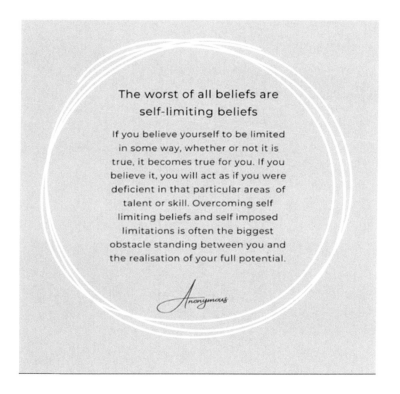

The worst of all beliefs are
self-limiting beliefs

If you believe yourself to be limited
in some way, whether or not it is
true, it becomes true for you. If you
believe it, you will act as if you were
deficient in that particular areas of
talent or skill. Overcoming self
limiting beliefs and self imposed
limitations is often the biggest
obstacle standing between you and
the realisation of your full potential.

Anonymous

You will keep learning things about yourself your whole life if you are open to it. I keep thinking to myself, how much more could I not know about myself and then 'bang' something happens and a new learning experience comes from it. It's mind blowing and I love it. I love RIGHT where I am now in my life because things just keep getting better and better. I'm evolving as a human, as a leader, as a friend and a lover.

Every week I'm learning new things and my affirmations are kicking in as manifestations all over the place and I'm just like 'I'm here for it'. Life is good because I have made it good. I am making it great, then excellent, then incredible, then ridiculously mind blowing – every day's an adventure in the mind. It's so awesome.

By knowing yourself, many wonderful things will happen. Also, some not so wonderful things may happen too – but that is part of our journey to confidence, through self-discovery. Be brave enough to study yourself. Be brave enough to love and accept yourself. Be brave enough to say to the world 'hey this is me, and I'm really OK with it!' Keep working on yourself every day, just like you would if you went to the gym every day – invest in yourself. You are the greatest project you will ever have!

Equation Part 2: (BIY) KY+BIY
Believe in Yourself

"Believe in yourself. Believe in your capacity to do good things. Believe that no mountain is so high that you cannot climb it. Believe that no storm is so great that you cannot weather it. Believe in youself.

Gordan B. Hinckley

The second area is believing in yourself...if you believe in yourself then whatever you tell yourself is the truth! if you believe you can do something, you can do it, if you believe you can't do something, then you can't do it. it's as simple as that – but if you know yourself really well, then you can believe in yourself. Let me say that again – if you know yourself then you can believe in yourself. This is because you're capable of, how far you can go and the fact that you can be pushed to go even further because you've been pushed before and that's what you know about yourself. what you've experienced. No, one else is you and that is your power!

Let me ask you a question – if you don't believe in yourself, why should anyone else?

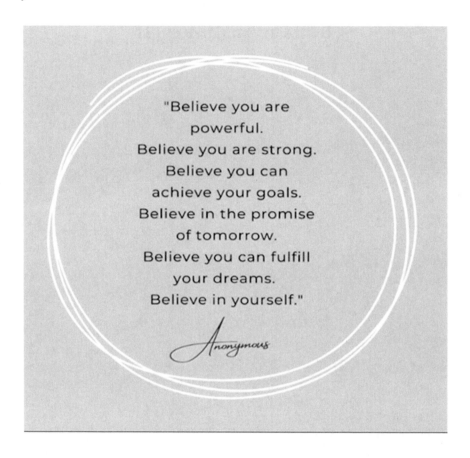

"Believe you are
powerful.
Believe you are strong.
Believe you can
achieve your goals.
Believe in the promise
of tomorrow.
Believe you can fulfill
your dreams.
Believe in yourself."

Anonymous

Believing in yourself means having faith in your own capabilities. It means believing that you CAN do something – that it is within your ability. When you believe in yourself, you can have the confidence to take action and make things happen. Believing in yourself is the key to your own leadership because self-confidence lets you inspire others with assurance, vision and direction.

So, knowing yourself is the first step, then you can really start to believe in your abilities, your powers, your potential, your character and what you really truly bring to the table.

You need to believe in yourself – in your abilities, skills and passions to take a leap into the unknown. Take for example, when I left my husband of 10 years, I had always wanted to renovate property but had zero experience. Yet I **believed** in my heart I could do it, and I **believed in myself** and knew I could do it, so I did it. I bought a rundown house that an elderly person had died in, and literally gutted the whole house. I planned and dealt with the trades myself, ripped up carpets, walls, got quotes, striped walls, tore out fireplaces, grouted tiles, painted, managed a budget solo, fired some trades and kept it all on track. I literally did it all within four months and I was absolutely thrilled, so much so I caught the bug and went on to do another two houses! But my point here is that I told myself I could do it and I didn't let anything stand in my way, I believed in my abilities and my strengths. This is because I know myself and what I am capable of. Even though I had never done anything like this before, I knew in my heart I could do it. Yes, at times it was testing and hard work but I learned so much from doing it…and I continue to learn about myself. Learning about yourself never stops never.

Believing in yourself also means that when times get hard or if you feel rock bottom, you know in your heart this feeling isn't permanent and that you believe in yourself enough to know that you will bring yourself back up. It may take a day, a week or even a month, but you know you believe in yourself to bring it back round.

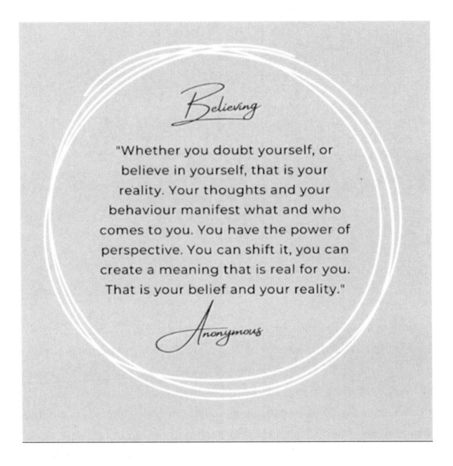

Believing

"Whether you doubt yourself, or believe in yourself, that is your reality. Your thoughts and your behaviour manifest what and who comes to you. You have the power of perspective. You can shift it, you can create a meaning that is real for you. That is your belief and your reality."

Anonymous

Where do I lack belief in myself?

_____

_____

Why do you lack belief in what you wrote above?

_____

_____

How Do You Start Believing in Yourself?

First things first, you have to tell yourself every damn day!

Positive self-talk also known as positive affirmations can manifest themselves in your life as a reality. Believe me, it is a thing!

A quote from health-line 2021 states:

'Affirmations can help strengthen self-worth by boosting both your positive opinion of yourself and your confidence in your ability to achieve your goals. They can also help counter the feelings of panic, stress and self-doubt that often accompany anxiety.'

Every morning, when I walk the dog, I do my positive affirmations. I am speaking it into existence. You have to say the affirmations as if you already have them.

It goes something like this:
- 'I am beautiful, I am strong, I am powerful'
- 'I believe in who I am'
- 'I do not chase, I attract'
- 'I am excelling in my work and in my career'
- 'People trust me and want to work with me'
- 'My listening skills get better every day'
- 'Money comes easily to me'
- 'Universe, show me how good it gets'

The biggest difference I've noticed between successful people and unsuccessful people isn't intelligence or opportunity or resources. It's the belief that they can make their goals happen.

Affirmations

1. I am grateful for this moment
2. I am resilient
3. I am stronger than I think
4. I am equipped with all the tools I need to succeed
5. I am determined to succeed
6. I am intrinsically motivated to achieve goals, overcome challenges and live with passion
7. I am growing through every experience
8. I aspire to be a blessing and an inspiration to other
9. I challenge myself to grow
10. I strive to be the best version of me
11. I have a voice which matters
12. I am capable of making choices in my life
13. I live for those I love
14. I choose compassion and cooperation over competition
15. I am kind
16. I am enough
17. I choose to be positive and optimistic
18. I am faithful
19. I honour my commitments and promises
20. I am blessed
21. I know my worth
22. I am energised by my passion
23. I strive to listen more than I speak
24. I strive to read more than I write
25. I am the author of my story

You can say whatever you want – and the internet has lots of ideas, or you can buy a journal – which you can spend 5 minutes a day on, and keep you focused on your confidence journey. You can have them written and pinned on the wall, or you can make it into a song (totally recommend 'I am woman' by Emmi Meli) or they can come from memory. Just make sure you do them every day as part of your routine, and I promise, YOU will notice a difference.

If you are a fan of social media, I would encourage you to explore the community that lives and shares on these platforms. Their content is inspiring and it challenges my thinking. I love it!

If you use Instagram, pop the # in the search bar for either 'affirmations' or 'manifestations' – some of these communities demonstrate lots of other ways to manifest your dreams, it's really interesting! Also, the platform TikTok, they are always discussing different affirmations and the results, it's worth a look.

Essentially, rather than telling yourself all day every day that you aren't good at this or you can't do that, it's a way of readjusting that lense and telling yourself positive things about yourself.

There are also lots of books on the subject, The Secret being a popular one, but there's a huge variety. It's the key to start believing in yourself – so start today and don't look back.

If you don't believe in yourself – how do you expect anyone else to? Would you believe in someone who had no faith in themselves?

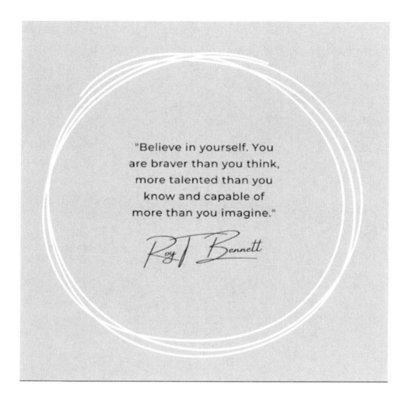

"Believe in yourself. You are braver than you think, more talented than you know and capable of more than you imagine."

Roy T Bennett

My daily affirmations:

1. _____
2. _____
3. _____
4. _____
5. _____

If you look back at your past achievements, think about how and when you succeeded – what did you do then? How did you feel? Drawing from past experience can start to help you with that belief system.

Where have you believed in yourself before where it worked out?

Who are you surrounded by? People, friends, colleagues, associates – are they cheerleading for you? Or do they tell you it can't / won't be done? Outside negative sources can stop you from believing in yourself – so take a look around – are they helping and supporting you, or the opposite?

The thoughts that you think and the way you speak to yourself is so important. Are you telling yourself kind and supportive words? Or do you speak negatively to yourself? Remember, if you had a friend that said the words you tell yourself inside your head – would you be friends with them?

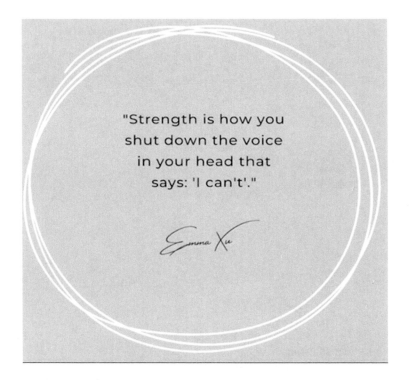

"Strength is how you shut down the voice in your head that says: 'I can't'."

Emma Xu

Help Build Your Self-Belief

- Work on your areas of strengths. Ask your family and friends what they are. Ask for (honest) feedback at work. Take it gracefully, even if it's hard to hear. Figure out what you are good at and work on it and become amazing at it. When you are struggling with confidence, you might focus on things you can't do. These can be painfully highlighted in your mind shame, weakness and failure. "I'm bad at this" quickly escalates to "I'll never be good at anything". So, focus on your strengths and excel at them. Ask others what they trust about you, what do they believe in you for? This is where your strengths will shine through.

- Try to see the positive in the negative… when things go wrong or don't go as planned, usually there is a positive to be found somewhere…One example I have of seeing the positive in every situation is when my 2nd Reno went up for sale. It had been up for a while and I had not sold it yet. Then the detached house opposite went up for sale and it was only £20K more than mine, I was furious! I knew that any potential buyers of mine would see mine and want the house opposite. (mine was a semi) Gutted. Then about an hour later, I thought to myself, you know what Adele, that house being for sale might drive MORE people to see yours…boom positive found in the negative. You have to practice!

- Be your own cheerleader and coach.

  o I describe myself as a cheerleader. I'm always encouraging and cheering my friends on. I don't see any competition, just pure love and well wishes for them to achieve their best. Why wouldn't you want the best for yourself? Why wouldn't you treat yourself like you treat your friends?

  o I coach myself all the time in any situation. I work through different outcomes and how I might deal with each situation. I work out the impact of each action on the situation or other people before I decide what to do. It helps stop overthinking and creates a plan.

- Embrace who you are

  o How can you have faith in yourself when you don't know who you really are? Or worse, you are trying hard to be someone you're not. Self-confidence comes from embracing who you are and what's important to you. It does not come from being inauthentic or trying to impress people. So, if you don't like yourself, you probably won't embrace yourself. That's something this book will help you with, but it starts with your-self acceptance.

- So, part of this book is about knowing yourself and once you have that figured, you can embrace who you are. Remember to be honest with yourself. Really honest, raw honesty is best.
- Recently I got into crystals, tarot, spirituality, chakras, sound baths, wild swimming and crystal healing. This isn't for everyone and when I tell people about it, I get some comments or funny looks, but I have decided that is who I am and what makes me, me. It's not harming anyone and I totally own it – if someone doesn't like it, as far as I'm concerned, that's their problem not mine! I'm not hurting or harming anyone!

- **Be uncomfortable**

  - Good things never happened in your comfort zone did they? You have to be able to push yourself to try new things and this means stepping outside of your comfort zone.
  - Experimenting with different skills, approaches, and tactics in your life is one of the best ways to build confidence and foster mental toughness. Sure, it's uncomfortable! New things always are.

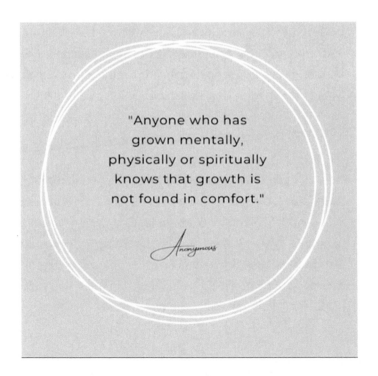

"Anyone who has grown mentally, physically or spiritually knows that growth is not found in comfort."

Anonymous

'When I was kicked off a train in the middle of the night while travelling through Hungary, I was lost and confused. I couldn't find anyone who spoke English, so as the train pulled away, I ran alongside, hopped back on, and trusted that I would figure it out anyway. When I've discovered an opportunity that sounds awesome but that I'm not qualified for (which happens often), I trust that I'll figure it out and go for it anyway. I believe in myself. This confidence has made the difference for me again and again. I didn't need intelligence or opportunity or resources. Just a simple belief in myself.'

– James Clear

- Past experience

  o Where in the past have you done something when you believed you could do it? We all learnt to walk as children, we just didn't stop trying, we fell over again and again but not at one point did we say, 'I keep falling over, I guess I'll give up.' Did we? You have achieved something and you believed in yourself to do it!

The magic happens by simply believing it's possible. Your belief in possibility is necessary to the work, the experimentation, and the consistency needed to change your life.

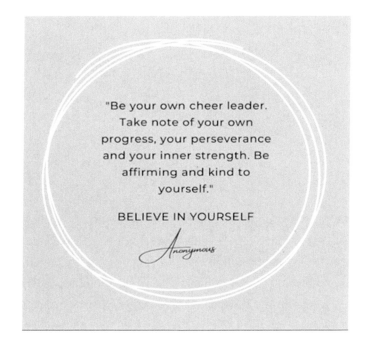

"Be your own cheer leader.
Take note of your own
progress, your perseverance
and your inner strength. Be
affirming and kind to
yourself."

BELIEVE IN YOURSELF

Anonymous

I promise YOU if you believe in yourself, anything is possible.

Have fun and enjoy!

Visualization – What Is It?

Visualization can be described as the following:

Visualization is any technique for creating images, diagrams, or animations to communicate a message. Visualization through visual imagery has been an effective way to communicate both abstract and concrete ideas since the dawn of humanity.

You need an imagination!

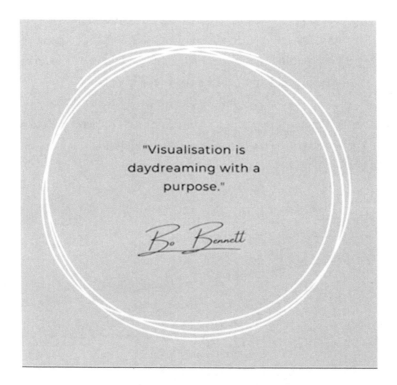

"Visualisation is daydreaming with a purpose."

Bo Bennett

Visualization is something I do a lot. It's imagining, or seeing your future self-doing / saying or being is incredibly powerful. Let me give you an example:

If you want to feel and be confident, – you have to "see" yourself in that way. You can't aim to be confident if you don't know what that looks like for you.

One thing I do with my coaches is to ask them where they would rate their confidence now on a scale of 1–10. If they say they are at 3 now and they want to be a 7… I would ask them what a 7 looks like for them. To aim for something, you have to know what it looks like.

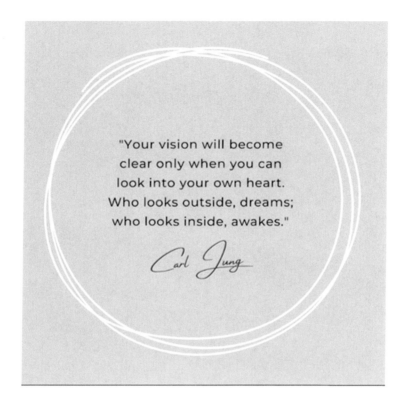

"Your vision will become clear only when you can look into your own heart. Who looks outside, dreams; who looks inside, awakes."

Carl Jung

Try this exercise:

You are walking into a room full of people, and you are feeling confident. How do you walk? (Do the walk for me please, actually get up and walk how you would walk)

How do you hold yourself? What is your posture like? How does it make you feel?

When you speak, how do you speak? Notice your tone, pitch and pace. Now you know what you are aiming for – so start practicing the walk.

Posture, words and feel – visualize it and start doing it each and every day.

Remember – practice makes permanent. Only by visualising our future selves can we show up as that person!

"To bring anything into your life, imagine that it's already there."

Richard Bach

These are tips from the coaching academy 2021 around visualization:

1. Visualize the Familiar

If you don't feel experienced in visualization then look at what is familiar to you. Think about what you had for lunch? Think about the colour of your front door? Who was your favourite teacher? What was your first pet? Where did you go for your last holiday? Start in those familiar places and relive the experience. That is Visualization!

2. Visual Navigation

Close your eyes and begin to remember journeys that you have made before, now in your mind. Positive journeys. Perhaps start with a walk around your favourite place and re-notice all the landmarks – the smells, the sound, and the feelings. Perhaps around your old school, a place where you worked, somewhere that you visited. Notice as much as you can in your mind. Revisit this place often and notice new things. This will help you to develop your neurological pathways and create the basis for change. For re-visiting places in Visual Navigation, make sure that you only revisit places that are kayak for you psychologically.

When I am renovating houses, I use this method. I visualize myself walking into the house when it is all done, I look around, I see how it looks, the colours, the textures, how I visualize myself using the sink or the cooker, hanging my coat. I walk through the entire house. It's an amazing way to be there in 3D with VR! Its future visualization, as I am not familiar with it as it's not finished, but if I don't see it in my mind, how will I know what it will turn out like?

3. Self-Talk

Look at the language that you use to yourself. Is it full of demands; should, musts, have to do? These put unnecessary pressure on yourself and make the journey towards your goal much more demanding. Think of converting your demands to preferences, have a desire for action and create a new language to yourself that is more helpful.

4. Repetition, Repetition, Repetition

The key to success in goal achievement is repetition. Eventually new behaviours become new habits and unhelpful behaviours are extinguished. Regular practice of new behaviours, such as Goal Visualization, lays down new neurologists as 'templates' in the brain that you access from new memory. The name of the game is Repetition; new behaviours become habits over time.

5. Short-Term Goals

Practice regular short-term goal visualization, perhaps 5 minutes twice every day. Imagine the Stepping Stones that you will take towards your goal and make the images as vivid and as real as possible. Think about When, Where and With Whom?

6. Familiar Anchors

Use familiar objects to "Anchor" or "Fix" the images and the feelings of your new goals. Use things such as trees, steps, buildings, traffic lights. Things that you will encounter on a regular basis and that will remind you of the steps along your journey and your goal.

7. Outcome or Process

Research has shown that if you focus on the Process (The Steps), as well as the Outcome (your Final Goal), that the end result will be more durable and effective than focusing only on the Outcome (Pham & and Taylor 1999). Visualizing and imagining the steps along the way as well as the final goal will make the result much more successful.

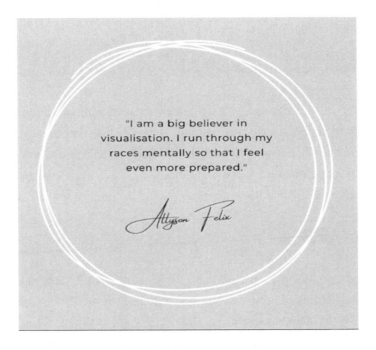

"I am a big believer in visualisation. I run through my races mentally so that I feel even more prepared."

Allyson Felix

Another of mine is a visualization board. I have LOTS of Pinterest, but recently after talking to a close friend, he encouraged me to make one and have it in my office where I look at it every day, – so I did just that!

A vision board is simply a visual collage of images and words that represent your goals and dreams in life. A vision board is also a powerful way to activate the manifestation to attract the people, resources, and opportunities that will help you achieve your goals and make your dreams come true.

Create a board, one that you will see daily and add what represents you feeling confident. Keep adding to it and reviewing it daily, make it part of your routine. It will manifest into reality!

Pinterest is great for on the go, – I use Pinterest for my interior design ideas, however feeling materialist, I started a board of all the luxury things I could never afford to buy – this included designer gloves, a Rolex, fancy hair dryers, bespoke trainers, Hollywood mirrors and a G-wagon! Well, I can tell you that I now have all of these except a G-wagon (I'm working on that right…!)

What if we did the same with ***our mindset instead of material things?*** I post quotes daily about the life I want to live – and I am living my dream life, so what can get better than that? Remember, happiness is a state of being, not a destination.

Visualize your best, confident self, turning up everyday day and it WILL start to happen.

How I will start to visualize my best confident self:

_____

_____

_____

Visualisation:

- Ensure your goals are one of the first things you think of every day
- Write down your mantras, create a routine to say them daily
- Helps you remember your focus and what you want out of life
- Creating your vision board can be a powerful, meditative process that brings clarity on what you really want your life to look and feel like
- Inspires you and boost your mood & expands your sense of what's possible
- Helps you remember what's most important and not sweat the small stuff
- You can share them with others to enlist their support in helping you achieve your vision

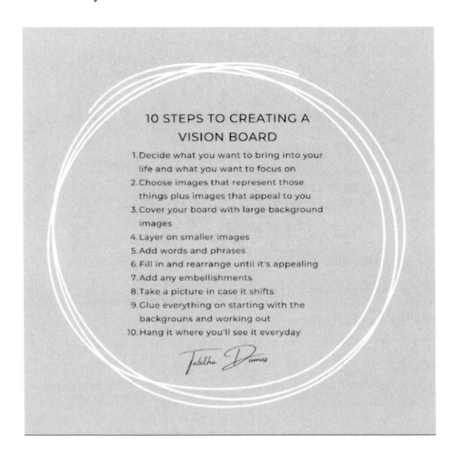

10 STEPS TO CREATING A
VISION BOARD

1. Decide what you want to bring into your life and what you want to focus on
2. Choose images that represent those things plus images that appeal to you
3. Cover your board with large background images
4. Layer on smaller images
5. Add words and phrases
6. Fill in and rearrange until it's appealing
7. Add any embellishments
8. Take a picture in case it shifts
9. Glue everything on starting with the backgrouns and working out
10. Hang it where you'll see it everyday

Tabitha Dumas

Another way to visualize, and it's my favourite, is when I'm renovating. I often visualize myself walking around the new kitchen or the bathroom when I'm designing, as I want to make the best use of the space, so I have to transport myself there. I walk through the front door, down the corridor and walk into the room – what are the first things I see? What is the lighting like?

What do the countertops feel like under touch? I arrange the furniture and I see different colours on the walls, where pictures will go and where the TV and bar cart will be placed. The best way for me to do that is usually when I go to bed, totally relaxed, and I close my eyes and off I go. It's great to do it with anything I want to "'see" 'like a presentation at work, or a piece of work I need to do, or a difficult conversation I might have to navigate. It can be used for a whole host of things!

Something else to try is to remember a time when you were at your most confident. You radiated it from every pore. Take yourself back to that space – what made you feel so confident? What were you wearing? What perfume did you have on? How did you walk? How did others respond or react to you?

Dr Gia Marsdon states: Visualisation has many benefits backed by studies. When done right, a regular visualisation practice can help you:

- Gain confidence
- Decrease anxiety
- Enhance performance
- Boost your motivation
- Adopt healthier behaviours, such as eating more fruit
- Increase muscle strength
- Reduce pain
- Relieve stress
- Speed up healing
- Improve prospective memory, or remembering to do something in the future
- Spark inspiration
- Spark inspiration
- Improve mood
- Declutter your mind
- Determine what you want

Visualisation is a great way to enhance and instill confidence. This is because you have spent time thinking about the person you want to be, who you want to show up as, where you want to go with your life… this means you have thought things through and feel confident around your decision making, your life choices and the life you choose to live. You know what you want your life to look like and you are creating it. This creates true confidence in yourself. You are the captain of your ship and you know where you are headed!

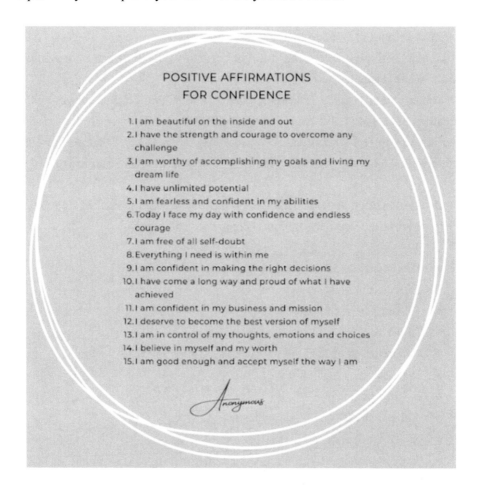

POSITIVE AFFIRMATIONS
FOR CONFIDENCE

1. I am beautiful on the inside and out
2. I have the strength and courage to overcome any challenge
3. I am worthy of accomplishing my goals and living my dream life
4. I have unlimited potential
5. I am fearless and confident in my abilities
6. Today I face my day with confidence and endless courage
7. I am free of all self-doubt
8. Everything I need is within me
9. I am confident in making the right decisions
10. I have come a long way and proud of what I have achieved
11. I am confident in my business and mission
12. I deserve to become the best version of myself
13. I am in control of my thoughts, emotions and choices
14. I believe in myself and my worth
15. I am good enough and accept myself the way I am

Anonymous

Imposter syndrome

Impostor syndrome is a belief in which an individual doubts their skills, talents, or accomplishments and has a persistent internalized fear that they will "get found out".

This is where believing in yourself is key. If you have the full equation to confidence, then it's likely you have imposter syndrome. If you have imposter syndrome, it's likely because one of the 3 are missing from your equation to confidence. Which one is missing for you?

Healthiness 2020 state:

'Imposter feelings represent a conflict between your own self-perception and the way others perceive you. Even as others praise your talents, you write off your successes to timing and good luck. You don't believe you earned them on your own merits, and you fear others will eventually realize the same thing. Over time, this can fuel a cycle of anxiety, depression, and guilt.'

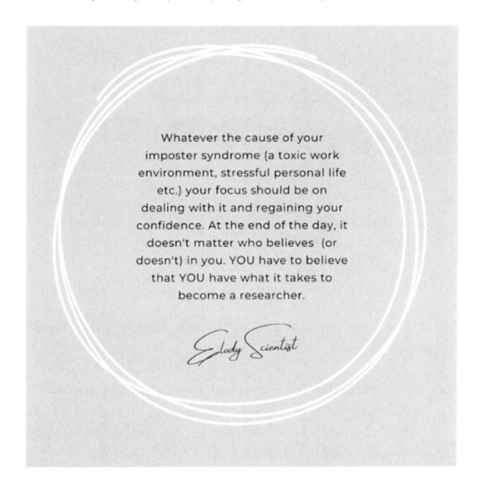

Whatever the cause of your imposter syndrome (a toxic work environment, stressful personal life etc.) your focus should be on dealing with it and regaining your confidence. At the end of the day, it doesn't matter who believes (or doesn't) in you. YOU have to believe that YOU have what it takes to become a researcher.

Elody Scientist

Very Well Mind 2022 state:

'You might have imposter syndrome if you find yourself consistently experiencing self-doubt, even in areas where you typically excel.1 Imposter syndrome may feel like restlessness and nervousness, and it may manifest as negative self-talk. Symptoms of anxiety and depression often accompany imposter syndrome.'

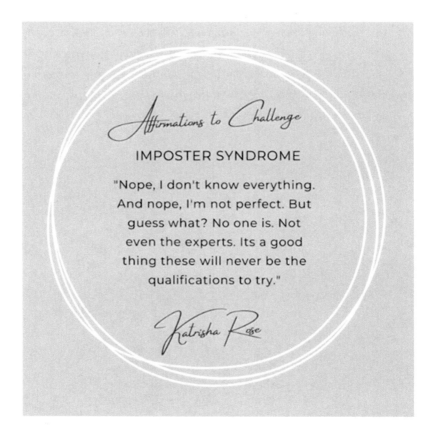

Affirmations to Challenge

IMPOSTER SYNDROME

"Nope, I don't know everything. And nope, I'm not perfect. But guess what? No one is. Not even the experts. Its a good thing these will never be the qualifications to try."

Katrisha Rose

Accordingly, to Very Well Mind 2022 – these are the 5 types of Imposter Syndrome:

- **The Perfectionist**. This type of imposter syndrome involves believing that, unless you were absolutely perfect, you could have done better. You feel like an imposter because your perfectionistic traits make you believe that you're not as good as others might think you are.
- **The Expert**. The expert feels like an imposter because they don't know everything there is to know about a particular subject or topic, or they haven't mastered every step in a process. Because there is more for them to learn, they don't feel as if they've reached the rank of "expert".

- **The Natural Genius**. In this imposter syndrome type, you may feel like a fraud simply because you don't believe that you are naturally intelligent or competent. If you don't get something right the first time around or it takes you longer to master a skill, you feel like an imposter.
- **The Soloist**. It's also possible to feel like an imposter if you had to ask for help to reach a certain level or status. Since you couldn't get there on your own, you question your competence or abilities.
- **The Superperson**. This type of imposter syndrome involves believing that you must be the hardest worker or reach the highest levels of achievement possible and, if you don't, you are a fraud.

I am not a doctor, so please seek the help you need if you feel this may be rooted in a medical issue. If it is not a medical issue, then we need to explore how we can believe we are in the right job because you have the right abilities.

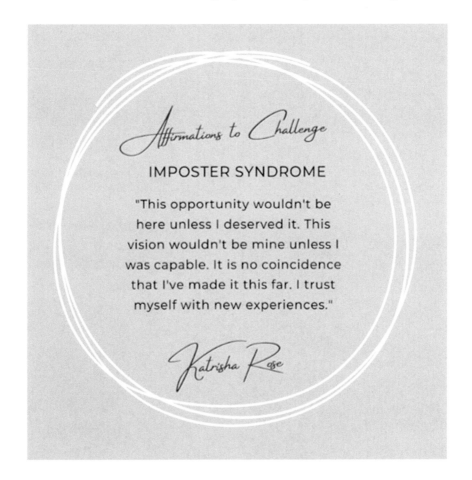

Affirmations to Challenge

IMPOSTER SYNDROME

"This opportunity wouldn't be here unless I deserved it. This vision wouldn't be mine unless I was capable. It is no coincidence that I've made it this far. I trust myself with new experiences."

Katrisha Rose

What do I think about myself that I know is not true?

_____

_____

Why do I believe my thoughts about myself on Imposter Syndrome?

_____

_____

What steps do I need to take to reframe my thoughts?

_____

_____

How will I know when I have achieved this?

_____

_____

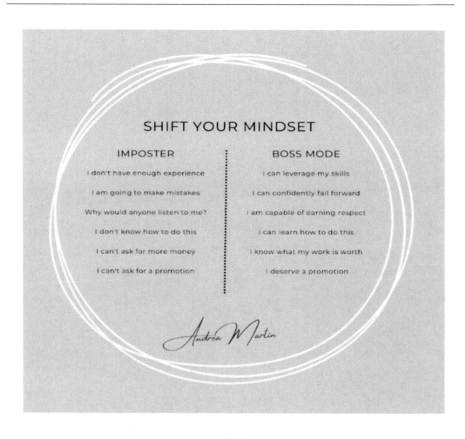

SHIFT YOUR MINDSET

IMPOSTER	BOSS MODE
I don't have enough experience	I can leverage my skills
I am going to make mistakes	I can confidently fail forward
Why would anyone listen to me?	I am capable of earning respect
I don't know how to do this	I can learn how to do this
I can't ask for more money	I know what my work is worth
I can't ask for a promotion	I deserve a promotion

Andrea Martin

Write your new statement about how you feel about yourself:

Old imposter statement:
New boss statement:
Old imposter statement:
New boss statement:

Old imposter statement:
New boss statement:

Old imposter statement:
New boss statement:

Old imposter statement:
New boss statement:

By embracing confidence, you can really make a difference to your thinking, which in turn will help you with your thoughts about yourself in the workplace. Remember – you have to practice! There is no magic wand!

"Imposter syndrome: ' I don't know what I am doing. It's only a matter of time until everyone finds out.'

Growth mindset: ' I don't know what I a doing. It's only a matter of time until I figure it out.'

The highest form of self confidence is believe in your ability to learn."

Adam Grant

Comfort Zones

'Life begins at the end of your comfort zone'

Comfort zones are where it's easy, comforting and stable. Nothing challenges you here or forces you to grow. It's our safe space. Our sanctuary. But it is also our prison. Fear keeps you locked up in there. YOU HAVE to push yourself out of it if you truly want to start being confident. I have a saying in life "Practice makes Permanent", start with practicing one small thing to make you feel confident, do it daily, push yourself and make yourself do it. You will see the difference in yourself and please observe the reactions of others when you try. Notice how they react vs. what you assumed they would do. Notice how you feel after you have pushed yourself out, notice how you feel in a few days, a week, a month, keep trying and challenge yourself to try someone new every day that pushes you further outside your comfort zone. If you want to be confident, you have to make it happen, no one else can do it for you. It's your responsibility and yours only.

Recently, I feel like I am at the top of my game in my work role. I have been thinking about this a lot and wondering what this means for me. I feel this is dangerous and I'm aware of this as I do not want to become complacent...I started a discussion with my coach (yes I have a coach and if you don't I highly recommend you get one…more on that later) about how I want to be surrounded by people who challenge me (in the right way) and push me to expand my mind.

I want my thinking to be challenged by others and I want to always explore the art of the possible. I want to be stretched and challenged and pushed. This will all bring out new learning and new thoughts and I'm excited for it. I love the thought of what might come from a conversation where my thinking is challenged and I'm exposed to new ideas. I have a very open mind and because I know myself well, I know how I would respond in these situations (not attack or get upset, but curious to understand) and this is why I loved being pushed out of my comfort zone. I am comfortable with being uncomfortable.

Start by thinking about when you last stepped outside your comfort zone… what happened? How did it feel? Are you glad you did it?

Experience is what life is all about, learning, growing, trying new things, having fun…

How will we ever know if we will love something if we don't ever try it? We all have the strength and curiosity to do it…but we hold ourselves back…why?

Try something new, even if it is just practicing gratitude every day. Why not?

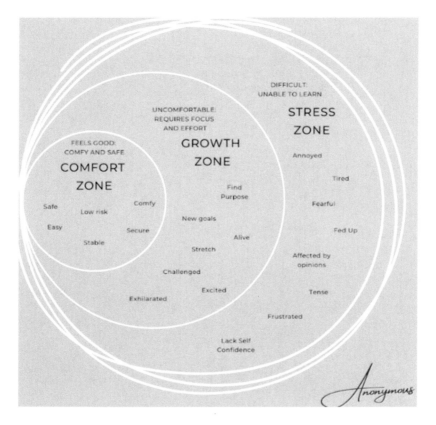

To believe in yourself is true inner confidence. In you, your abilities, your mindset, what your capabilities are, your strengths, weaknesses, and vulnerability – all of it!

The only person who can truly believe in you is yourself. So, go do it, show the world how incredible you are! I BELIEVE IN YOU!

Do you believe in yourself???

Equation KY + BIY + TIY
=Trust in Yourself

The Third Area Is Trust in Yourself (TIY)

If you know yourself, and believe in yourself, then you have to TRUST yourself.

Trust in your skills, your knowledge, your beliefs, what you bring to the table, how you conduct yourself, respect, loyalty, reliability, you know if a situation were to arise, you would 100% trust yourself to show up and do the right thing.

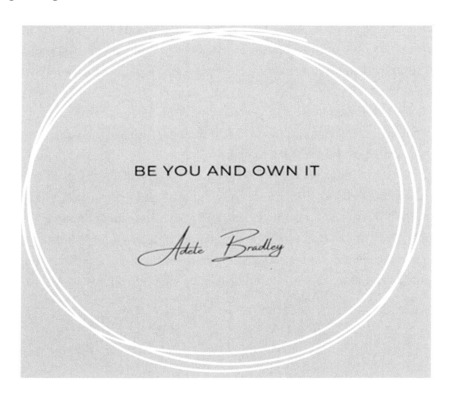

BE YOU AND OWN IT

Adele Bradley

Since of People 2022 state:' *Self-trust means consistently staying true to yourself. At its very core, trusting yourself means you look after your own needs and safety. You treat yourself with love and compassion, rather than strive for perfection. You know, deep down, that you can survive difficulties (and you refuse to give up on yourself). People who trust themselves stay true to their values and beliefs, regardless of their situation. They know they are capable of overcoming obstacles and surviving difficulties. When life throws lemons at them, they refuse to give up or lose hope.'*

Read more at: https://www.scienceofpeople.com/trust-yourself/

You know the imitations in which you operate and you are aware of your capabilities (hidden or otherwise as you know there is always more back there, right!)

I know that I trust my decision-making process. I trust myself because I know myself and I believe in myself, I have experience and I know I am good at making decisions under pressure. I know how to make a decision quickly and stick with it, usually with a 100% success rate of no regrets. I trust my reliability (I can always be relied on, one of my core values) and I trust my gut implicitly. I trust how I choose to show up and I trust my work ethic, my morals and value set. I trust how I show up to every meeting at work, because I believe in myself because I know myself.

I really LIKE who I am! Yes, part of being confident means you have to like who you are – warts and all. I trust myself to always get the job done, and to a high standard, I trust myself not to make mistakes but to forgive myself if I do and learn from it. I trust myself to pay my mortgage and bills every month (never missed a payment in my life), I trust myself to walk and feed my dog every day. I trust myself that if I go on a night out, and I have something important in the morning, that I trust myself to go home and not pull an all-nighter. More than likely, after reading this, you trust yourself more than you realize. You probably just got up "and did it" but it's part of trusting yourself to do this.

"Self trust is the first
secret of success."

Ralph Waldo Emerson

People who trust themselves, have tools and techniques that they use as mindset tools, day in, day out. For example, those who worry, you can spend hours, days, months even years worrying about things that you have NO control over. What's the point in worrying about things you can't change? It's like walking around with a brolly up waiting for it to rain. Pointless.

Psychology today state:

"Self-trust is not trusting yourself to know all the answers, nor is it believing that you will always do the right things.
It's having the conviction that you will be kind and respectful to yourself regardless of the outcome of your efforts"

The best way to combat this? Write down everything that you are worrying about, cross the things out you have no control over and then do something about what is left on the list that you can do.

Why is Self-Trust So Important?

'Trusting yourself is one of the most helpful things you can do for yourself in your life. It can help build your confidence, allow others to trust you more, and make the process of decision making much easier. To trust yourself, all you need is to make a little effort, create self-love, and find the ability to look inward.'

(Healthline, 2022)

To look inward, we have to really look. Not only about how we think, but how our bodies react too. How do our bodies react to situations, people, work or life? How do you feel when you are around certain people, events or situations?

If we are going to look inward, we have to learn to trust what our bodies are telling us... our gut feelings, feeling dizzy or sick, a knowing feeling, a tingly feeling or all other sorts of messages that our bodies use to try and communicate to us.

Let's talk about 'gut feeling' …

Trust your "gut"

When you trust your gut, what does that mean? Healthline 2022 states, '*A sixth sense, hunch or gut feeling. Whatever you choose to call it, the sudden flash of insight from deep within can inspire plenty of faith. The old saying "Trust your gut" refers to trusting these feelings of intuition, often as a way to stay true to yourself.*'

Some people call it Spidey senses. Some people, intuition, some others, trusting the universe. Whatever you call it, we all have and we need to get to know this feeling better.

Healthline 2022 also states, '*Ever experienced a nagging feeling of unease about a situation? Suddenly felt suspicious about someone you just met? You can't explain your feelings logically, but you know something isn't quite right. Or maybe a rush of affirmation or calm floods you after a tough decision, convincing you that you're doing the right thing.*'

That our gut, our six-sense telling us exactly what to do, get out of danger! Move! Don't trust that person! You can trust this person!

I trust my gut implicitly; it never lets me down. But to be able to trust it, I had to get to know myself and understand that "sixth sense" and what it is trying to tell me. I trust her because based on previous experiences on how I have made my decisions, every single one of them has been right with no regrets, so therefore experience dictates I am doing the right thing by listening and trusting her.

Note: There is a difference between wishful thinking and gut feeling. You have to establish the difference so you aren't kidding yourself!

How to Recognise a Gut Feeling?

- A flash of clarity
- Just feeling like "you know"
- Tension or tightness in your body
- Your body feels in tune with it
- A warm feeling across your body

- Goosebumps or prickling
- A feeling of agreement
- A sinking sensation in the pit of your stomach
- A "feeling" in the pit of your stomach
- A feeling of sickness / nausea
- Sweaty palms or feet
- Butterflies
- A "rush" that comes over you
- Thoughts that keep returning to a specific person or situation
- Feelings of peace, safety, relief or happiness (after making a decision)

What are yours?

_____

_____

Gut Feelings Lead You in A Clear Direction

That sense of knowing you recognize as a gut feeling tends to come up in specific situations or when thinking about a certain person. This intuition usually leads you toward a concrete decision or action. Anxiety, on the other hand, tends to focus on the future and often has less definition.

With anxiety, you might find yourself worrying about all manner of concerns, particularly those you can't change or control. You might come up with several solutions to cope with potential negative scenarios but not feel certain about any of them. My advice? If it makes you feel anxious or any sort of way, it's a warning from your gut. Listen to it!

Confidence matters. Self-trust from your own abilities and mental / physical preparation can literally be a game-changer.

An example of where I used and trust my gut feel the most:

- Viewing and buying houses: My instinct / gut feels / tells me instantly. I was thinking about how to explain it and it got me thinking. It's a feeling, and once you hone into these feelings, you can start to understand what they are telling you. I just "know". The feeling tells me. It's like it says, 'Yes, this is the one, I know and you know.' However, sometimes these things don't work out – I and my best friend have a saying we have always used 'if it's meant to be, it will be.' When I was looking to buy my first renovation property, I found a place and it was just behind my mum and dad's house. I thought it was perfect, and even more perfect too if I was working away, my parents would let the trades in and out. I decided to go for it, and I got it! But then my sale fell through on my house and I had to let it go. I knew if I was meant to have it, I would. I was gutted. But these things happen right. I was sure that house was meant for me, but alas it seemed not (if it's meant to be, it will be, right) so there was nothing I could do until I re-sold my house. Then, I sold my house luckily to proceed again with my sale. My mum mentioned about a month later that the house I had lost, it had gone back on the market. Apparently, the sale had fallen through! so, as I had a new buyer on my property, I got the house. My gut knew I would, I had to trust the process.

People and relationships

- I always trust people until they give me a reason not to but sometimes, I meet people and my gut literally screams at me. I feel people's "vibes" that" they give out. I can tell a lot about a person by only spending a few minutes within their company. I can tell if they are a "good" soul or a "damaged" soul. We all watch those programs like Sherlock Holmes or James& Bond, where the main character "knows" things about that person and can provide intricate detail. I'm not saying I am there yet to that level of detail but I have started to recognize some real signs into how people operate.

- We've all been there, we have all met people that just instantly turned us "off" (mood hoovers, energy vampires, people who are just out to find fault, argue or pick at things, negative people, doom and gloom people, people with bad intentions, angry people, I can go on...) They all give out energy / vibrations and it's these we pick up on. Trust what your gut tells you. It's telling you for a reason.

- It's the same with you and your partner – you can pick up if they behave or act differently or even just pick up that their "vibration" is not the same as usual and you "feel" this.

- Or you might have said in a conversation, 'I just feel it' and you just "know", that is your gut feeling.

- Whatever it looks like for you, listen to it! If your feeling has always proved to be right, it's time to start trusting it and listening to it more. It's there for a reason!

Decision Making

If I'm totally honest, my gut makes all my decisions. I use logic where required, but I will get an instant reaction in the form of a feeling that tells me exactly what I need to do. I completely trust myself in every way possible. This is because I know myself! During a renovation, I have to make about 15 plus decisions a day, so I have to know myself to trust myself in my decision-making process. This takes time, experience and practice, remember!

Sandy Woznicki tells us "Let's talk about how freaking hard it is to make confident decisions without worrying all night that someone is going to misinterpret your email...Or trusting yourself to make a choice without fear of missing out because maybe the other option "might be better" Or not feeling guilty when you need to choose time for yourself instead of time for your kids once in a while...Or pushing through your overthinking and get to work instead of procrastinating another month or 2 (or year or 2) before writing that book because you "must do it perfectly from the get-go...Or to make quick decisions instead of feeling like an idiot when you can't make a simple choice. At the height of my anxiety, I remember several times having to abandon my half full grocery cart in the cereal aisle and leave because I felt so overwhelmed and like such an idiot because I didn't have a shopping list, and I didn't have the capacity at the time to make simple decisions. Because here's the truth: The reason you have a hard time making decisions isn't because you aren't smart enough. It isn't because you don't have enough information.

Smart people have a hard time making decisions because overthinking FEELS like problem solving. And we are problem solvers! But in reality, it's a protection strategy giving you the illusion of control. The real problem is that you don't trust your empowered action to make decisions and trust doesn't mean that you know beyond any shadow of doubt that you are right or that everything will work out perfectly. It's about betting on yourself to be right while also knowing that if things don't turn out, you trust "future you" will be able to figure it out."

By tuning into your 'gut instinct' when it comes to decision making, you can start a 'test and learn'. Did you get it right? And if you didn't, why was that and what happened? Start to recognize and observe how you make decisions, it's a game changer. It's part of your reflective practice.

"Wanting to be right is a signal that you're not trusting yourself to make the right decision."

Listening to the universe and its signs

- I still don't always do this but I need to. Remember the so-called "fuel" crisis when panic buyers bought all the petrol? I was due to be at a work meeting that was 2hrs away – the fuel crisis happened and I wasn't sure if I should go or not (if I am not sure, I have now learnt, don't do it.) I went, barely managing to get some fuel and that evening a lorry crashed into the back of me. If I had stayed at home, that wouldn't have happened. I get signs quite often but I choose to ignore them, usually at my own peril. Another sign from the universe was recently, I was due at another work meeting 90 mins away, I set off and also immediately I got a call to say there had been a Covid outbreak at the site we were due to be at. So, we changed venues. Then 5 mins after that, they shut the motorway due to an accident and I had to divert off and take all the backroads, which turned the trip into 3hrs. I massively felt like both these things were signs not to go – my boss even suggested virtual but by this time we had agreed on the new venue. 3 days later, me and my boss tested positive for COVID – which we picked up in the venue. I knew I should have just turned around and gone home.
- I am listening more and more to the signs. You have to learn how to tune into them and what they mean. I am getting better at seeing them, I need to be better at doing something about it! I know that if I am EVER unsure, that means my gut is telling me DON'T DO IT or TAKE CAUTION, for example, I was invited somewhere recently that I have ALWAYS wanted to go to but it's been years since I have thought about it and recently came in conversation about going there. Initially I was like OMG, yes, I want to go – but my gut feel didn't match what was going on in my head. Weird, I wondered why and sat and thought about

it. I was 10 years younger when I wanted to go to this place, and 10 years ago I was a completely different person to who I am now. I have different priorities, lifestyle and mentality. The thought of going to this place is nice but if I'm truly honest with myself, that time has passed. I'm totally okay with not going, and actually, even had a tiny bit of anxiety at the thought of going. I really did let my gut, totally make that decision, because I trust my gut. She is always right.

How to Develop Self-Trust

- Give yourself space to feel your feelings.
- It's okay to be sad, lonely, and hysterical or however you feel, you trust yourself that you won't dwell and the feeling will pass through as they need to. Having a real sense of awareness of your feelings is key to trusting yourself.
- Create a positive relationship with your inner critic.
- Looking for the positive in every situation, challenging the inner voice with positive affirmations and being kind to yourself. Learn how to silence that inner voice.
- Make self-care a priority.
- Lots of walking, breathing, good eating, exercise, sleep, drinking water, reading, less TV, hair, nails and home.
- Choose your advice sources and friends carefully.
- Who is a good influence and who is not in your circle? Toxic or people who don't have your best interests at heart may not always have your best interests at heart when they advise you. Choose your circle carefully. Keep it close and healthy.
- Notice how it feels when you don't trust yourself.
- Become self-aware of when this happens and make a mental or journal note. Why happened to cause it and why has it happened?
- **Let go of habits / routines that undermine your self-trust. Things such as;**
  - Look like you're not listening / you don't follow through on promises / you use the wrong tone of voice.
  - Or it could be putting yourself last, accepting less than you deserve or you just focus on your flaws.

o   Think what yours might be and start to work on them one day at a time, step by step…

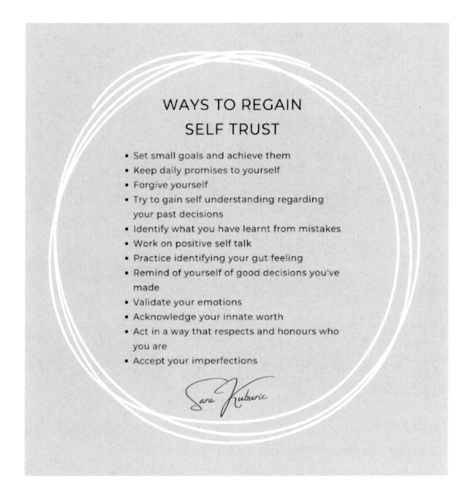

WAYS TO REGAIN
SELF TRUST

- Set small goals and achieve them
- Keep daily promises to yourself
- Forgive yourself
- Try to gain self understanding regarding your past decisions
- Identify what you have learnt from mistakes
- Work on positive self talk
- Practice identifying your gut feeling
- Remind of yourself of good decisions you've made
- Validate your emotions
- Acknowledge your innate worth
- Act in a way that respects and honours who you are
- Accept your imperfections

Lauren Jenson (The streaking app 2022) states:

'Often, we find a cognitive dissonance between who we are and who we would like to be. The journey from where we are to where we would like to be feels too long and we feel unable to make the attempt. In order to strengthen our confidence and ability, we need to build our self-trust. We need to keep promises to ourselves.'

"Self trust is the essence of heroism."

Ralph Waldo Emerson

She talks about keeping our promises to ourselves – but where do we start? There is only one place to start from – by being consistent.

Do you trust yourself to create a routine and stick to it? Do you tell yourself you will go to the gym / eat healthy / go for a walk, actually to never do it?

Lauren goes on to then say:

"When we see ourselves keeping our word every day, we begin to see ourselves as someone who can do the things, we set out to do. Even as things fall apart around us, we know at least one person that we can trust. This radiates into our relationships, both business and personal. Flipping what Stephen Covey said, "If you trust yourself, then others can trust you."

Do others trust you? If so, how do you know this and what is your evidence?

_____

_____

Am I consistent?

_____

How can I be more consistent with myself?

_____

What does that look like for you?

_____

Tips for consistency:

- Develop consistent habits
- Be realistic with yourself
- Stick to a schedule
- Use reminders
- Focus on one thing at a time
- Don't over complicate it
- Are you listening to the inner critic or the inner cheerleader?
- Increase your willpower – do you want to do it really?
- Get enough sleep
- Get support in form of motivational tools
- Only make promises you can keep

Often, if we know ourselves pretty well, but we don't trust that fact because we've disappointed ourselves too many times. If you have a list of regrets or bad decisions under your belt, we have to begin the process of letting them go and forgiving yourself.

1. Write down all of the mistakes you have made the past few months:

_____

_____

2. Are you overgeneralizing from a couple of bad recent decisions, or is this an enduring pattern across many different situations?

_____

_____

Sometimes cringe-worthy blunders can seem way more impactful than they actually are.

Seeing them written down can help you remember that you make good decisions way more often than the bad choices that live rent-free in your mind.

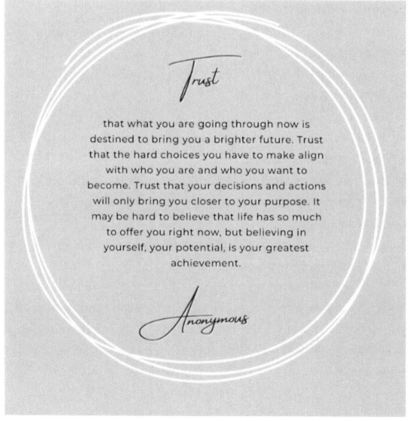

Trust

that what you are going through now is destined to bring you a brighter future. Trust that the hard choices you have to make align with who you are and who you want to become. Trust that your decisions and actions will only bring you closer to your purpose. It may be hard to believe that life has so much to offer you right now, but believing in yourself, your potential, is your greatest achievement.

Anonymous

What happens if you don't trust yourself?

1. You hesitate to priorities your needs and safety
2. You struggle to treat yourself with unconditional love and compassion
3. You're always listening to the knaggy, criticizing voice in your head
4. You doubt yourself
5. You stress yourself out
6. You feel uncomfortable spending time alone
7. You struggle to hold the mirror up to yourself
8. You dwell on the past
9. You worry about things that are outside your control
10. You don't trust your emotions / gut feel
11. You make bad decisions
12. You need constant reassurance
13. You ignore your curiosity

Not having trust in your abilities and in others can lead to:

- Broken relationships (Where are YOU going tonight all alone, honey?)
- Bad workplace experiences (Are you SURE you can complete it by the deadline?)
- An overall disturbing life (If I can't trust myself, who CAN I trust at all?) Read more at: https://www.scienceofpeople.com/trust-yourself/

Why might you not trust yourself?

_____

_____

Tips for trusting yourself

- Be you! No one else is you and that is your power!
- TRUST your GUT! Instinct is everything and it is always right. Tune into it and make it your best friend.
- Be authentic.
- Be decisive and learn from your decision making
- Know your decisions making processes are right and true for you

- Write down where trusting yourself has paid off
- Ask for feedback from others. Do they trust you? Why?
- Enjoy being alone
- Look at the past times you trusted yourself and how that worked out for you
- Push yourself
- Keep a note of compliments you receive
- Be kind to yourself
- Manage your own expectations
- Stick to your guns
- Know what you want and stick with it
- Allow space for your growth
- Visualize your success. I'm a MASSIVE fan of visualization and I want to share some tips with you all.

Growth Mindset

Do you like learning? Do you apply the learning to yourself?

A growth mindset means that you believe your intelligence and talents can be developed over time. A fixed mindset means that you believe intelligence is fixed, so if you're not good at something, you might believe you'll never be good at it.

Mindset is everything. I believe this to my core. How you think about yourself is so important but you HAVE to believe it, in you, to your core.

Intelligent changes ask:

- How do you rate your life so far?
- Do you enjoy learning new stuff? Or would you rather stick to your well-known routines?
- Are your relationships based on mutual love, trust and respect? Or do you feel like you're constantly competing with someone?
- Are you having fun and taking risks? Or do you fear failure?

If you relate more to the "or" questions and problems, perhaps it's time to change your mindset. Trust yourself to find out how to switch from a fixed mindset to a growth mindset and achieve your goals in every area of your life.

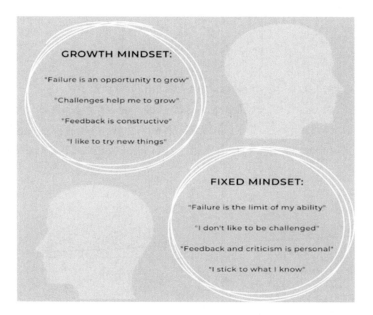

Mindset Quiz

1. Circle the number for each question which best describes you
2. Total and record your score when you have completed each of the 10 questions
3. Using the SCORE chart, record your mindset

	Strongly agree	Agree	Disagree	Strongly disagree
Your intelligence is something very basic about you that you can't change very much				
No matter how much intelligence you have, you can always change it quite a bit				
Only a few people will be truly good at sports, you have to be born with the ability				
The harder you work at something, the better you will be				
I often get angry when I get feedback about my performance				
I appreciate when people, parents, coaches or teachers give me feedback about my performance				
Truly smart people do not need to try hard				
You can always change how intelligent you are				
You are a certain kind of person and there is not much that can be done to really change that				
An important reason why I do my school work is that I enjoy learning new things				

Score Chart

22–30 = Strong Growth Mindset
17–21 = Growth with some fixed ideas
11–16 = Fixed with some growth ideas
0–10 =Strong fixed mindset

- What did I learn about myself from doing that quiz?

_____

_____

_____

- What changes do I want to make?

_____

_____

_____

- When will I start my changes?

_____

_____

_____

I have a growth mindset, I would even say I'm hungry to keep learning, evolving and changing. If I have an opportunity where I can get better, improve myself and the impact of that is only good for me, then I'm going to do it!

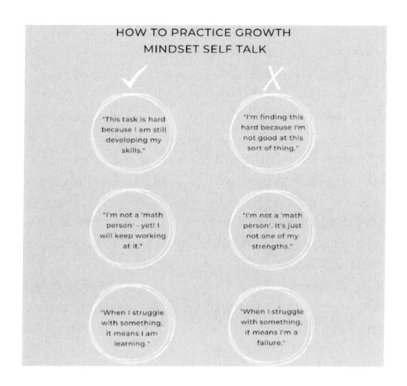

HOW TO PRACTICE GROWTH
MINDSET SELF TALK

✓	✗
"This task is hard because I am still developing my skills."	"I'm finding this hard because I'm not good at this sort of thing."
"I'm not a 'math person' - yet! I will keep working at it."	"I'm not a 'math person'. It's just not one of my strengths."
"When I struggle with something, it means I am learning."	"When I struggle with something, it means I'm a failure."

Thrive Global states: 'Carol Deweck, who studies human motivation, talks about her inquiry into our beliefs in her book – Mindset: The New Psychology of Success. The book takes us on a journey into how our conscious and unconscious thoughts affect us and how something as simple as wording can have a powerful impact on our ability to improve. Deweck's work shows the power of our most basic beliefs. Whether conscious or subconscious, they strongly "affect what we want and whether we succeed in getting it." Much of what we think we understand of our personality comes from our "mindset". This both propels us and prevents us from fulfilling our potential.'

In Mindset: The New Psychology of Success, Deweck writes:

'What are the consequences of thinking that your intelligence or personality is something you can develop, as opposed to something that is a fixed, deepseated trait? If you have only a certain amount of intelligence, a certain personality, and a certain moral character. Well, then you'd better prove that you have a healthy dose of them. It simply wouldn't do to look or feel deficient in these most basic characteristics. I've seen so many people with this one consuming goal of proving themselves in the classroom, in their careers and in their relationships. Every situation calls for a confirmation of their intelligence,

personality, or character. Every situation is evaluated: Will I succeed or fail? Will I look smart or dumb? Will I be accepted or rejected? Will I feel like a winner or a loser?' https://thriveglobal.com/stories/carol-dweck-a-summary-of-the-two-mindsets-and-the-power-of-believing-t hat-you-can-improve/

Essentially what Carol is saying is that it's about the way in which you view yourself and your mindset. If you tell yourself you aren't intelligent – then you are likely to believe this. I call being "open minded" and it's a trait I have always had. If you can be open minded to YOURSELF. This is where the magic can happen! Try to avoid "putting in a box". This is where you say, 'Oh, I'm always impatient, that will never change' and then you put it in a box and hold firm to that belief. Your growth mindset would say, 'I know I'm impatient and I will work on it as much as possible.'

There are probably lots of things you "put in a box" over the years and I would invite you to examine these and see if you can view them differently. If you can, you know you are on your way to achieving a growth mindset. Below is a way of challenging those thoughts…

Those who adopt a growth mindset are more likely to:

- Be okay with life's ups and downs
- Embrace lifelong learning
- Be resilient and can deal with backs
- Believe intelligence can be improved
- Want to try
- Put in more effort to learn
- Believe effort leads to mastery
- Failure does not stop them as it is not failure, but lessons learned
- Believe failures are just temporary setbacks
- View feedback as a source of information and WANTS it
- Willingly embraces challenges
- View others' success as a source of inspiration
- View feedback as an opportunity to learn
- Inspires others

Start to create this mindset for your daily thoughts and behaviours, I promise you it will change your life. You will be drama free from your own internal damming thoughts and you will feel free.

Why does a growth mindset matter to confidence? If you want to be confident you have to have a growth mindset…

CoreConfidence state: A fixed mindset is trying to keep us safe, the downside is that it also keeps us small. Confidence is a powerful resource when developing and sustaining a growth mindset. When we lack confidence, it's easy to get stuck in our own heads, limiting our opportunities and what we believe is possible for us. To grow and leverage the opportunities presented to us, a shortcut is to adopt a growth mindset and to do this in a gentle and self-compassionate way. This means challenging and expanding our thinking, asking ourselves some good questions;

What is holding me back from trying something new?
Why is my identity / sense of self so tied to my expertise and being right?
How can I get more comfortable with failing and taking healthy risks?
How can I ask for help with confidence?
There is a difference between the things we cannot do…and the things we cannot do …yet!

The things we cannot do yet, are the things we can be shown to do, or the things we can learn to do (e.g., learn to speak a different language). Things we cannot do, are the things we will never ever be able to do (e.g., grow wings and fly, grow flippers and swim under water). Using the Growth Mindset and the power of yet, will change the way you view the world.

Negative phrases like 'I can't, I won't and I don't – can be turned into positive phrases simply by adding the word…yet. The word yet, has a massive impact on performance and persistence.

In the space below, make a list of all the things you can't do…yet;

What you tell yourself inside your head, matters. One of these thoughts we have is called a **"Limiting belief"** they sound like this:

'I can't do that,' 'I will never be good enough to try that,' 'I am not good enough,' 'I am not pretty or thin enough,' 'I am too old or I am too young,' 'I am not smart enough or don't know enough,' 'I don't have enough time,' 'I don't have enough money.'

Sound familiar? Try writing down all your limiting beliefs and then asking yourself the following question about it:

- Is the thought true?
- Is it really true?
- If it is true, what is your evidence to support this?
- How do you react when you think that thought? Who are you with that thought? How do you treat yourself and others?
- Who would you be without that thought? How would you treat that person? How would you treat yourself? How would you live differently? What would happen if you thought the opposite?

I can *recognize and identify*
negative thought patterns
and limiting beliefs when
they arise in my mind,

**AND I HAVE
THE POWER TO
change THEM.**

My limiting belief is:
Is it true? Is it really true? Where and what is your evidence?

_____

_____

_____

My limiting belief is:
Is it true? Is it really true? Where and what is your evidence?

_____

_____

_____

My limiting belief is:

Is it true? Is it really true? Where and what is your evidence?

_____

_____

_____

My limiting belief is:

Is it true? Is it really true? Where and what is your evidence?

_____

_____

_____

Give it a go and let me know over on Instagram @adelebradleygram and tell me if those helped. Remember, you have to be honest with yourself.

If you wish to be truly confident, breaking through the limiting beliefs will enable this and set you free. Use your growth mindset to keep learning and keep evolving – and JUST WATCH your confidence change!

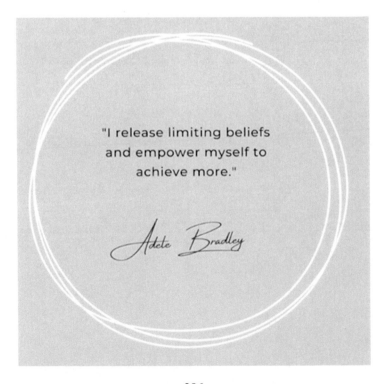

"I release limiting beliefs
and empower myself to
achieve more."

Adele Bradley

Gratitude

What matters to you the most in life? What are you most grateful for?

Gratitude is a thankful appreciation for what you receive, whether tangible or intangible. With gratitude, people acknowledge the goodness, happiness and what they are thankful for in their lives.

I give gratitude every day at 4.30 pm (I set an alarm) and I say 3 things that I am grateful for. I love it as it makes me stop and reflect on the day and fills me with a warm fuzzy feeling as it's all the good stuff I'm thinking about. I enjoy practicing it. I would encourage you to do the same. After all, there are so many things in life to be grateful for…here are some examples:

- Grateful for my puppy dog Mia, she brings joy to my life
- Grateful for my Mum & Dad who looks after Mia when I work away
- Grateful for the fact I have enough money in the bank so I can afford to heat my house in winter
- Grateful for my amazing job and the people I work with
- Grateful I have food to eat every day and a lovely home to live in
- Grateful for my drive and focus that keeps me resilient and driven
- Grateful for my health (Honestly, it's only when you are ill you really realize how much we take our health for granted)
- Grateful for my amazing, incredible and beautiful friends
- Grateful for my car and the fact it works like a dream

These are general though; I try to be more specific each day my alarm goes off based on what has happened that day.

If you have never done it before, give it a try and start to say thank you for all the amazing things / people you have in your life. Get specific by writing 'Today my partner gave me a shoulder rub when he knew I was really stressed' or 'my sister invited me over for dinner so I didn't have to cook after a long day.'

Or one that I used recently: 'I'm amazingly grateful to my friends for arranging a shopping delivery to my house as a surprise when I caught Covid.'

Happily states, *'The benefits of practicing gratitude are nearly endless. People who regularly practice gratitude by taking time to notice and reflect upon the things they're thankful for experience more positive emotions, feel more alive, sleep better, express more compassion and kindness and even have stronger immune systems. And gratitude doesn't need to be reserved only for momentous occasions: Sure, you might express gratitude after receiving a promotion at work, but you can also be thankful for something as simple as a delicious piece of pie. Research by UC Davis psychologist Robert Emmons, author of Thanks! How the New Science of Gratitude Can Make You Happier, shows that simply keeping a gratitude journal, regularly writing brief reflections on moments for which we're thankful, can significantly increase well-being and life satisfaction. You'd think that just one of these findings is compelling enough to motivate an ingrate into action. But if you're anything like me, this motivation lasts about three days until writing in my gratitude journal every evening loses out to watching stand-up comics on Netflix.*

https://www.happify.com/hd/the-science-behind-gratitude/

And I agree. Every New Year I convince myself I'm going to write in my journal. It lasts about 2 weeks and then I just stop. I did the same thing this year and I couldn't figure out why, so I guess I had to "get to know myself" as to why I was doing this. It turns out when I write journal notes, I write bullet points that are high level that don't really mean anything. It's just gibberish to anyone else even gazing at it and it wasn't really doing anything for me. However, I have found myself picking up my phone and leaving voice memos for myself. If I was happy or sad, I would record what happened that day and why and I also added detail which was more than the bullet points in my journal.

So now I have figured I write short but record voice notes in detail longhand and I like listening to my voice memos back, so I have decided to start my journaling that way. Who knew? Not me until I tried it and I learnt something new about myself!

You could write a gratitude letter to someone who had an impact on you whom you've never properly thanked. You could also share the day's grateful moments around the dinner table. The conversations that follow may give you even more reasons to give thanks.

Once for a whole year, every day I wrote something in a post it note that had gone well that day and popped in a jar. Someday I write up to 5 or 6, other days just one. They got put in the empty jar and at the end of the year, I had a whole jar of amazing things to read about and jog my memory of all the things I should be grateful for that year! I really enjoyed doing that and I would thoroughly recommend it. It made me feel amazing...

Happify back this by stating *'So how can you cultivate a growing sense of gratitude and its positive side-benefits on your own? It turns out that the tools used by psychologists in research studies, namely a gratitude journal and some thank you notes, are some of the best ones for boosting gratitude both in and out of the lab. By writing down positive things that happen to you and actively acknowledging those who have helped you, you become better at recognizing the good in your life, which naturally helps you feel more grateful and thankful more often* (Happily, 2022).

When was the last time you wrote a thank you note letter or a complimentary email to anyone?

What makes you feel good? What stirs good feelings?

As a reminder, here are some of the best feelings in the world...

- A love interest telling you that they want to be your partner and they want to make it work with you
- Freshly made bed with clean sheets
- Getting a job that was really important to you or a promotion
- Passing your driving test / degree / exams / qualifications
- Being proposed to / proposing to someone
- Buying / renting your first home
- Getting married / declaring your love / first kiss
- The smell that hits you when you step off a plane on holiday
- Doing work for cause that is close to your heart and making an impact
- Achieving something you have been planning / practicing for a long time
- Being in nature
- Getting great feedback on a job / performance
- Rescuing an animal
- Being seen as you are
- Giving birth to your baby / being a parent / adoption / fostering

- Going to a concert and it turns out to be the best night of your life
- Eating your favourite meal in the world after being very hungry
- Seeing your children achieve their dreams / Celebrating with them
- Waking up without anxiety / having the best sleep possible

I am grateful for:

1. _____
2. _____
3. _____
4. _____
5. _____
6. _____
7. _____
8. _____
9. _____
10. _____
11. _____
12. _____
13. _____
14. _____
15. _____

The small things that make me happy are:

1. _____
2. _____
3. _____
4. _____
5. _____
6. _____
7. _____
8. _____
9. _____
10. _____
11. _____

12. _____
13. _____
14. _____
15. _____

What has gratitude got to do with confidence? Insider.com states, '*Gratitude increases self-esteem. Research shows that people who are more grateful also tend to have higher self-esteem. This may be because when you intentionally notice the ways other people are good to you, you develop a stronger sense of your own value.*'

So, by practicing gratitude, you raise your self-esteem, which in turn increases your confidence. It helps you to stop comparing yourself to others, and helps ground you in the amazing things you have around you already – and I'm not just talking about materialistic items.

You will walk a little taller when you realize you are so rich in love, friendships, family, pets, career, being in nature, health, talent and so many more things than personal possessions! Remember, it's all about perspective. Change your thinking, change your life!

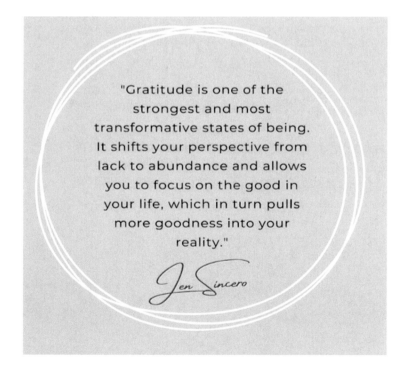

"Gratitude is one of the strongest and most transformative states of being. It shifts your perspective from lack to abundance and allows you to focus on the good in your life, which in turn pulls more goodness into your reality."

Jen Sincero

Perspective

'Though similar, perception and perspective stand on their own and knowing the difference can help you pinpoint areas you need to improve. Perception is what you interpret. It is your understanding of a given situation, person, or object. It is the meaning you assign to any given stimulus. Perspective is your point of view. It's the lens you see the world through and determines how you view yourself, others, and everything else around you.'

Pauline Rose Moore 2022 – Maxwell Leadership

Perspective

Life will throw so many obstacles at you, ones that will create new opportunities and others that will test your strength but never anything you cannot handle. In the end, it's not about what these obstacles are, but instead how you respond and view them. There is so much you can do, even when you feel as though your circumstances hold you back. Maybe it's about focusing less on what or who you have and more on everything you can do, the opportunities life will bring and those that want to spend thier life with you. Your perspective can build you up or tear your down.

Tiffany Moule

Perspective is EVERYTHING! It's the lenses you choose to view the world through.

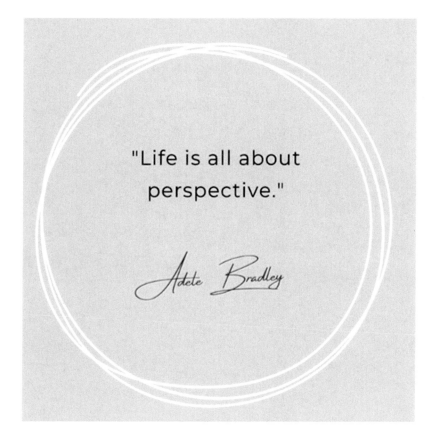

"Life is all about perspective."

Adele Bradley

But first, let's define what perspective actually means... Merriam Webster dictionary definition:

1. The angle or direction in which a person looks at an object.
2. Point of view.
3. The ability to understand what is important and what isn't. I know you're disappointed but keep your perspective.
4. An accurate rating of what is important and what isn't. Let's keep things in perspective.

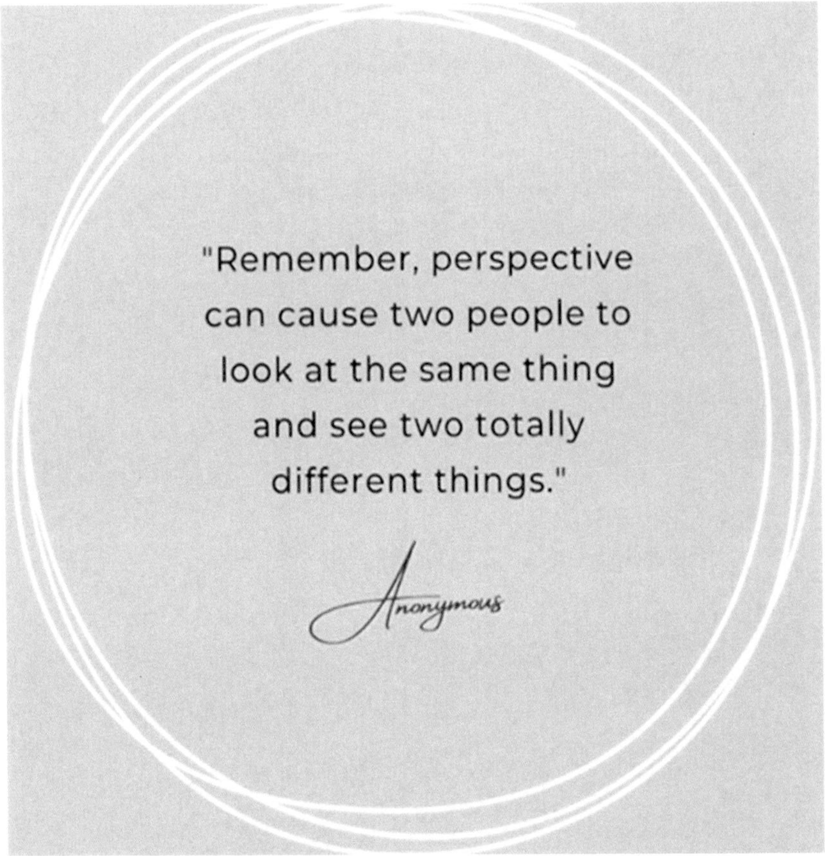

> "Remember, perspective
> can cause two people to
> look at the same thing
> and see two totally
> different things."
>
> *Anonymous*

Perspective is how we take information in on a situation and process it. For example, from my perspective, things may have looked completely different to how my friend saw it.

If you look at a railway track and it looks like it's bending in the horizon, or a piece of art that has depth and distance that changes on the paper. It's the same with people, things look different to different people.

Has anyone ever said to you, 'You need to get some perspective?' It is essentially somebody saying you need to adjust your point of view.

You can help someone see a different perspective by sharing yours, having a conversation about what you have both seen and interpreted always helps.

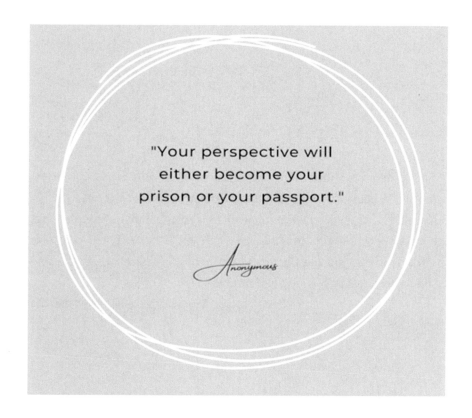

"Your perspective will either become your prison or your passport."

Anonymous

And guess what? You get to choose the lens you view the world through. If a situation happens, play a few different scenarios through in your head. Put yourself in someone else's shoes and view the experience from their lens.

It takes practice, so remember before you blow up a situation, try and view it from all perspectives first. It's about looking at something through a fresh pair of eyes. It will help you change your thoughts if you practice it enough and this in turn, will help you feel more confident.

How am I going to work on my perspective:

_____

_____

_____

_____

_____

Perception

'Though similar, perception and perspective stand on their own and knowing the difference can help you pinpoint areas you need to improve. Perception is what you interpret. It is your understanding of a given situation, person, or object. It is the meaning you assign to any given stimulus. Perspective is your point of view. It's the lens you see the world through and determines how you view yourself, others, and everything else around you.'

Pauline Rose Moore 2022 – Maxwell Leadership

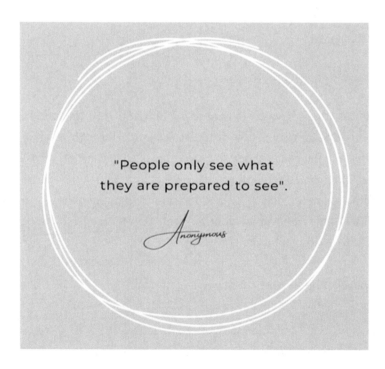

"People only see what they are prepared to see".

Anonymous

Perception is about what is regarded, understood, or interpreted by you. It is how you see the situation and this can be perception through feelings or perception through evidence. You can sense something and this is either through vision, touch, sound, taste or smell.

Perception

YOU SAY	I SAY
Agressive	Steadfast in approach
Impulsive	Decisive decision maker
Impatient	Quick to move forward
Rebellious	Stepping outside of the norm
Hyperactive	Exhilarated by everything
Demanding	In tune with what I want
Stubborn	Certain of the outcome

Anonymous

People's behaviour is based on their perception of what reality is, not on Reality itself.

That's a big statement, right? And it's so true. Have you ever had an argument with a partner or a friend and their perception of what happened is completely different to yours? How can that be so? It's because we all see the world differently, and interpret situations differently based on who we are, our values, morals, the way in which we see the world. It's crazy that two people can experience the same situation but have completely different perceptions of it. No one's reality is ever the same!

If you are going to work on your confidence, perception is important. You will ultimately doubt yourself and it will cloud your judgment in perception if you are not confident. Knowing how perceptive you are will help increase your confidence because you will TRUST yourself with your judgment.

Learn to tune into your mind and learn how it perceives things around you.

My perception of situations for a long time was dramatic and exaggerated. I realized this didn't help with my reputation, and that I needed to be authentic and real. So I view things through logic and trusting my gut. I trust myself but THAT doesn't mean my perception is always right. Sometimes you need somebody to challenge your thinking and help you see things in a different way or from another point of view. And I welcome this! I want to see the lens that someone else looked through. It's so important.

Being able to hold that balance is confidence in itself. Understanding that the way you see the world differently to everyone else is hugely freeing from a negative mindset.

What do you see in this picture?

An old lady or a young woman? What is your perception?

A rabbit or a duck?

 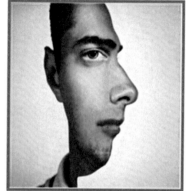

So perception can totally change a thought, a situation, a mindset summarise being. A good question to ask others? Tell me your perception of what just happened? You might be shocked by their answer! Challenge yourself daily on the way your perception is and how it affects your life. You won't regret it.

To achieve confidence, viewing your perception as just one version of events will help free you from any chains that hold you down. This is where your confidence will grow!

How am I going to work on my perception:

_____

_____

_____

_____

_____

Reflecting

"We do not learn from experience. We learn from reflecting on experience."

John Dewey

I talk a lot about reflecting in this book. It can be called "reflective practice" or "reflective learning" and it involves looking inwardly about experiences and understanding what it means to you and what you have learnt from it. Toolshero state: (https://www.toolshero.com/personaldevelopment/reflective-learning/)

'Reflection then becomes a learning process known as reflective learning, which is the conscious way in which a person thinks and analyses the situations in which they are involved, leading to Reflective Practice.'

I 100% recommend reflective practice – it's one of my favourite ways to learn. I usually do it on dog walks, in the shower or in bed before I go to sleep.

Toolshero also states, *'According to Dewey, it is important to reflect on the events that happened and to be able to have self-criticism and to think from different points of view of a situation in order to have a variety of knowledge and to be able to lead to positive learning from the actions and decisions an individual made. Reflecting on what happened and how it happened, for Dewey, is the analysis of eventualities that human beings experience but at the time of experiencing certain situations cannot understand what is happening. This understanding comes as a result of the reflection after the event that was lived and which can lead to answers to important questions.'*

And I couldn't agree more. I often think about conversations I have had, would I have changed anything and if so what, and what will I do next, or differently. I often use this knowledge to try new and different approaches and I keep learning from it. If you have a disagreement with your partner, before blaming them or kicking off, it can be worthwhile looking inwardly to see if there was anything you did that may have caused this.

Getting into a habit of reflective practice will make you a better person all round. If you reflect on your parenting skills, your skills as a partner, as a sibling, co-worker and much more, you will keep leveling up. Keep wanting to be the best version of yourself. This is all part of being confident. You are getting to know yourself better and better which in turn will increase your confidence.

One way I do reflective practice at work is to keep what is known as "WLC", which means "Win Learn Change".

If you are starting reflective practice for the first time, this is a great way to start.

After any major work event (depending on what you do, it might be after a big meeting with key customers at work, or presentation – ANYTHING really) sit down and ask yourself the following:

- What were the big wins? What did we do well? What went well?
- What did we learn? What did we learn about each other? What did we learn about the situation?
- What would we do differently next time? What changes do we need to make?

This will start you off on your reflective practice journey. You can also apply these questions to personal situations and events too.

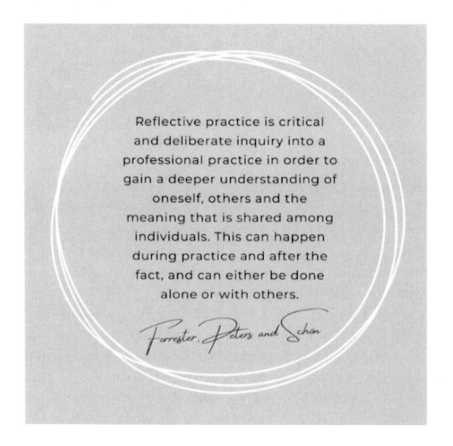

Reflective practice is critical and deliberate inquiry into a professional practice in order to gain a deeper understanding of oneself, others and the meaning that is shared among individuals. This can happen during practice and after the fact, and can either be done alone or with others.

Forrester, Peters and Schon

Some others say that these 6 steps also help with reflective practice:

- **Read** around the topics you are learning about or want to learn about and develop
- **Ask** others about the way they do things and why
- **Watch** what is going on around you
- **Feel** pay attention to your emotions, what prompts them, and how you deal with negative ones
- **Talk** share your views and experiences with others in your organization
- **Think** learn to value time spent thinking about your work

Skillyouneed also state the huge benefits around reflective practice: ·https://www.skillsyouneed.com/ps/reflective-practice.html

'Reflective practice has huge benefits in increasing self-awareness, which is a key component of emotional intelligence, and in developing a better understanding of others. Reflective practice can also help you to develop creative thinking skills, and encourages active engagement in work processes.

In work situations, keeping a learning journal, and regularly using reflective practice, will support more meaningful discussions about career development, and your personal development, including at personal appraisal time. It will also help to provide you with examples to use in competency-based interview situations.'

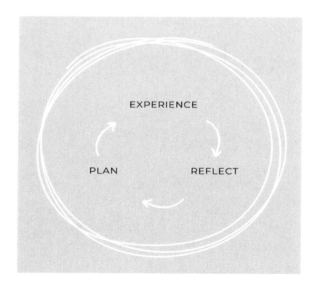

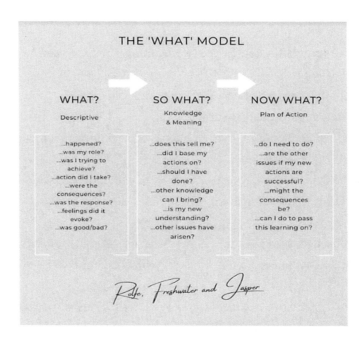

THE 'WHAT' MODEL

WHAT?	SO WHAT?	NOW WHAT?
Descriptive	Knowledge & Meaning	Plan of Action
...happened? ...was my role? ...was I trying to achieve? ...action did I take? ...were the consequences? ...was the response? ...feelings did it evoke? ...was good/bad?	...does this tell me? ...did I base my actions on? ...should I have done? ...other knowledge can I bring? ...is my new understanding? ...other issues have arisen?	...do I need to do? ...are the other issues if my new actions are successful? ...might the consequences be? ...can I do to pass this learning on?

Rolfe, Freshwater and Jasper

By reflecting on your actions, situation and thinking, it will help you develop more self-awareness which in turn will help increase your confidence. This is due to the fact you are learning from your experiences, the impact you have on others and changing this – this is growth! This is confidence!

My reflective log:

What was the experience / situation / event?

How did it make me feel?

What were my key learnings about myself?

How will I use this new information?

What did I find important & useful? And why?

What will I do differently as a result of this learning?

My reflections of the situation in total:

Strength

I feel like I have a rod of steel through my core. That is what I call my strength. I know I am strong. I know this to my core. I know when I make a decision I stick with it, I have my core values and I know what I stand for, what my views are on things and I have my moral compass. I am completely secure in who I am.

"Strength grows in the moments when you think you can't go on but you keep going anyway."

Anonymous

I think my strength comes from lots of places. One of them being my resilience, my upbringing, my independence and I also think I was born with it. Who you are, your DNA is you, like whether you are hopeless romantic or really sexy or an adrenaline junkie or always late to everything. Sometimes I believe it is just your makeup, your DNA, you. I believe that my strength and confidence is part of my DNA, whereas being terrible at DIY and having limited patience is also part of my DNA!

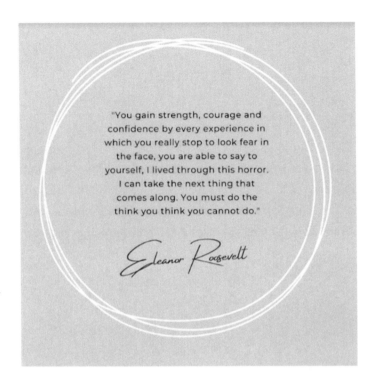

"You gain strength, courage and confidence by every experience in which you really stop to look fear in the face, you are able to say to yourself, I lived through this horror. I can take the next thing that comes along. You must do the think you think you cannot do."

Eleanor Roosevelt

I know I can do anything I put my mind to and I know no one can stop me doing anything I want to do. I hate being told what to do and I have a huge rebellious streak. Hehe!

I am human, I get run down and exhausted, I get tired and I cry but I always know that no matter what, I will be ok. No other option other than to survive! The positive mindset and the strength are a lethal combo! In my most recent role, when I asking for feedback, this is what I received:

- A force of nature
- Inspirational
- Passionate
- A force to be reckoned with
- Unstoppable

And that made me smile. Those words made me feel awesome and let's face it, if I wasn't confident, I wouldn't get that feedback, would I?

Being confident can and will change your life. Imagine walking into somewhere, head held high, shoulders back, eyes forward and feeling like you are totally in control with zero anxiety … imagine it! You have to really **TRUST** in yourself, really **BELIEVE** in yourself and you will do all the things you never thought you could do … You are unstoppable!

"Getting your shit together requires a level of honesty you can't even imagine. There is nothing easy about realising you are the one thats been holding you back this whole time."

Jayde

My thinking changes and evolves every day. I know today that I thought differently just 1 year ago… When I reflect back, I see my journey and my evolution over the years. I observe how I react and deal with situations now, compared to how I used to. I think back to how judgmental I used to be, how much I used to think everyone thought the way I did! I have invested years and years into my mindset, through reading books, taking courses and gaining qualifications that force you to hold the mirror up, learning from others, looking at things through a different lens, understanding how complex people are and how we are all so different.

If you truly, truly want to change your life and become the most confident, self-assured person ever, please commit to it. Commit to the journey for you and for no one else other than you want to be the best role model of a parent / brother / sister / friend / cousin / aunty / uncle or partner you can be!

I have grown so much as a person and it's because I WANTED to and I still do – Life is all about learning, experiences and memories! It's not been easy and I am far from perfect – I have to challenge my thinking every day and course correct it where needed – and I don't always get it right. It's a full-time commitment to yourself.

I hope you enjoyed reading this book. I know I really enjoyed writing it, it was a lot of fun and I feel like I've just handed over my mindset in a journal book. This is me in a book!

If I have helped you anyway by sharing my stories and helping you think, then I am honoured. Keep this book with you. Keep reading and revisiting it. If you find a question hard, come back to it in 6- or 12-months' time, see if you still feel the same. Evolution will happen if you open your heart and mind and let it – grow with yourself. Learn about yourself. Accept yourself. Love yourself. Respect yourself. Take care of yourself. Live your life to the fullest. Enjoy the moments. Accept and be.

You have just one short life on this earth. Why wouldn't you want to try and live the most wonderful life?

FINDING COURAGE

Let this be the year. Let this be year you go after courage. For years, your heart desired it, but worry held you back. You allowed yourself to dream courageously, but you forced yourself to end it at that. But after all this time, let this be year. Let this be the year you take those deeper breaths, with eyes wide open, say *yes*, running with total abandon in the direction of the courage you have longed to find for years. Go after it on the mountain. Go after it in the valley. Go after it in the silence between the words in your late night prayers. Go after courage everywhere, for wherever you pursue it, God will be there. Ever-Loving, ever-guiding, He will bring you out of hiding, dispelling every fear, giving courage, giving strength. Let this be the year. — *Morgan Harper Nichols*

The End